W9-BYW-974

BUTTERFLY ON ROCK

A STUDY OF THEMES AND

Butterfly on Rock

IMAGES IN CANADIAN LITERATURE

D. G. JONES

UNIVERSITY OF TORONTO PRESS

Reprinted 1971

Printed in Canada by

University of Toronto Press, Toronto and Buffalo

ISBN 0-8020-5230-4

LC 75-133438

Contents

for Stephen, Skyler, Tory, and North & Sheila

Acknowledgments

Atheneum Publishers, New York, for quotations from LOREN EISELY's *The Firmament of Time*. Copyright © by LOREN EISELEY. Copyright © by The Trustees of the University of Pennsylvania. Reprinted by permission of Atheneum Publishers.

MARGARET AVISON, for quotations from "Neverness, or The One Ship Beached on One Far Distant Shore," "The Local and the Lakefront," "The Butterfly," *The Dumbfounding* (New York: W. W. Norton 1966).

EARLE BIRNEY, for quotations from *Ice Cod Bell and Stone* (Toronto: McClelland and Stewart 1962), *Selected Poems* (Toronto: McClelland and Stewart 1966).

GEORGE BOWERING, for quotations from *Points on the Grid* (Toronto: Contact Press 1964), *The Silver Wire* (Kingston: Quarry Press 1966).

ERNEST BUCKLER, for quotations from *The Mountain and the Valley* (Toronto: McClelland and Stewart, NCL Series 1961).

Canadian Literature, University of British Columbia, for quotations from LOUIS DUDEK's "Groundhog Among the Stars" (No. 22, 1964); JOSEPH GOLD's "The Precious Speck of Life" (No. 26, 1965); D. G. JONES's "The Sleeping Giant" (No. 26, 1965); WARREN TALLMAN's "Wolf in the Snow" (Nos. 5 & 6, 1960); PAUL WEST's "Pratt's Four-Ton Gulliver" (No. 19, 1964).

LEONARD COHEN, for quotations from *Selected Poems: 1965–1968* (Toronto: McClelland and Stewart 1968), *The Favourite Game* (New York: The Viking Press 1963), *Beautiful Losers* (Toronto: McClelland and Stewart 1966).

Crown Publishers, New York, for quotations from HOWARD O'HAGAN's *Tay John*. Copyright © 1960 by HOWARD O'HAGAN. Used by permission of Clarkson N. Potter, Inc., New York.

MRS. F. P. GROVE and A. LEONARD GROVE, for quotations from FREDERICK PHILIP GROVE'S *Fruits of the Earth* (Toronto: McClelland and Stewart, NCL Series 1965), *Settlers of the Marsh* (Toronto: McClelland and Stewart, NCL Series 1966), *Our Daily Bread* (New York: Macmillan 1928), *The Master of the Mill* (Toronto: McClelland and Stewart, NCL Series 1961), *In Search of Myself* (Toronto: Macmillan 1946).

RALPH GUSTAFSON, for quotations from *Sift in an Hourglass* (Toronto: McClelland and Stewart 1966).

IRVING LAYTON, for quotations from *Collected Poems* (Toronto: McClelland and Stewart 1965).

GWENDOLYN MACEWEN, for quotations from *The Rising Fire* (Toronto: Contact Press 1963), *Breakfast for Barbarians* (Toronto: The Ryerson Press 1966).

HUGH MACLENNAN, for quotations from *Each Man's Son* (Boston: Little, Brown and Company 1951), *The Watch that Ends the Night* (Toronto: Macmillan 1959).

The Macmillan Company of Canada Limited, Toronto, for quotations from MORLEY CALLAGHAN'S *The Loved and the Lost* (1951); HUGH MACLENNAN'S *The Watch that Ends the Night* (1959); COLIN MCDOUGALL'S *Execution* (1958); E. J. PRATT'S *Collected Poems* (1958); ANNE WILKINSON'S *The Collected Poems of Anne Wilkinson* (1968), edited by A. J. M. Smith; ADELE WISEMAN'S *The Sacrifice* (1956).

ELI MANDEL, for quotations from *An Idiot Joy* (Edmonton: M. G. Hurtig 1967).

COLIN MCDOUGALL and Blanche C. Gregory Inc., New York, for quotations from *Execution* (Toronto: Macmillan 1958).

McClelland and Stewart Limited, Toronto, for quotations from EARLE BIRNEY'S *Selected Poems* (1966), *Ice Cod Bell and Stone* (1962); BLISS CARMAN'S *The Selected Poems of Bliss Carman* (1954); LEONARD COHEN'S *Beautiful Losers* (1966), *Selected Poems: 1956—1968* (1968); RALPH GUSTAFSON'S *Sift in an Hourglass* (1966); MARGARET LAURENCE'S *The Stone Angel* (1964), *A Jest of God* (1966); IRVING LAYTON'S *Collected Poems* (1965); STEPHEN LEACOCK'S "The Rival Churches of St Asaph's and St Osoph's"; DOUGLAS LEPAN'S *The Deserter* (1964); JOHN NEWLOVE'S *Black Night Window* (1968); P. K. PAGE'S *Cry Ararat* (1967); A. W. PURDY'S *The Cariboo Horses* (1965), *Wild Grape Wine*

(1968); THOMAS H. RADDALL's *At the Tide's Turn* (NCL Series 1959); JAMES REANEY's *The Red Heart* (1949); SIR CHARLES G. D. ROBERTS' *The Last Barrier and Other Stores* (NCL Series 1958); GABRIELLE ROY's *The Hidden Mountain* (1962), *The Cashier* (NCL Series 1963); SHEILA WATSON's *The Double Hook* (NCL Series 1966).

JOHN NEWLOVE, for quotations from *Moving In Alone* (Toronto: Contact Press 1965), *Black Night Window* (Toronto: McClelland and Stewart 1968).

ALDEN NOWLAN, for quotations from *The Things Which Are* (Toronto: Contact Press 1962).

Oxford University Press, Toronto, for quotations from MARGARET ATWOOD's *The Animals in that Country* (1968); JAY MACPHERSON's *The Boatman* (1957); A. J. M. SMITH's *Collected Poems* (1962), *The Oxford Book of Canadian Verse* (1960); *A Choice of Critics* (1966), edited by George Woodcock.

A. W. PURDY, for quotations from *Poems for All the Annettes* (Toronto: Contact Press 1962), *The Cariboo Horses* (Toronto: McClelland and Stewart 1965), *Wild Grape Wine* (Toronto: McClelland and Stewart 1968).

JAMES REANEY and Sybil Hutchinson, for quotations from "The Horn," *The Red Heart* (Toronto: McClelland and Stewart 1949), *Twelve Letters to a Small Town* (Toronto: The Ryerson Press 1962).

LADY JOAN ROBERTS, for quotations from "The Moonlight Trails," "As Down the Woodland Ways," "At the Tidewater," *The Selected Poems of Sir Charles G. D. Roberts* (Toronto: The Ryerson Press 1955).

SINCLAIR ROSS, for quotations from *As For Me and My House* (Toronto: McClelland and Stewart, NCL Series 1957).

The Ryerson Press, Toronto, for quotations from PATRICK ANDERSON's *The White Centre* (1946); A. M. KLEIN's *The Rocking Chair* (1948); GWENDOLYN MACEWEN's *Breakfast for Barbarians* (1966); DESMOND PACEY's *Ten Canadian Poets* (1958); JAMES REANEY's *Twelve Letters to a Small Town* (1962); SIR CHARLES G. D. ROBERTS' *The Selected Poems of Sir Charles G. D. Roberts* (1955); PHYLLIS WEBB's *The Sea Is Also a Garden* (1962).

MRS ELISE A. SCOTT, for quotations from DUNCAN CAMPBELL SCOTT's "Night Hymns on Lake Nipigon," "A Night in June,"

Selected Poems of Duncan Campbell Scott (Toronto: The Ryerson Press 1951).

F. R. SCOTT, for quotations from *Overture* (Toronto: The Ryerson Press 1946), *Selected Poems* (Toronto: Oxford University Press 1966).

RAYMOND SOUSTER, for quotations from *A Local Pride* (Toronto: Contact Press 1962), *The Selected Poems* (Toronto: Contact Press 1956).

Yale University Press, New Haven, Conn., for quotations from PAUL TILLICH'S *The Courage To Be* (1952).

This book has been published with the help of a grant from the Humanities Research Council of Canada, using funds provided by the Canada Council and with the assistance of the Publications Fund of the University of Toronto Press.

BUTTERFLY ON ROCK

Introduction

Having reached the Pacific, Canadians have begun to turn back on themselves, to create that added dimension Teilhard de Chardin calls the noosphere or, to put it more simply, Canadian culture. Of course, we have been at this for some time, but to use the words of Robert Frost quoted elsewhere in this study, more than ever before we have arrived at a point where we recognize, not only that the land is ours, but that we are the land's.

The north remains, and the cultural implications of that future settlement have hardly been felt. But our westward expansion is complete, and in the pause to reflect upon ourselves we become increasingly aware that our identity and our view of the world are no longer determined by our experience of Europe, but by our experience of life as it is lived between two oceans in a stretch of land that has been referred to as a few acres of snow and, more recently, as America's attic. It is apparent that we must now move into our own cultural house, for we are no longer at home in the houses of others. As John Newlove says in his poem "The Pride":

> we stand alone,
> we are no longer lonely
> but we have roots,
> and the rooted words
> recur in the mind, mirror, so that
> we dwell on nothing else, in nothing else,
> touched, repeating them,
> at home freely
> at last, in amazement.[1]

This book dwells deliberately on some of the words that have taken root in Canadian poetry and fiction during the past three generations. It is not primarily a survey, nor does it attempt to deal fully with any single author or work. Rather, by isolating certain themes and images it attempts to define more clearly some of the features that recur in the mind, the mirror of our imaginative life.

Undoubtedly there are other important themes and images to be studied in Canadian literature, but those explored here have been singled out by virtue of their recurrence in a wide variety of authors and often over a period of several generations. The study touches on most of the principal poets writing between 1880 and the present as well as on many of the novels that have provoked serious discussion. Still others might have been cited. Thus, though there may be individual writers who ignore these themes or who treat them quite differently, there can be little doubt that they are central and characteristic themes in Canadian literature. To study them closely should reveal essential features of both individual writers and the literature generally. It may also reveal something of the Canadian temper.

As the last remarks suggest, the approach here is cultural and psychological rather than purely aesthetic or literary. It parallels that of such critics as Northrop Frye and Warren Tallman, and the present discussion can only hope to confirm and amplify many of their observations. Such an approach has its dangers, too. It can lead into a discussion of general ideas that may blur the distinctions between individual authors or grossly simplify the complex perceptions of an individual work. It assumes a relationship between literature and life that can never be defined with precision and that invariably involves one in a maze of circular arguments. One can never be sure that, as one reader suggested, the result is not simply another poem. If so, it is a possible poem, and one that is well worth writing. In other words, it seems worth the risks. And whatever we call the result, it must be judged on the basis of the evidence it presents and the experience of readers over a period of time.

Meanwhile, the persistent concern of widely different authors with similar themes and images certainly suggests that the individual writers share a common cultural predicament. It may also suggest that they participate in and help to articulate a larger imaginative world, a supreme fiction of the kind that embodies the dreams and nightmares of a people, shapes their imaginative vision of the world, and defines, as it evolves, their cultural identity.

Louis Dudek does not go that far. In his article "Nationalism in Canadian Poetry," he argues that many Canadian poets, both French and English, share a common cultural predicament, but that it is one defined almost exclusively by an inherited literary tradition.[2] Their preoccupation with the theme of a national identity is simply a reflection of the nineteenth-century Romanticism within which Canadian poetry first developed. Undoubtedly there is some truth in this argument, but it strikes me as superficial and as involving a rather narrow conception of what is meant by a national identity. Quite apart from the fact that the spirit of nineteenth-century nationalism is by no means dead, in Canada as in other parts of the world, the question of a national identity is not to be equated with simple national pride, political independence, or some inevitably chauvinistic self-assertion. For Canadians, as for others, it is a question of recognizing and articulating a view of life within which they can live with some assurance, or at least with some conviction. That is, it is less a question of nationalism than of an imaginative stance towards the world, towards nature and culture, past and present, the life of the body and the life of the mind, the fact of death. It is a question of finding a satisfying interpretation of these fundamental elements in human life so that one can take a stand, act with definitive convictions, have an identity. As John Newlove puts it, it is a question of feeling at home.

Such are some of the questions explored in the work we shall study. Their treatment there should make it evident that the cultural predicament prompting different writers to take up the same themes is not defined simply by a literary tradition, but by the actual experience of many Canadians. It suggests to begin with that we have not always felt freely at home here, partly because of the influence of such traditions.

The first part of this study is devoted to the expression, in prose and in poetry, of a sense of exile, of being estranged from the land and divided within oneself. A number of voices have made the point that the conventional culture, largely inherited from Europe, fails to reflect the sometimes crude but authentic experience of our lives and that this experience is in urgent need of expression in native terms. There is something that grows in us, says John Newlove:

> and idles about and hides
> until the moment is due –
>
> the knowledge
> of our origins, and where
> we are in truth,
> whose land this is
> and is to be.[3]

Though Newlove asserts that this knowledge will spring upon us out of our own mouths when the moment is due, many have felt the moment to be long overdue. They attest to a failure to give voice to this knowledge, and they dramatize the sense of frustration that attends such a failure.

The knowledge of our origins to which Newlove's poem refers is a knowledge of our American rather than our European roots. "The Pride" centres upon the life of the North American Indians, and it is our North American inheritance embodied here in the Indians that idles about and hides, waiting to be given a voice. On that point many of the writers we are to study agree: the voice that demands to be heard is the voice of the land.

Chapters 2 and 3 might well have been called the mirror of landscape. The analysis of various novels and poems in which the land plays a prominent role reveals that the land is associated with the most vital elements in the lives of the characters and that these vital elements are frequently suppressed by the conventional life of the community. Frustrated, they remain inarticulate or unconscious. The drama then centres upon the division or, more seriously, the antagonism between culture and nature. Society and its official representatives are pitted against the land; men are divided against each other and against themselves.

In his "Conclusion" to *Literary History of Canada*, Northrop Frye offered an explanation for the antagonism between culture and nature that informs a good deal of our literature. It is, he suggested, a literary reflection of the colonial mentality, which is, practically by definition, a garrison mentality. Again and again we are confronted by a garrison culture confronting a hostile wilderness. The present study confirms and illustrates this point. But it would also suggest that Frye's metaphor may be extended.

The division between culture and nature dramatized in some of the literature goes far beyond any purely Canadian colonialism; it can only be considered to reflect an antagonism towards nature characteristic of western culture generally. It will not disappear with the disappearance of the colonial mentality in Canada. A book like Leonard Cohen's *Beautiful Losers* implies that western culture is itself a garrison culture confronting a hostile wilderness.

Given the tendency to discriminate the whole range of our experience into light and dark, western man has shown a marked inclination to ally himself wholly with the so-called forces of light in an all-out attack on the so-called forces of darkness. In the name of various spiritual or intellectual ideals he has embarked on a kind of holy war against the material world, the world of the flesh and the devil. Whether his ideal has been secular or divine, he has set himself against all that is mortal and seemingly irrational in nature, human and non-human. It is in this perspective that the hostile wilderness becomes, not just a Canadian wilderness but the whole natural universe. Only within such a perspective can the antagonism between culture and nature evident in the work of Leonard Cohen or Frederick Philip Grove, E. J. Pratt or Archibald Lampman, be fully appreciated.

Here Canadian writers take up themes common to western literature. It is interesting to note how such themes are developed in native terms, to see the great flour mill in Grove's *The Master of the Mill* performing the same symbolic function as the coal mine in Lawrence's *Women in Love*, to see the Indian or the half-breed in various poems and stories playing something of the same role as the Congolese native in Conrad's "Heart of Darkness." For it becomes clear that the world symbolized by D. C. Scott's Powassan, by Newlove's Indians, as by the half-breed in a novel such as Howard O'Hagan's *Tay John*, is not only the undigested raw material of Canadian experience but all that is primitive in nature and man.

The need to make a transition from a garrison culture to one in which the Canadian will feel at home in his world makes itself felt at a time when western man generally feels compelled to make a similar transition. In this perspective the search for a Canadian identity cannot be divorced from that larger search for identity that provides a common theme in so much contemporary writing. Modern literature is filled with images of the exile, the outsider, the alienated man. The same man appears in Douglas LePan's *The Deserter* and, indeed, in Jay Macpherson's image of Adam wandering in the waste wood while Eve lies abandoned on the barren shore.

The weakness of the colonial mentality is that it regards as a threat what it should regard as its salvation; it walls out or exploits what it should welcome and cultivate. The same weakness is inherent in the assumptions of western culture that lead man to view the universe as an enemy. Though he may be less inclined to view it, in a religious sense, as the playground of the devil, he is still inclined to regard it with a wary eye.

Not infrequently modern man stands like Job before a creation that, however magnificent, appears violent, irrational, and without justice. For no apparent reason it has given him birth and at the same time sentenced him to death. The Old Testament Job may be said to face two problems: he must contend with his comforters, each of whom is the mouthpiece of a conventional wisdom that is no longer convincing, and he must contend with Jehovah, with a universe that evinces an awesome creative exuberance and an almost equally awesome disregard for the creatures it has produced. More precisely, it lacks any human sense of justice and fails to discriminate between the lion and the lamb. The problems are as alive as ever and occupy the imagination of a good many Canadian writers. The chapter entitled "The Problem of Job" focusses particularly on the paralysis that results from a failure to resolve one or the other or both of these problems. Actually they cannot be divorced, for the conventional wisdom of an inherited culture is itself an answer to the question of how to take the universe. When it has become unconvincing, it tends on the one hand to stifle life through the perpetuation of moribund attitudes and purely ineffectual gestures and on the other to increase the difficulty of life through the often more desperate assertion of inappropriate but materially effective attitudes and gestures. Grove and Cohen, Lampman and Pratt, Douglas LePan and Jay Macpherson, all point out that the more completely man sets himself against nature and her imperfections the more completely he alienates himself from his world. And when he turns his theological or his technological weapons upon nature in the hope of completely walling out or annihilating the threats of disorder, suffering and death, he only adds to life's violence and pain. He quickly reaches a point where the supposed instruments of his salvation become rather the instruments of his death.

In a recent poem called "The Progressive Insanities of a Pioneer," Margaret Atwood writes:

> If he had known unstructured
> space is a deluge
> and stocked his log house-
> boat with all the animals
>
> even the wolves,
>
> he might have floated.[4]

The only effective defence for a garrison culture is to abandon defence, to let down the walls and let the wilderness in, even to the wolves. This is the advice that Miss Macpherson's Ark gives to an apprehensive Noah in the midst of the deluge. If he would but accept rather than defy the engulfing sea, his exile would end and he would discover instead his community with an apparently hostile universe. He would become Miss Macpherson's "Anagogic Man," discovering that he was not contained by, but himself contained the whole of creation. The majority of writers examined in the later chapters of the book appear to move towards a similar resolution of the problem of man's alienation from his world.

Again and again these writers dramatize the difficulty of affirming life in a world constantly threatened by absurdity, suffering, and death. Again and again they end by emphasizing the necessity of affirming life despite these threats. Particularly they emphasize the necessity of courage, not the courage to resist so much as the courage to accept, not the courage to defy but the courage to affirm, to love, and celebrate a world that sooner or later demands of them the sacrifice of their lives. Only within such an affirmation can man discover his identity and community with the rest of nature. The sense of threat may never entirely disappear; yet whether these writers share or do not share Louis Fréchette's sense of divine providence, they say as he does in "Les oiseaux de neige":

> Allez, tourbillonnez autour des avalanches;
> Sans peur, aux flocons blancs mêlez vos plumes blanches.[5]

With one exception, this book does not deal with the work of French-Canadian writers, largely because I did not feel competent to do so when I began. A closer acquaintance with French-Canadian literature, the poetry in particular, has convinced me that a combined study would have been profitable. Gilles Marcotte, in his book *Une Littérature qui se fait*, characterizes French-Canadian poetry as a poetry of exile. Here again the sense of exile springs from a garrison mentality. Here again it reflects both a purely French-Canadian reaction to an apparently hostile North American environment and a larger western reaction to an apparently hostile natural world. Two main differences between English- and French-Canadian literature reflect differences in their cultural and historical development. Compared to their English-Canadian counterparts, many French-Canadian writers have themselves been more deeply infected by the garrison mentality, and that mentality has been reinforced by the weapons of western culture that French Canada has traditionally emphasized for use against a hostile world, namely the spiritual weapons of detachment, of mortification and renunciation. English-Canadian culture has generally placed more emphasis on the material weapons for transforming the world, on technology and scientific technique. Both are satirized in Leonard Cohen's *Beautiful Losers*, for both may produce equally sterile results in their extreme form. But whereas English-Canadian literature tends to be haunted by the sterility of a materially abundant but overly mechanical order imposed upon life, French-Canadian tends to be haunted by the sterility of an overly ascetic order resulting from a complete withdrawal from life. Such a withdrawal is evident in French-Canadian poetry from Octave Crémazie through Emile Nelligan, Alain Grandbois, and Saint-Denys-Garneau to the early Anne Hébert. The disillusionment of the individual in his personal life, the French-Canadian in his national life, and the spiritual man in his worldly life, all lead to a withdrawal from the actual world of the present into a world of the ideal. It may be a world of the past, either a collective past of the *ancien régime* or an individual past, the world of childhood. It may be a world of memory or of dream, of the religious or of the artistic vision, but it tends in any case to become an ever more enclosed and barren ideal. Nelligan journeys to *le château de nos Idéals blancs* under a *clair de lune intellectuel*. Grandbois tends to become *le veuf d'une invisible terre*. Saint-Denys-Garneau withdraws to a bare room where he would strip himself to the bone and even prune the skeleton as one would prune a tree, lopping the branches from the top down. Anne Hébert moves through the rooms of her "Vie de châteaux" which are empty except for the mirrors from which spectres of the past emerge to embrace her in a barren shiver imitating love. The garrison mentality leads here from a closed garden to a closed room to the narrow world of the grave, where the only communion is the communion of saints, or of shades. The more recent work of Anne Hébert and of a generation of younger writers rejects this mentality, moving outward towards the world and towards action. It takes up anew the attitude of Louis Fréchette that would affirm life and celebrate the world whatever its imperfections or threats. These writers too insist that the voice that now needs to be heard must be the voice of the land and that the new pioneer must stock his log houseboat with all the animals, even the wolves.

Gabrielle Roy, the one French-Canadian writer actually discussed in this book, arrived at such a point of view very early in her career, and without having to go through the same painful disengagement from an oppressive garrison mentality that typifies so many writers in Quebec. No doubt because she was born in Manitoba, not Quebec. This fact, along with her talent, may help to explain why she was so quickly translated into English and recognized by English-speaking readers – long before the recent widespread interest in all things French-Canadian had begun to develop. Her work is included in this study partly because she has always assumed a place in Canadian literature, for English-speaking as well as French-speaking Canadians, and partly because the problems she explores, the way in which she resolves them and her over-all vision of life place her within the same imaginative world as that inhabited by the English-speaking writers discussed here. She speaks for Canadians, both English and French. For despite some very real differences in emphasis and in their literary language, both tend increasingly to speak in the same terms. Both would abandon the garrison mentality, knock down the walls and let the wilderness in, even to the intractable sea. Both have increasingly emphasized the creative role of language in the recovery of all that is inarticulate in their lives and in the life of the universe: its role in the creation of a larger community, not only between man and man, but between man and his world.

In "Le chevalier de neige," Gatien Lapointe declares that his country has surmounted the barriers of its fears and its defensive walls: "Mon pays a franchi ses frontières d'exil ... Mon pays a franchi ses frontières de mort."[6] His country stands erect on the threshold of a new spring. The sea, he tells us, has taken his country by the hand for the delights and torments of the world. Similarly Anne Hébert states that her country has arrived at a point in time analogous to the first days of the creation: "Notre pays est à l'âge des premiers jours du monde." Like the figure of A. M. Klein's anonymous poet in "Portrait of the Poet as Landscape," the writer and indeed everyman becomes the nth Adam taking a green inventory of a world but scarcely uttered. As Miss Hébert puts it: "Life here is a matter of discovering and naming: the obscure features we possess, the silent heart that is our own, all the land that extends before us waiting to be inhabited and possessed, and the confused words that issue in the night, all these seek to find expression in the light of day."[7] It is the same sort of world that seeks to find expression in Ernest Buckler's *The Mountain and the Valley*, in F. R. Scott's "Laurentian Shield," in John Newlove's "The Pride." For though the country of Anne Hébert or Gatien Lapointe, of Jean-Guy Pilon or Yves Préfontaine, is French Canada, the land of the Québécois, it is also North America and finally the world of Man, the Terre des Hommes that was the theme of Expo '67. The point is made by Yves Préfontaine in the introduction to his 1964 volume of poetry, *Pays sans parole.* Although he celebrates Quebec's rediscovery of itself as the birth of a country in specifically nationalistic terms, he insists that it must go beyond that to become the rediscovery of man and his world, "cette Terre que l'on dit être des hommes."[8] He sees in the new poetry in French Canada the first stammerings there of the North American as opposed to the European man. He agrees with Gilles Marcotte that to build a country one must do more than build roads, mines, and cities: one must reinvent Man.[9] That is the work of culture, and of a whole people. As F. R. Scott puts it in "Laurentian Shield," "what will be written in the full culture of occupations/Will come, presently, tomorrow,/From millions whose hands can turn this rock into children."[10] Yet the writer may symbolize the larger process. It pleases Yves Préfontaine to see the poet as total man, as a symbol of the whole man rooted in the earth as much as in any purely technical, narrowly human order. When Gatien Lapointe says the sea has taken his country by the hand, he sees the long arm of the St. Lawrence reaching in to where the five fingers of the Great Lakes grasp the heart of a continent.

The present vitality of Canadian literature in both languages, particularly of Canadian poetry, may be partly ascribed to a growing conviction as to the power of language in the recovery and definition of our experience, in the re-creation of our cultural vision, and in the articulation of a more profound and inclusive communion between man and the universe he lives in. In recent work we may detect something of the excitement of contributing to the full culture of occupation, an excitement that springs from a sense, as Irving Layton describes it in "The Birth of Tragedy," that someone from afar off blows birthday candles for the world. For Irving Layton as for Gabrielle Roy, the whole inarticulate creation cries out for expression. To give it expression is the job of the poet, the artist, the makers of human culture. And it must find that expression in a cultural vision that grows out of the rock, whether the rock is the Laurentian Shield or the globe itself. As Layton says in his poem "Butterfly on Rock":

> ... the rock has borne this;
> this butterfly is the rock's grace,
> its most obstinate and secret desire
> to be a thing alive made manifest.[11]

It is in this wider perspective that I should hope the present study might be read, for it sees the writers who are discussed here as contributing to that new birth and, whatever its inadequacies, would help to make their contributions manifest.

CHAPTER ONE

The Sleeping Giant

Neither capons nor pullets nor hens
Can wake the sun and the world;
Only the prophets of the Old Testament
Huge old cocks, all speckled and barred,
Their wings like ragged pages of sermons,
Only they from their roosts in the henhouse
Can rouse the bread from its oven-sleep,
Raise the smoke from the haunted chimney.
JAMES REANEY, "The Horn"

Many voices now agree that our chimneys are haunted. Mr Brian Stock, writing in the *Atlantic Monthly* (November 1964), argues that he cannot be accused of betraying Canada by leaving it; on the contrary, Canada has betrayed him by failing to provide him with a sense of identity, a sense of *patria*. "The trouble with you Canadians," says M. Pierre Bourgault, President of the Rassemblement pour l'Indépendance Nationale, "is you have no identification with your country."[1] Earle Birney begins a poem, "Once upon a colony/there was a land that was/almost a real/country called Canada."[2] Elsewhere he tells us, "It's only by our lack of ghosts we're haunted."[3] Leonard Cohen in *The Favourite Game* brings us back full circle to Mr Stock when he writes, "Some say that no one ever leaves Montreal, for that city, like Canada itself, is designed to preserve the past, a past that happened somewhere else."[4] In *Cité Libre* (mai-juin 1965) André Rosinger presents a very similar analysis of the Canadian mentality as it has developed historically, and he concludes his discussion of Canada's present situation by saying categorically, "Le Canada n'a que deux choix: ou grandir ou mourir."[5]

A small but growing line of criticism is concerned about the haunted character of the life reflected in Canadian literature. It is represented by W. P. Wilgar's "Poetry and the Divided Mind in Canada,"

Warren Tallman's "Wolf in the Snow," and most recently T. E. Farley's thesis submitted at Carleton University, "Love and Death in Canadian Poetry."

Whether they look at poetry or the novel, such critics uncover a picture of irresolution, of isolation and frustration, of exile. All suggest that Canadians have developed a kind of cultural schizophrenia, a division between their conscious aspirations and their unconscious convictions, which undermines their lives and leads to the development of a profoundly negative outlook.

For example, Mr Farley's reading of English-Canadian poetry presents a world in which the past is to be preserved whereas the future is to be resisted; in which intellect and will must rule over all passion and spontaneous impulse; in which, even so, human ideals, human loyalties, and love itself are constantly betrayed; in which man is burdened by a sense of guilt, and God, if he appears, becomes a God of Vengeance rather than a God of Love; in which frequent symbols of vitality and abundance, such as the sun and the sea, become more often symbols of paralysis and death, the Medusa sun, the capacious tombs of the sea. Death alone is both triumphant and final. English-Canadian poetry is a poetry of exile, increasingly negative to the point of being neurotic.

This view has been "suppressed, officially denied." So far I have not heard that Mr Farley has been shot, "as a precautionary measure." Still, whatever the weakness of his thesis, the point of view which he presents is not to be easily dismissed. It is an extreme development of Mr Wilgar's earlier essay. It comprehends or confirms in the poetry what Mr Tallman has observed in the novel, and it is supported by the comments of Mr Stock, M. Rossinger, and others quite outside the literary universe.

At any rate, it is clear that a number of critics have been able to characterize Canadian literature as essentially negative, even neurotic, and that they have suggested that this negative character reflects the absence of a positive national myth or a sense of identity. As Mr Wilgar would put it, it reflects "the inability of the Canadian to decide what he is or, more dangerous what he wants to be."[6]

My point is not that this view is wrong, but that it is a partial view. A closer study of Canadian literature reveals both positive and negative characteristics; more especially it reveals not only the anxiety which results from the lack of any clearly defined identity, but also, and sometimes simultaneously, a confidence that such an identity exists and is to be realized. Later I will illustrate how this duality reveals itself in a number of recurring images in Canadian literature, but first I would like to suggest a general way of looking at Canadian literature which would allow us to acknowledge the many negative characteristics and yet maintain that the literature has a basically positive character.

If we were looking for a single large or archetypal pattern in terms of which Canadian literature could be placed in perspective, the pattern of the Old Testament might suit us best. It is a pattern that would comprehend the critical view so far presented, but that would also allow us to modify that view. For if the world of Canadian literature is a kind of Old Testament world, if the literature to date is a kind of Old Testament of Canadian literature, we can say that it is finally no more negative and no more neurotic than the Old Testament of the Bible. And we can suggest that the poets and novelists who produced this literature are not simply the advanced victims of a national neurosis, but also the prophets of the Old Testament who can raise the smoke from our haunted chimneys.

If the world of Canadian literature is an Old Testament world, it is a world of Adam separated from his Creator and cast out of Eden to wander in the wilderness. It is a world of the scattered tribes of Israel, in exile from the Old Kingdom and not yet restored to the New, in bondage to foreign powers, aliens in their own land, tied to the law of the fathers from which their hearts tend nonetheless continually to turn away. It is a world of angry patriarchs and rebellious children, and of the prophets of the wrath of God. It is a world in which life in all its fullness remains distinctly a promise rather than an actuality. Its prophets go into the desert to listen to the still small voice, to wrestle with the angel, or to discover the mountain of God, the Sinai, Ararat, or Eden from which a Moses, Noah, or New Adam shall bring down the word and reveal the new order of the world. It is an Old Testament world which implies, sometimes without much hope, sometimes with great confidence, its completion in the New.

That Canadian history bears some resemblance to this Old Testament archetype is, I think, self-evident. Later chapters should reveal that the world of Canadian literature often does. Both Mr Farley and Mr Tallman make clear that it is often a world of exile and isolation, of guilt and conflict, a world in which the jealous God of the Old Testament is very much at home.

For the present, however, I would like to examine a number of images which are quite clearly related to this Old Testament archetype, and which illustrate the point that Canadian literature exhibits not only a sense of exile, or alienation from a vital community, but also a sense of expectation, or restoration to that community. Here we find the exiled Old Adam. Here we also find the sleeping Adam or dreaming Adam, who is a somewhat different figure. He is the sleeping giant, the major man, or, if you like, the personification of a world order, lost or as yet undiscovered. If there is a Canadian identity as yet unrealized, he is it. He embodies what James Joyce called the uncreated conscience of the race. Associated with this figure are the images of the Ark and of the Mountain, also potential symbols of a world order. These images appear in a variety of forms throughout Canadian literature, with varying degrees of positive and negative feeling, and reveal in a purely formal or archetypal manner something of the drama of the uncreated conscience of the race.

The images of Adam, Ark, and Mountain are practically all announced, if we include the title, in Margaret Avison's poem "The One Ship Beached on One Far Distant Shore."

> We sprawl abandoned into disbelief
> And feel the pivot-picture of old Adam
> On the first hill that ever was, alone,
> And see the hard earth seeded with sharp snow
> And dream that history is done.[7]

Here we are placed in exile. Our pivot-picture is that of Adam, once the major man at home in Eden but now cast out in the wilderness. In moments of despair (or perhaps of rational clarity) we dream that history is done, that our exile from a unified world, from a universal spiritual community in any traditional sense, is permanent. The one ship, the ark of life, is beached on some other shore, and the first hill that ever was, the World Mountain and seat of Eden, is seeded with barren snow. This is the negative form of the image. The same general image reappears in other contexts, and with only slight modification takes on a much more positive character.

Jay Macpherson's book *The Boatman* provides us with a kind of skeleton key to the equations and permutations into which these images may enter. With "Eve in Reflection" we begin, as in Miss Avison's poem, with an image of exile. Adam and Eve have been cast out of the garden, which is here symbolized by Eve's own reflection, "the lost girl gone under sea." And while Eve, "the mother of all living," lies contemplating her image locked behind the mirror of ocean, Adam wanders alone.

> The beloved face is lost from sight,
> Marred in a whelming tide of blood:
> And Adam walks in the cold night
> Wilderness, waste wood.[8]

The image of the garden, nature unified and restored to community with God and man, becomes in the fallen world a mirror image, a world locked behind glass, frozen in ice, or drowned in the sea. Interestingly, Eve, in some sense, tends to be locked in, Adam out. The garden is either unattainable or becomes a travesty of itself as the garden of the isolated ego, the garden of the little king as opposed to the garden of God, or the big king. This is Miss Macpherson's "Garden of the Fall."

> The garden where the little king
> Contemplates his loves in stone,
> Breathless, branching, in a ring,
> All for his delight alone.[9]

These negative images of exile appear elsewhere in more or less obvious form. James Reaney's "The Katzenjammer Kids" and "The School Globe" both present us with Edens from which the speaker has been locked out. Instead of the happy paper world of the school globe, he has inherited "The great sad real one/That's filled/Not with a child's remembered and pleasant skies/But with blood, pus, horror, death, stepmothers, and lies."[10]

In the strange poem "Arras" by P. K. Page, and in Phyllis Webb's poem "Marvell's Garden," we are presented with gardens of the fall where the speakers have been locked in. Miss Page says, "No one joins those figures on the arras."[11] And of her version of Marvell's Garden Miss Webb concludes:

> And I have gone walking slowly in
> his garden of necessity
> leaving brothers, lovers, Christ
> outside my walls
> where they have wept without
> and I within.[12]

More distant in time and in their connection with the Old Testament archetype are certain images in the poetry of Charles G. D. Roberts and Archibald Lampman. Roberts' poetry reveals a progressive withdrawal or deepening sense of exile, and though such poems as "The Brook in February" or "Ice" are ostensibly no more than occasional descriptive pieces, I would suggest that they are also symbolic, and that here again we find the image of the frozen garden from which man has been expelled. For example, the poem "Ice":

> When Winter scourged the meadow and the hill
> And in the withered leafage worked his will,
> The water shrank, and shuddered, and stood still, –
> Then built himself a magic house of glass,
> Irised with memories of flowers and grass,
> Wherein to sit and watch the fury pass.[13]

In a like manner I suggest that the image of Adam and the lost garden lies behind several of the poems of Archibald Lampman. In the longer of his poems, "In November," the speaker wanders through a waste wood and comes upon a circle of dead mulleins looking like hermits who have died at their prayers. In a brief moment of sunshine they revive within him a kind of spectral happiness. He is the exiled Adam who here finds intimations of the lost paradise. Other poems, such as "In October," "Winter Solitude," or the sonnet "In November," present related images. At the end of the sonnet the speaker says:

> Fast drives the snow, and no man comes this way;
> The hills grow wintry white, and bleak winds moan
> About the naked uplands. I alone
> Am neither sad, nor shelterless, nor gray,
> Wrapped round with thought, content to watch and dream.[14]

We may be reminded here of the man on the hill, alone, while the hard earth is seeded with sharp snow. Yet there is a difference. There is a sense of optimism here that was lacking before. Miss Macpherson provides an illumination of this image.

She presents the lost Eden as a memory, an ideal, a dream in the fallen mind. It is the "lost traveller's dream under the hill," as Blake identifies Satan. Thus the garden becomes identified with the dreaming Adam or, in pastoral terms, with the sleeping shepherd, which is the title of Miss Macpherson's poem.

> The gold day gone, now Lucifer
> Lights shepherds from the eastern hill.
> The air grows sharp, the grasses stir.
> One lies in slumber sunken still.
>
> Oh wake him not until he please,
> Lest he should rise to weep:
> For flocks and birds and streams and trees
> Are golden in his silver sleep.[15]

A related poem, "The Faithful Shepherd," identifies the sleeping figure with the ark, also a symbol of the totality of life unified and preserved from destruction.

> Cold pastoral: the shepherd under the snow
> Sleeps circled with his sheep.
> Above them though successive winters heap
> Rigours, and wailing weathers go

Like beasts about, time only rocks their sleep,
An ark upon a deep.
And drowsy care, to keep a world from death,
Maintains his steady heartbeat and warm breath.[16]

The speaker in Lampman's poems frequently becomes just such a faithful shepherd in whose dream, as in an ark, a world is kept from death. In Miss Macpherson's "The Anagogic Man" the same figure is identified as Noah.

Angel, declare: what sways when Noah nods?
The sun, the stars, the figures of the gods.[17]

We can now turn to a series of images which have been related already by Milton Wilson in his article "Klein's Drowned Poet." For as Eden becomes Ark, Adam in the snow becomes the poet in the sea. A vivid transition is provided by Duncan Campbell Scott's "The Piper of Arll." The piper in the little cove of Arll is a lonely shepherd. With the arrival of a mysterious ship, he hears the music of a larger life (associated in the poem with the more dynamic elements in his own little world). He strives to learn the music, but when the ship sails away without him he is heartbroken and accordingly breaks his pipe. Yet he mends it again, and as the mysterious ship returns he sings his soul out and expires. The crew takes his body to the ship, whereupon piper, crew, and all sink beneath the sea. Thanatos overcomes Eros. Negative as it may be, the conclusion remains haunting, rich, and beautiful.

The ship is another ark, and the sunken ark and the piper are one, just as in the case of the dreaming shepherd in whose faithful sleep the plenitude of Eden is preserved. Here too, the ship, the shepherd, and the crew become jewelled and "golden in their silver sleep."

Tendrils of or and azure creep,
And globes of amber light are rolled,
And in the gloaming of the deep
Their eyes are starry pits of gold.

And sometimes in the liquid night
The hull is changed, a solid gem,
That glows with a soft stony light,
The lost prince of a diadem.

And at the keel a vine is quick,
That spreads its bines and works and weaves
O'er all the timbers veining thick
A plenitude of silver leaves.[18]

The struggle between Eros and Thanatos, which is here so decisively won by Thanatos, becomes more open and violent as Scott's poetry develops. If the sleeping shepherd may be said to wake, he often does so only to rise and weep. Nevertheless, there is a deliberate attempt to recover the dynamic life which here lies sunk and to affirm what Scott calls "the beauty of terror" as well as "the beauty of peace."

A similar affirmation characterizes the poetry of E. J. Pratt, where the ark becomes more realistic, more mixed or ironic, but always struggles fiercely to stay afloat, as in "The Titanic" or "The Cachalot." The *Titanic* is, of course, an actual ship; but it is also the symbol of a world, an ark, and in part at least a false ark. The cachalot is very like a whale, but he too is an ark, capable of containing rivers, islands, and the little boats of men, sounding the heights and depths, gold and beryl in the sun and brushed by the sea gulls with their silver wings.

The whale is capable of being related closely to our initial image of the dreaming Adam, as the beast tells us himself in Jay Macpherson's poem "Whale:"

> I am an ark to swim the perilous flood.
> With gold and spices, with candles burning sweet
> In wakeful silence at his head and feet,
> Vaulted in my sepulchre lies the first man.[19]

As in the case of the garden, the whale may also appear in a negative or demonic guise. In Earle Birney's poem "Mappemounde" he becomes "*Cetegrande* that sly beast who sucks in/with the whirlwind also the wanderer's pledges."[20] In Phyllis Webb's poem "A Tall Tale, or a Moral Song," it is a fantastic fish story that brings us back to the garden of the fall or "Eve in Reflection."

> The whale, improbable as lust,
> carved out a cave
> for the seagirl's rest;
> with rest the seagirl, sweet as dust, devised
> a manner for the whale
> to lie between her thighs.[21]

Lying for ages under the sea, "this coldest whale aslant this seagirl's thighs," and the seagirl herself have turned to stone. The story makes sense if we see here Eve, "the lost girl under the sea," embracing the lost order Eden, which is equally her major man, the dreaming Adam.

The attempt to catch the world by the tail in all its manifold variety is an unlikely business. A. J. M. Smith offers a few directions in his

"Plot Against Proteus," where the imagery is drawn from a different mythology and old Proteus takes the place of the whale.

There are echoes of this theme in other poems on swimmers which Milton Wilson notes in F. R. Scott, A. M. Klein, and Irving Layton. However, it is Klein's "Portrait of the Poet as Landscape" which brings us back most directly to the image of the sleeping Adam. The shepherd or piper is now the poet. He too remains as effectively sunk beneath the sea of modern life as Scott's piper of Arll. Yet he too carries the secret within him and is, with the piper, "the lost prince of a diadem."

> Meanwhile, he
> makes of his status as zero a rich garland,
> a halo of his anonymity,
> and lives alone, and in his secret shines
> like phosphorus. At the bottom of the sea.[22]

His Old Testament connections are established a little earlier in the poem where we are told

> Look, he is
> the nth Adam taking a green inventory
> in world but scarcely uttered, naming, praising ...[23]

The poet in his formal guise is Adam, who gives names to the creation. Though he may be sunk in anonymity, he holds the key to the new Eden or "world but scarcely uttered."

Irving Layton has adopted the formal role of the nth Adam in a number of his poems, notably "The Birth of Tragedy," in which the speaker proclaims:

> In me, nature's divided things –
> tree, mould on tree –
> have their fruition;
> I am their core. Let them swap,
> bandy, like a flame swerve
> I am their mouth; as a mouth I serve.

Not quite drowned under the sea, in this poem the speaker says, "I lie like a slain thing/under the green air the trees/inhabit." And the note of expectancy is heard at the end of the poem, where we are told that all the while "someone from afar off/blows birthday candles for the world."[24]

In "the Cold Green Element" the drowned poet is hauled from the water, but later in a reincarnation returns to it as an active swimmer. At the beginning of the poem the speaker sets out from the end of his garden walk towards a mystery and finds the undertaker going in the same direction.

> Hi, I tell him,
> a great squall in the Pacific blew a dead poet
> out of the water,
> who now hangs from the city's gates.
>
> Crowds depart daily to see it, and return
> with grimaces and incomprehension;
> if its limbs twitched in the air
> they would sit at its feet
> peeling their oranges.

The last image may suggest the crowd in the pit at a Shakespearean play, or any old-fashioned hanging. In the context of the biblical archetype, however, the hanged man is a Christ-figure; he is not really or finally dead, though that is incomprehensible to the crowd. He has, in fact, found his resurrection in the speaker. Though the undertaker has seen his heart in the grass, though he has seen himself in the eyes of old women, "spent streams mourning (his) manhood," he is not dead; what they have seen or mourned was but one of his "murdered selves" which, like the poet hanging from the city gates, can be seen everywhere "hanging from ancient twigs." At the end of the poem he tells us, "I am again/a breathless swimmer in that cold green element."[25]

The image of the mountain appears more fleetingly in both its positive and negative guises. It appears explicitly as Ararat in F. R. Scott's poem "Lakeshore," where the speaker becomes a kind of pessimistic Noah watching the modern rationalistic world – indeed, all exiles from the primal ocean – go down before the flood. Yet we tend to adopt the point of view of the speaker who stands safe on the world mountain and who has already allied himself as a swimmer with the underwater world.

The appearance, I suspect, of this image in two poems, one by Birney and one by Layton, would seem to confirm Birney's pessimism and Layton's optimism. In Birney's poem "Bushed" the isolated man is finally destroyed by an increasingly alien and hostile nature, which at the end of the poem takes on the form of the mountain in its darkest guise.

> Then he knew   though the mountain   slept the winds
> were shaping its peak to an arrowhead
> poised

> And now he could only
> bar himself in and wait
> for the great flint to come singing into his heart.[26]

Layton's "Mont Rolland" presents a more positive version by far. Here the mountain is opposed to a commercial and industrial society which tries to tame it. But the speaker is not an alien. Filled with pity for the trees which like monks climb the exhausted hillside, he is one of the chosen, a kind of Moses.

> While all around me, as for a favoured intruder,
> There's an immense silence made for primeval birds
> Or a thought to rise like a great cloud out of a crater,
> A silence contained by valleys,
> Gardes Civiles in green capes.[27]

Frequently enough Layton is an angry prophet crying for destruction; he tells us of his kin when he says that from time to time he will take his hot heart to Ezekiel and Jeremiah, to stand awhile "in aching confraternity." Yet in the context of this discussion, he is the most confident prophet of a new life.

The Mountain and the Valley is a realistic novel which nonetheless brings us back to Margaret Avison's image of Adam on the first hill that ever was, alone, while the hard earth is seeded with sharp snow, or perhaps more exactly to Jay Macpherson's cold pastoral: the shepherd under the snow.

Buckler tells the story of David Canaan from his childhood to his death in early middle age. As he grows up and the members of his family get married, move to the city, or die, we see him increasingly isolated on his Nova Scotia farm. His isolation is not simply an individual or family matter. It reflects the disintegration of the old rural ways of life and the final failure of the cultural community of the previous generations. David is also aware that a new cultural community has not developed simultaneously with the development of the cities. There is no point in simply following his sister or his brother-in-law into the towns. The people there are only superficially better off.

> The town people seemed to have only a thin personal topsoil. Nothing grew on it but a sparse crop of self-assurance. They were absolutely unresponsive to anything outside their own narrow communion.[28]

More or less intuitively he has come to write. He keeps an old copybook in which he chronically attempts to come to terms with his experience and give it significance within an order of words. At such moments he escapes from his isolation. When he is not trying to formulate his world anew in this way, he finds that his most immediate life becomes unreal and his alienation total.

> Even the sensations of his own flesh had become outside. The inside was nothing but one great white naked eye of self-consciousness, with only its own looking to look at. The frozen landscape made no echo inside him.[29]

If he is to escape from this growing sense of unreality, he must do no less than remake the world in his own image – in his own words. His realization of this fact is associated with the realization of another ambition.

Ever since he was a boy, David has wanted to go up the nearby mountain, but something has always prevented his going; the death of a neighbour, some division in the family. Several times he has hoped to go with his father to cut a particular tree, one marked out for a ship's keel. Interestingly, his father is killed on the mountain, cutting the keel-tree. Having set off abruptly in anger against his wife, he fails to concentrate adequately on the job of felling the tree and is struck down as it falls. What was to have been a kind of ceremonial becomes no more than a tragic accident. The ark with that particular keel is never launched.

At the end of the book David finally makes it to the top of the mountain by himself. There he looks out over the whole valley, and there the urge to describe every minute thing, to express its unique intensity and find precisely the right word for its individual character, sweeps over him again. To do this, to be at all, he must be these things.

> He must *be* a tree and a stone and a shadow and a crystal of snow and a thread of moss and the veining of a leaf. He must be exactly as each of them was, everywhere and in all times; or the guilt, the exquisite parching for the taste of completion, would never be allayed at all.[30]

So he resolves to take a green inventory of this world but scarcely uttered. It will be like the day in his youth when he composed a petition for some of the villagers: "When he read it back to them they heard the voice of their own reason speaking exactly in his." This time it will be the voice of their world, of their lives, speaking exactly in his.

Up to this point he has been intimidated by the overwhelming task of finding words for every minute detail in every light and in every season. Suddenly he sees that he need find only the core or central word.

> It wouldn't be necessary to take them one by one. That's where he'd been wrong. All he'd have to do ... oh, it was so gloriously simple ... was to find their single core of meaning.[31]

The single core of meaning would be nothing less than a complete cultural identity, a central myth or fundamental conception of the world. That is what will restore him to the community of his fellow men. That is what will allow them to find their real community with each other, with the land, and with the dead as well. For the word redeems not only the present but the past.

> He caught his breath. He felt like the warm crying of acquittal again. Even my mother and my father and all the others who are gone will know somehow, somewhere, that I have given an absolving voice to all the hurts they gave themselves or each other – hurts that were caused only by the misreading of what they couldn't express.[32]

One of the things Mr Farley noted in his study of Canadian poetry was precisely the lack of such a communion with the past, which is here to be restored only with the complete reformulation of the world in new terms.

Unfortunately, the effort of climbing the mountain has overstrained David Canaan's already weak heart. Like Moses, he shall not enter the promised land. He dies of heart failure, and he and his vision lie like the faithful shepherd on the top of the mountain under the falling snow.

One more example should make clear the persistence with which this image recurs in Canadian literature. Gabrielle Roy's *The Hidden Mountain* is a more deliberately symbolic novel about the artist's role in the recreation or rediscovery of his world. The central character is an artist named simply Pierre. He too sets out to take a green inventory of the world. His isolation and solitude are concretely rendered by the setting. He journeys across the Canadian sub-Arctic from the Mackenzie River to Ungava, where he too finds his mountain. It rises in the wilderness unknown to all but himself and a few Eskimos. Fascinated by its shifting lights and iridescent beauty, he sets to work to paint it, not all at once, but aspect by aspect, for like David Canaan, he cannot at first comprehend it as a whole. In his preoccupations he paints through the short summer season and is caught in the first snows. It is then that he encounters a great buck caribou which he must hunt down to survive. It leads him an exhausting chase through a stony landscape of hell, until he brings it down, finally, face to face, with an axe. In the night, nearly dead himself he becomes as it were the blood brother of the great animal lying beside him. He survives.

Later a priest arranges for Pierre to go to Paris to learn to paint the mountain as it needs to be painted: so that it may speak to all men. He lives meagerly; his painting goes badly; he becomes seriously ill. Yet he paints a final self-portrait in which a friend discovers a strange and haunting power which he had caught glimpses of in Pierre's earlier work. The head, in a tangled thicket of shadows, seems to be sprouting horns, antlers. Like the great buck caribou, or like Michelangelo's Moses, he wears the horns of primitive divinity, the symbol of godhead or power. For Pierre is also a kind of Moses who has come down from the mountain bearing a vision of the godhead or universal power.

At the very end, having been given a drug to stimulate his heart, he feels prepared at last to capture the whole mountain on canvas. He sets to work, but in the midst of laying on the background colours, he too suffers a heart attack and dies.

> Forms, beloved images, dreams, the witchery, and the colours – all spun about, snowflakes in the storm, snow seen in a kaleidoscope.
> The lofty mountain faded away.
> Who, in the mists, would ever find it again?[33]

Despite the fact that Patrick Anderson was moulded by England and by the universities of Oxford and Columbia before his arrival in Canada in 1940, and despite the fact that like many others during the next few years he was much occupied by the war in Europe, he was nonetheless drawn into this whole question of a national identity. It is as if there was something sufficiently compelling in the Canadian situation that it drew the newcomer into it and forced upon his poetry certain typical forms of expression. For here again, some years before the appearance of Layton's "Mont Rolland," Buckler's *The Mountain and the Valley*, or Roy's *The Hidden Mountain*, we find the same imagery and the same theme. *A Tent For April* appeared in 1945. In "Montreal Mountain," part three of "Canadian Scene," Anderson describes Mount Royal:

> Lonely, hauling down rain,
> or full of summer birds untying the air,
> carrying the ribbons of air away in their beaks,
>
> mountain, volcanic mound and mindlessness,
> central, empty, a windswept giddy crown.

The mountain with its pregnant silence does not exist only in the country or in the wild stretches of Ungava; it is here in the midst of the city:

We used to say the loneliness and the mystery
were somewhere on the rims, a distant suburb:
we were wrong. They are here. Here in the center.

Again, the loneliness symbolized by the mountain springs from the failure to articulate a community of belief, a shared world of experience. Just as for Buckler at a later date, that loneliness is evident in the cities as much as on the farms. As if anticipating Buckler's David and Roy's Pierre and as if to warn the reader against interpreting these figures as no more than eccentric writers and artists whose thirst for completion is more aesthetic than anything else, Anderson states:

We thought it empty outside, over the frontier,
going North by a needle, a painter's and poet's trek,
leaving home and then on the ridges a crystal luck,

but it is more lonely here in the wind-crazed grass
by the artificial lake, by the flag, in the vast view,
where the dream is political, and the strangers are you and you.[34]

The dream is political as much as it is anything else, and the failure to give it expression colours the whole fabric of our social life.

In *The White Centre*, which Anderson published the following year, the poetry is everywhere haunted by a sense of a cultural vacuum and by the inarticulate presence of a dream that resides in the silence of the snow-covered land. In the remarkable "Poem on Canada," Anderson explicitly equates that inarticulate dream with a Canadian identity that has yet to be realized. To the question, "What are you?" the land replies:

... I am the wind that wants a flag.
I am the mirror of your picture
until you make me the marvel of your life.
Yes, I am one and none, pin and pine, snow and slow,
America's attic, an empty room,
a something possible, a chance, a dance
that is not danced. A cold kingdom.[35]

Canadian literature has no priority on the imagery of the Old Testament, nor on the themes of exile and alienation, the loss of identity, and the search for a new community. Yet our discussion of the images of Adam, Ark, and Mountain, along with other related images, reveals a persistent element in the Canadian literary imagination as it is represented by a variety of writers from Confederation to the present. And it suggests a continuing and distinctly Canadian concern with the question of our cultural identity. We have not, it suggests, taken full possession of our own experience and asserted our own convictions. Or, as Patrick Anderson puts it: "And the land was. And the people did not take it."[36]

That this should be so is not altogether surprising. It was inevitable that for Canadians, as for Americans, "The land was ours before we were the land's." But unlike the Americans, Canadians have had no intention of giving the gift outright, of finding "salvation through surrender."[37] They have been colonials not simply from necessity, but from choice. The early Canadians, says William Toye in his *Book of Canada*, "were not, and did not want to be, wholly independent. The cultural standards and interests they developed had little to do with Canada." He goes on, quoting from Edward Hartley Dewart in an early collection of Canadian poetry:

> "Not only are our mental wants supplied by the brain of the Mother Country, under circumstances that utterly preclude competition, but the majority of persons of taste and education in Canada are emigrants from the Old Country whose tenderest affections cling around the land they have left." Thus the colonial state of mind was succinctly explained in 1864. It was probably the most potent single enfeebling influence on the native voice and character; it prevailed long after Canada ceased to be a collection of colonies, well into the present century, and can even be detected today.[38]

As M. Rossinger pointed out in his article in *Cité Libre*, for the English-speaking colonists, whether they were frustrated Loyalists, frustrated Scots, or frustrated Irish, Canada was only a place in which to establish a new residence, not a place in which to develop a new way of life or build a new nation. *Des Canadiens? Non, des Européens désenchantés.*

The intention of each separate group of colonists to preserve an inherited culture rather than create a new one, even if that inherited culture had little to do with Canada, Mr Farley has labelled "the Loyalist response." It is this response, he argues, that lies behind the cultural schizophrenia he detects in the poetry. Canadians, he contends, have ignored the implications of their actual experience to the point where their authentic identity lies stillborn in the unconscious, at any rate in the realm of the inarticulate, so that they remain divided within and against themselves. Precisely such a state of affairs is symbolized by the images we have been looking at, the images of the drowned poet, the sleeping shepherd, the dreaming Adam under the snow. One of the examples clearly implies that we shall continue to be plagued by feelings of guilt, by "an exquisite parching for the taste of completion," until we are willing to surrender ourselves to our authentic experience, until we are willing to be the tree and the stone and the thread of moss and the crystal of snow.

What Mr Tallman said of Hugh MacLennan's novel *Each Man's Son* represents what he said of all the novels he examined: at the heart of the novel lies a conflict between the cultural façade and the crude violence of place. Again, these novels imply that the conflict is to be resolved only by rejecting the façade and accepting the authentic reality of the characters' everyday experience. For this reason, Mr Tallman is led not only to condone but to recommend the behaviour of Duddy Kravitz in Mordecai Richler's novel. He explains:

> Duddy has ceased to care for appearances and this insouciance releases him from the nightmare. All of the other people in the novel cannot possess themselves because their vital energies are devoted full-time to maintaining the false appearances in terms of which they identify themselves. These appearances – the cultural, ethical, communal pretensions to which they cling – mask over but scarcely conceal the distinctly uncultured, unethical, isolated actuality in which they participate.[39]

Duddy Kravitz's cry of "I don't care" is the cruder North American version of Stephen Daedalus's "*Non serviam.*" "I will not serve that in which I no longer believe, whether it call itself my home, my fatherland, or my church."[40] It is on the basis of this apparently negative resolution that Joyce's character sets out to encounter "the reality of experience and to forge in the smithy of (his) soul the uncreated conscience of (his) race."[41]

Our predicament is not unique. Ortega y Gasset in an essay on Goethe says even more generally:

> However much a man searches heaven and earth, the past and the future, for his higher destiny, he remains the victim of a perennial vacillation, of an external influence which perpetually troubles him until, once and for all, he makes up his mind to declare that right is that which is in accord with him.[42]

It is not unique, but it may have a uniquely Canadian application.

The trouble is that even though Mr Dewart's brand of colonialism may well retire with Mr Diefenbaker, the colonial state of mind may not. Whereas our mental wants were long supplied by Great Britain, since the Second World War they have been increasingly supplied, along with our investment capital, by the United States. So argues M. Rossinger, who fears that Canadians may become confirmed in the mentality of a satellite country, the mentality of a *satellite à béquilles*, the word *béquilles* meaning "crutches." Canada's leaders, he writes, "being conditioned to the mentality of a *satellite à béquilles*, a mentality which had always sustained them on a national level throughout the periods of childhood and adolescence, the transition was effected without regrets, and with the blessing of Great Britain."[43] That is, we have simply exchanged one external influence for another. With the possible exception of the French Canadians, who may have decided once and for all to declare that that is right which is in accord with them, we remain the victims of a perennial vacillation.

Margaret Avison protests against the world of "Someone not at home. Exporters. Glutting us: with Danish spoons." In "The Local and the Lakefront" we heard the voice of the prophet raised against the false gods of Sumer and Babylon.

> I, stevedore of the spirit,
> slog day and night, picketing
> those barges and brazen freighters with their
> Subud, Sümerian ramsgate, entrails and altars.

She frames her grievance ironically, in an image that is at once technical and symbolic.

> Who that must die but man
> can burn a bush to make a bar of soap?

She directs us to our salvation, if only by asking us to recognize that we have created nothing that is authentically ours.

> Committeman:
> there are no ships or cargoes *there*.
> Believe me. Look. Admit it.
> Then we start clean:
>   nothing earned; a nowhere to exchange
>   among us few
>   carefully.[44]

However negative the situation, this is not a negative poem. To discover an illusion and to recommend the acceptance of a reality, however bleak, is a perennial theme and a positive achievement, in literature or in life.

Some of the images we looked at earlier are even more bleak; a few may be brighter; the majority are ambivalent. They too tell us of a world that has not been realized; they also tell us that it exists, inchoate. It is this ambivalence which Al Purdy exhibits in a poem explicitly entitled "On Canadian Identity: A Sentimental Monograph for the Daughters of the Empire." The paradoxical conclusion suggests very nicely the Old Testament mood of one whose kingdom has not come but who is sure that it is there waiting for him to possess it. He says:

> The worth of life being not necessarily noise
> we kept unusual silence, and then cried out
> one word which has never yet been said.[45]

We *have* kept unusual silence. And we have no doubt cried out in our hearts the word which we have never said with our mouths. We may even have cried out in our literature the word which has not yet been read. In fact, I suspect it may be possible to trace in the literature certain elements of a Canadian view of life, a view of man and his relationship to the universe of a fundamental kind, which is surely what we must mean by a Canadian identity if it is to be anything more than a parochial difference in accent or in the details of economic and political organization.

The images of Adam wandering in the waste wood are patently images of exile. And one could emphasize the persistently negative conclusion to which all but one of our examples lead. Yet I think such an emphasis would be perverse. There is a good deal of difference between the exiled Adam in some of these images and the sleeping Adam in others – or the figure of David and Pierre pregnant with vision at the moment of death. Despite the heart failures, despite the fragmentary success of a David or a Pierre, there is a conviction that the major man is alive, that he is, or can become, "again a breathless swimmer in that cold green element." At this point, then, when many are expressing their doubts about the existence of a Canadian identity, when Mr Stock and others have in fact given it up as a lost cause, it seems to me possible to detect its presence, in the conviction of certain voices if in nothing else.

Ou grandir ou mourir? In answer to this question, let me quote what I hope is the voice of a prophet. She often speaks with an Old Testament accent. It is from the final poem in Gwen MacEwen's book *The Rising Fire*, the poem entitled "Generation Cometh":

> the boy
> a coy root or
> bright among cities
> is growing you
> cannot stop him
> growing.

try to
pull him out
by the roots
from your loins he
is green like a tree
planted there

he is in your dark garden
he will eat your dark flowers
you cannot stop him old
men old women you
cannot stop him
growing.[46]

The figure who emerges here from the inarticulate ground of our experience has his own entelechy, at odds with the conventions of our public world. We may "send him to school/or macabre churches," says Miss MacEwen, but we shall not stop him growing, we shall not stop him from satisfying his own taste for completion. If we now turn to explore the dark garden in which he has his roots, perhaps we may also discover something of the character of the generation that grows there.

CHAPTER TWO

Eve in Dejection

Come, flaunt the brief prerogative of life,
Dip your small civilized foot in this cold water
And ripple, for a moment, the smooth surface of time.
F. R. SCOTT, "Surfaces"

Whether in snow scene or a green season
whether through whipping grass or foundering amongst swans
the emptiness is always the arena
where you are the one.

When bird like a bright pilot steers in the trees
or the snow's blossoms bulge in the shut pines
whatever is haunting there on the horizon
is wanting your mind.
PATRICK ANDERSON, "Landscape"

The conflict between the world of appearances and the world of spontaneous feeling is frequently reflected in Canadian literature in a conflict between nature and culture, between man and the land. The life of the land has been central to the experience of most Canadians and to the literature which reflects their experience. It is the very warp upon which the early travellers wove the individual accounts of their experience in diaries and journals. But it also makes up much of the weave of the distinctly more "literary" writing. Yet in contrast to popular sentiment and much official publicity, this literature often records a marked resistance, even antipathy to the land. As Patrick Anderson says in "Poem on Canada," "And the land was. And the people did not take it."

Anderson's Aunt Hildegarde is representative of this failure to possess the land. She owns five thousand acres, including three unnamed lakes, but she has never seen them. She lives on Lincoln Terrace, "one of the genteel poor, unmarried, playing at patience." The trees and the streams, the birds, beaver, and butterflies–all the abundant life of her five thousand acres remains unknown or unavailable to Aunt Hildegarde. Its life lies buried in her unconscious. It inhabits the world of her dreams and stirs when she sleeps.

> When she sleeps, I thought, beside her medicine bottles,
> *It* does not sleep. Maybe the Indians cross it
> as shadows slur her features when she nods
> by the parlour fire, reading the *Globe and Mail.*

The land embodies the unrealized inner life of Aunt Hildegarde, and of Canada itself.

> When I grew older, I thought of those lakes as mirrors
> in which Aunt Hildegarde had never seen herself–
> brisk pits to show her soul and Canada's.[1]

Until we possess the land, says Anderson, we shall never possess that much lamented sense of *patria*, or, more radically, our own souls.

The land is both condition and reflection, both mirror and fact. Particularly in literature it comes to symbolize elements of our inner life. As these elements are ignored or repressed, the land becomes a symbol of the unconscious, the irrational in the lives of the characters. And the more powerful those elements are, the more disturbing and demonic the land and the figures associated with it may become.

Northrop Frye has remarked that he has "long been impressed in Canadian poetry by a tone of deep terror in regard to nature. ... It is not a terror of the dangers or discomforts or even the mysteries of nature, but a terror of the soul at something that these things manifest."[2]

What these things manifest, according to Anderson, is nothing less than our own vital instinctual life. Only too often, he argues, Canadians have looked into the land simply to confirm preconceived notions, commercial, political, or religious, of what they were, ignoring anything in the reflection which did not fit. If they did sometimes pay attention to what the mirror had to say, it was often in the manner of the wicked queen in Snow White, refusing to accept as final what her mirror told her. To extend the analogy, the attempt on the part of the wicked queen to eliminate Snow White is equivalent to the attempt on the part of the Canadian to suppress or eliminate his native impulses, his most authentic life. To the extent that he is successful, it will then lie in his unconscious, like a sleeping beauty in the heart of the forest, as in the case of Aunt Hildegarde. More actively, it may haunt his dreams and play the devil with his waking life.

We may see in this refusal to accept the land a particular aspect of that refusal to accept what Mr Tallman has called the crude violence of place, the attempt to live in terms of various communal, ethical, and cultural pretensions while ignoring the distinctly uncultured, unethical, isolated actuality in which the characters participate. More profoundly we may see in it a suspicion or even a fear of the irrational and instinctual that may be characteristic not only of Canadian but of western culture generally. There is no doubt that the land performs such symbolic functions in Canadian literature. And the drama that often unfolds around the divided attitudes towards the land would seem to reflect a real division within Canadian culture.

A certain ambiguity in his attitude towards the land is no doubt typical of the pioneer. For a time at least he must feel a certain sense of exile in the new world to which he has come. But from the very beginning there has been a real question as to the intentions of many who came here towards the land which is Canada. For some of the early explorers, as Patrick Anderson puts it, it was simply the wrong country. For many fur traders and timber merchants it was an economic resource to be exploited rather than a country to live in. As A.R.M. Lower points out in *The Making of Canadians*, well into the twentieth century many business families lived neither in Canada nor in Europe but, as it were, in between, crossing and re-crossing the ocean and erecting colonial outposts in their clubs in Montreal or Quebec. Even among those who came deliberately to settle and cultivate the land, its specific character, apart from the fact that it might be a British possession, seems frequently to have been secondary. The point might be illustrated by the story of Tarleton's Legion, men of the Carolinas, Georgia, and Florida, who fought on the side of the king in the American Revolution and lost.

As Thomas Raddall tells it in "The Harp Among the Reeds," they arrived in Nova Scotia in November 1783, three thousand men, women, and children determined to settle a section of that rocky coast simply because it had been given to them. They were warned against the attempt, but settle it they did, during one terrible winter, sawing logs at a sawmill several miles away, hauling the lumber by water, from which it emerged coated with ice, and erecting homes in December and mid-January. They established themselves until spring, when a forest fire drove them into the sea. From the shore they watched their winter's work and all they possessed reduced to a smoking ruin. Anyway, as the melting snow had revealed, no one could have farmed that patch of rock, sand, and bush and they had all been farmers, plantation owners, in the south.

Their example is suggestive. These men struggled fiercely to settle the land, but not precisely for the land's sake. They would have done the same had it been created by the devil himself, as perhaps it seemed to them it had. Raddall pictures them gathered for the last time to sing the old songs celebrating their martial exploits and the land they had left behind them in the south. "It had in it," he writes, "the pathos of that exiled Israelite beside the waters of Babylon, and when they sang of the sweet, the cool, the lovely Wateree, the tears sprang in all their eyes."[3]

For many of the Loyalists Canada was simply the prize of war, the booby prize. At best she was a sort of *fille du roi*. And not infrequently, as in the above case, they found that she had something of the devil in her. For later settlers like Susanna Moodie, the Loyalists themselves were often associated with the fallen character of the land. The Yankee farmer and his slattern daughter were for Mrs Moodie as insolent, scheming, and uncouth as any of the Indians. For a type of middle-class English gentry, the French and the Irish, the Italians, the Poles, and various others could be lumped together among the children of the devil, to be ignored or refashioned in the image of their betters.

For some of the explorers and trappers, voyageurs and settlers the land meant freedom and independence. They might embrace it with a passion. For a man like John Hornby, who died trying to winter in the barrens, the more difficult it became the more it was loved. But these were not the men and theirs were not the values which established the tone of cultivated life in the towns and villages. It was more the type of Mrs Moodie and the Anglican orthodoxy which established the tone of urban society. At a slightly more popular but also more pervasive level of society, especially in the more rural areas, it would appear to have been the Presbyterian and Methodist counterparts of Mrs Moodie who, in the long run, dyed the wool and wove the fabric of Canadian culture. In either case, whether inspired by taste or by morality, by religious or by social standards, it tended to be exclusive rather than inclusive, genteel or pious, or both, in a way that the majority of men and women and the lives they led were not. They created what Northrop Frye has called a garrison culture. For Hugh MacLennan, writing in *The Watch that Ends the Night*, the English-speaking community of Montreal as late as the 1920s could still be characterized in the words of a seventeenth-century traveller as an English garrison encysted in a large French village. The more strongly such a culture becomes entrenched and the longer it lasts, the more completely at odds with the world outside its walls it is likely to become. Less and less able to reflect the actual life of the land, it loses its authenticity and becomes mere pretension. What is vital and authentic in the experience of the community disappears from the conscious culture – goes underground. The official culture becomes more and more willed, more and more threatened by hostile forces without and by subversive forces within. The only real defence is to abandon defence, to surrender the garrison and embrace the life of the land. It is to give, as Robert Frost put it, the gift outright and surrender ourselves. It is by such a surrender that David Canaan in *The Mountain and the Valley* escapes from the isolation and unreality of his life. There the garrison is largely invisible. It subsists in his self-conscious awareness of other possibilities, of a different mode of life from that of his parents and neighbours, which sets him against his family, the farm, and the life of the land to which he is tied. But he realizes at last that his salvation lies not in leaving, but in accepting and articulating the very world that had seemed to threaten him. The joy which he feels just before his death springs from his resolve to become the voice of the land.

The struggle between a garrison culture and the land provides the basic pattern for W. O. Mitchell's *Who Has Seen the Wind*. Here the struggle between an authentic and an inauthentic way of life is dramatized as a struggle between the power élite of a small prairie town and the varied assortment of friends and mentors of the young boy, Brian O'Connal, all of whom tend to be associated with the land, with the life of the open prairie and, above all, with the prairie wind. Mrs Abercrombie, the banker's wife, and the Rev. Mr Powelly of the Presbyterian church, represent the official culture of the town. In their opposition to the Bens and to the school principal, Mr Digby, they reveal at length the essential hypocrisy and the final sterility of their attitude. Living outside town on the open prairie, the Bens embody the apparently amoral, animal vitality of nature. The Young Ben, completely indifferent to anything that is to be learned in school, is almost wholly identified with the life of the prairie, its gophers, grasshoppers, wind, and grass. As Brian observes, he always has the wind on his hair. The Ben keeps the semblance of a farm, does odd jobs, and brews moonshine in a still which he hides in his manure pile. The opposition to the Bens on the part of Mrs Abercrombie and the Rev. Mr Powelly is clearly an opposition to the land. In attempting to suppress and lock up the Bens they attempt to suppress and lock up the spontaneous vitality of nature. The result is likely to be precisely what happens when the minister tries to suppress the Ben's still. Driven further underground by continual harassment, the Ben pretends to join the church and to hold a steady job as caretaker, but the gesture is primarily a camouflage; he moves his still into the basement of the church itself. And there it explodes right in the midst of Divine Service.

The wind bloweth where it listeth and the authentic life of the spirit, as of the body, cannot be entirely suppressed. However, its representatives are, for the most part, outcasts from the established community and the official culture. From the point of view of the minister or the wife of the banker, they are delinquents, criminals, buffoons, or madmen. They and the authentic culture they potentially embody fail to find adequate expression. They are all wise fools, silent and inarticulate as the Young Ben, bitter and given to curses as Brian's Uncle Sean, mad and given to biblical raving as Saint Sammy, who lives appropriately enough in an unstrung piano box on the open prairie. There Saint Sammy pastures a magnificent herd of Clyde horses, not for any utilitarian purpose, but simply as "God's hired man."

The story centres on the growth of the boy, Brian. To further his education and complete his apprenticeship to life, it is to these outcast figures and to the school principal, Mr Digby, that the boy turns. Both their words and their example are more convincing than those of the established pillars of the society. Even the religious ravings of Saint Sammy are more convincing than the Rev. Mr Powelly's sermons, and they are backed up conveniently by nature itself. When the hypocritical Baptist, Bent Candy, who exploits the land with an impersonal army of tractors, covets Saint Sammy's Clydes and tries to drive him off the prairie in order to get them, Sammy calls down the wrath of God on the offender. The wind obliges with a tornado that flattens Bent Candy's barn and, like the Ben's natural spirits, explodes within the garrison of the town itself, causing fifty thousand dollars worth of damage and forcing the Rev. Mr Powelly and Mrs Abercromie to their knees in prayerful submission. Significantly, it does no damage to the farm of Brian's Uncle Sean.

The book has a happy ending since those who oppose the land are defeated and since Brian's education has been an education to the land. It is Uncle Sean who reveals to the boy his true vocation. Throughout the book Uncle Sean has fought to carry out a project to irrigate the land, a project for which he has found no support, but which he has initiated in a small way on his own. Uncle Sean is not only an embodiment of the land, but an active and intelligent human being concerned to preserve and cultivate it. At the end of the book Brian declares that he intends to go to the university to become a soil conservationist, "a dirt doctor." Except for the flatness of the prairie, the moral of the book might be summed up in the final verse of Patrick Anderson's "Landscape":

> O welcome the medicine man with the gay moral
> whose lovely politics are entirely love,
> who says that he is responsible to these hills–
> in him they shall move.[4]

In him they shall move whether he welcomes them or not. The same drama which unfolds in largely external fashion in *Who Has Seen the Wind* unfolds in internal fashion in Sinclair Ross's *As for Me and My House*. Here the characters are divided within and against themselves. And the land which embodies the authentic life of the

Rev. and Mrs Bentley becomes the more sinister and haunting as it reveals unconsciously their own suppressed vitality.

Philip Bentley has become a minister more or less by accident. Himself a bastard, child of the outcast culture, he was taken into the community and trained by the Church. Though he has never been convinced of either the Church's motives or its theology, he accepted its offer to send him to divinity school. He did so in order to escape from the prairie town in which he was born, and with the hope that in the city he might learn to become an artist. That hope was never realized. Ironically he has been sent back to precisely the type of prairie town he had hoped to escape. As the official representative of its culture, he is forced to lead a life that is a daily lie. A self-confessed hypocrite, he goes on serving a society and a religion in which he continually denies his own convictions. Though he has the talent to paint, he does not have the heart.

His wife is no better. Mrs Bentley has given up her career as a pianist for the sake of her husband's, which she diligently serves. Yet she knows the hypocrisy of his position. She knows he is a true artist and a false minister. Nevertheless she devotes herself entirely to maintaining that false position. It is in large part owing to her skill in dealing with people that her husband has been able to go on living a lie. She is in this respect divided against her husband as well as herself.

Alienated from themselves, from each other, and from the world around them, they suffer the same intense isolation as David Canaan in *The Mountain and the Valley*. They live under enormous tension, by force of will. Their creative energies are more and more paralysed, yet make more and more urgent demands upon them, finally shattering the superficial order of their little world. Throughout the novel that authentic but inarticulate life is associated with the world of the open prairie which lies outside and appears opposed to the world of the town. Mrs Bentley's attitude to the land is consequently ambiguous. It both draws and repels her.

The terror in regard to nature which Northrop Frye sensed in the poetry is distinctly felt and articulated in Ross's novel. Mrs Bentley and her husband spend a holiday at the ranch of a friend. Finding herself on the open prairie not far from the foothills of the Rockies, she writes in her journal:

> The wilderness here makes us uneasy. I felt it first the night I walked alone along the river bank – a queer sense of something cold and fearful, something inanimate, yet aware of us. A Main Street is such a self-sufficient little pocket of existence, so smug, compact, that here we feel abashed somehow before the hills, their passiveness, the unheeding way they sleep. We climb them, but they withstand us, remain as serene and unrevealed as ever. The river slips past, unperturbed by

> our coming and going, stealthily confident. We shrink from our insignificance. The stillness and solitude – we think a force or a presence into it – even a hostile presence, deliberate, aligned against us – for we dare not admit an indifferent wilderness, where we may have no meaning at all.[5]

The landscape and the flowing river do not pose here a metaphysical so much as a psychological question. The wilderness has become the mirror of Mrs Bentley's suppressed vitality. It is naturally hostile and deliberately opposed to her conscious will and to that conception of herself which her will sustains. It frightens her by revealing to her just how frail and superficial that conscious ego is when opposed to the power of nature, which is not to be denied. The dark river flows through her own unconscious and the terror that lies in the hills springs from herself. She does not wish to acknowledge these facts, but she is aware that what haunts her in the landscape is a reflection of herself: we think a presence into it, she says. In an earlier passage she suggests even more distinctly the nature and origin of this presence. She had gone out to where her husband was at work on a painting, trying to give expression to that part of his life which both he and his wife have persistently denied. She feels his rejection and leaves. Yet she feels in the land around her the same rejection.

> When I rounded a point and looked back and couldn't see the fire I was afraid for a minute. The close black hills, the stealthy slipping sound the river made – it was as if I were entering dead, forbidden country, approaching the lair of the terror that destroyed the hills, that was lurking there still among the skulls. For like draws to like, they say, which makes it reasonable to suppose that, when you've just walked away from a man because you feel he doesn't want to be bothered with you, you're capable of attracting a few ghouls and demons anyway.[6]

Fundamentally, however, Mrs Bentley cannot help but sympathize with the very forces that threaten her. They are the springs of her vitality. They have become demonic primarily because they have been forced underground. Were she completely successful in damming them up her life would become a dry riverbed. As it is, she invites a kind of paralysis or living death, and towards the end of the novel she notes that her fingers are becoming more and more wooden and that she feels as if she were slowly turning to lead. Intuitively, then, she aligns herself with the land against the world of her public personality.

The division between the land and Mrs Bentley's conscious self is repeated on a larger scale in the division between the land and the town.

The false fronts of the town are the concrete symbols of the public lives of the Bentleys. Both are garrisons besieged by the hostile forces of the wilderness. The whole situation is unmistakably revealed in terms of landscape early in the novel. Looking at one of her husband's sketches, Mrs Bentley comments:

> It's a little street again tonight, false-fronted stores, a pool hall and a wind. You feel the wind, its drive and bluster, the way it sets itself against the town. The false fronts that other times stand up so flat and vacant are buckled down in desperation for their lives. They lean a little forward, better to hold their ground against the onslaughts of the wind. Some of them cower before the flail of dust and sand. Some of them wince as if the strain were torture. And yet you feel no sympathy, somehow can't be on their side. Instead you wait in impatience for the wind to work its will.[7]

Mrs Bentley herself noticed that "the little town was too much like a mirror." In trying to escape from it on long walks to the railroad bridge, she has more or less unwittingly been trying to escape from her own false front. But if she secretly waits and hopes for the wind to work its will, it is through her husband that it finally does so. The wilderness enters their lives in the form of a girl named Judith.

Judith is a shy, almost inarticulate country girl who works as a maid in town and sings in the church choir. Like the Young Ben, she too has the wind on her hair. It is during a service quite early in the story that this connection with the wind is clearly established. There has been a long stretch of dry weather bringing drought. The community is depressed and the persistent wind that moans about the buildings and blows dust into faces and clothes makes the people edgy. Though still intent on "seeing that all the little proprieties of the service were carried out with nicety," the congregation is filled with anxiety and "an apprehensive sense of feebleness and isolation." They have all come into the official ark, but it fails to reassure them. Mrs Bentley shares their feelings. "I found it hard myself," she writes in her diary, "to believe in the town outside, houses, streets, and solid earth. Mile after mile the wind poured by, and we were immersed and lost in it. I sat breathing from my throat, my muscles tense. To relax, I felt, would be to let the walls around me crumple in." Their conventional Christianity cannot sustain them. Judith is the only one who does not sink before the flood, the only one for whom the wind is not an enemy.

> The wind was too strong for Philip or the choir, but Judith scaled it when she sang alone again before the closing hymn.
>
> The rest of us, I think, were vaguely and secretly a little afraid. The

> strum and whimper were wearing on our nerves. But Judith seemed to respond to it, ride up with it, feel it the way a singer feels an orchestra. There was something feral in her voice, that even the pace and staidness of her hymn could not restrain.[8]

Judith haunts the Bentley household in much the way that the wind haunts the congregation. Pale and timid on the surface, she is felt to be dark and passionate. Philip appears to ignore her, though each is obviously aware of the other. Like the land, Mrs Bentley both likes her and fears her. Uneasily, she keeps her around. When Mrs Bentley becomes ill, Judith comes in to help out. She does so by seducing the Rev. Mr Bentley.

As the wife becomes weak, Judith becomes strong. The passion which was exiled from the parlour finds expression in the shed. The shed at the back of the parsonage houses Philip's true life. It was prepared to make a room for an orphan boy whom Philip had tried to adopt, and it becomes finally the nuptial bed on which he begets a son of his own. In embracing Judith he embraces the wind and the wilderness within himself. In begetting a son in this embrace he is himself reborn.

Judith conveniently dies in childbirth. Since she represents equally the unconscious side of Mrs Bentley, there is a sense in which she does not die at all, but simply fades out as a separate figure. Symbolically she lives on in Mrs Bentley, who, having discovered her husband's affair, accepts it and, above all, accepts the child. In adopting him and giving him the name Philip they declare, in their own fashion, that they shall be responsible to these hills, to Judith and the feral vitality she embodies. A new wind blows through their lives, which now get off to a fresh start like the life of their child. They resolve to leave the church and lead a life which, though uncertain, is authentic. Even so, Mrs Bentley remarks in regard to Judith, "She'll haunt us a long time with that queer face of hers."[9]

In an unpublished discussion of pastoral imagery in literature, Jay Macpherson remarks on the tendency for landscape to become a mirror which generates "spectres and soul-mates, images of horror and desire." Of the latter as they appear in Canadian literature, she says, "The fleeing nymph, the elusive dream of the union of what is creative in man with what is idyllic in his vision of nature, is in this setting both the untouched wilderness retreating before him and the human Arcadian city he hopes to shape it into."

The figure of Judith may be seen as such a figure generated by the mirror of landscape. She clearly represents what is creative in the Bentleys and what is most potent, if not exactly idyllic, in nature. However, though inarticulate, she is hardly elusive, and though inconspicuous she can hardly be said to be fleeing.

Of various such figures that appear in Canadian literature, a few might be described as elusive, but a number are either silently pleading or plainly importunate. They offer themselves to the protagonist only to be rejected, sometimes temporarily, sometimes absolutely. In any realistic context these figures tend, like Judith or like the Bens and Saint Sammy, to be marginal members of society, outcasts or Indians. The half-breed is a particularly apt symbol of the divided mind. It is in terms of these figures and the reaction of the various protagonists to them that the quarrel between nature and culture continues to work itself out.

The figures are frequently feminine, but not always, especially if the central character is a woman. This is the case in Margaret Laurence's novel, *Stone Angel*, which centres around the formidable but terribly frustrated old woman, Hagar Shipley. Early in life Hagar had married Bram Shipley, despite the opposition of her father and of the community as a whole, only to reject him later on. In doing so she rejects the land and the spontaneous joy and creative fulfilment which she might have known in her own life. She embraces instead the barren security and respectability of the garrison culture, becoming the living embodiment of the stone angel which her father has placed over her mother's grave.

Hagar Shipley's father is a man of property, an energetic and successful merchant. He teaches his children the Scottish traditions of the family: clan, pipe-tune, and motto, "Gainsay who dare." He is a god-fearing man who fears no one, not even God. "God might have created heaven and earth and the majority of people, but," says Hagar, "Father was a self-made man, as he himself had told us often enough."[10] Still, he owns a pew in the church and never misses a Sunday service. He puts his real faith, however, in maxims such as, "God helps those who help themselves." One of the first things he teaches his daughters is the system of weights and measures. It is he who brings the stone angel, carved in marble, all the way from Europe as a proper memorial to place on his wife's grave. It is the petrified symbol of his cultural ideal.

Bram Shipley is his opposite, a bearded, ungrammatical, rudely virile ne'er-do-well, who swears better than he farms, keeps horses for the horses' sake and not for profit, likes to ride, drink, make love, and have children. He is a man who doesn't give a damn about property or proper appearances, though he loves the land as it is.

Hagar meets Bram at a dance. She discovers in him a passion and gaiety her own world lacks and marries him. But despite her marriage to Bram against her father's wishes, Hagar is made in her father's image. She cannot accept her husband as he is and tries to change him: to polish his grammar, correct his dress, furnish his house, and turn him into a successful farmer. She would refashion him in a style that the community respects. But Bram remains unfashionable, and when Hagar realizes she cannot remake him she rejects him. She leaves and goes to Vancouver, where she continues to serve the world of appearances working as housekeeper for a wealthy old man with a great houseful of furniture. Only towards the end of her life does she again reject the ideals embodied in the stone angel and welcome the world she had known in Bram. An old woman, ill, but utterly fed up at last with the neat, respectable, and yet perfectly barren life which her one surviving son continues to serve, she walks out of his house and goes down to the sea. It is one of her great and last adventures. Struggling down a steep bank, labouring through the underbrush and finally collapsing in what is, for her, a wilderness, she is yet intent upon rediscovering her identification with the land and the minute, teeming life of nature. Self-exiled from the streets and houses of the town, she spends the night in an abandoned fish cannery. Here she unbends, accepting the company of an unknown man, sharing his wine and his warmth, until she becomes so ill she must be taken to the hospital. Hagar Shipley has, in effect, returned to Bram and accepted what that masculine figure stands for.

To return, however, to that more purely feminine figure described by Miss Macpherson as arising from the mirror of landscape, let us take another look at Patrick Anderson's "Poem on Canada," where she appears in what may be her pure or pristine form. We see her there emerging from the continent at the moment of her first encounter with the European discoverer. Anderson's version of this encounter might well be compared with Louis Fréchette's in "La découverte du Mississippi." Whereas Jolliet's encounter with the North American wilderness has the character of an initiation into a religious mystery, that of Anderson's Renaissance man, *l'uomo universale*, has more the character of an operatic farce. The one is intent upon a sacred marriage, the other upon a profane seduction or rape. But some mix-up has occurred and *l'uomo universale* suddenly discovers he has got the wrong girl. Thus Anderson describes the moment of discovery:

> That moment when *l'uomo universale*
> crying with von Hutten "It is a joy to be alive,"
> captain and cousin of the Roman world,
> coined in the delight of the Medici banks, leapt
> upon the white sand of the continent!
> Yet shall we be in error if we say
> that then – as though by arrow shot – he fell
> down on his knees, God's cripple,
> and the clean sands were
> disordered by prayer and greed, as though by the wounded?

Planted a cross, claimed for a King, and stole
natives like curios, and hid his face
in the great purse of his soul?
For his America and Newfoundland
was not, after all, soft China like a girl's
expert monopoly in a lover's Trades,
but really the wrong country.
O here
in vast intervention island America
green as a tyro imposed her giant innocence
huge as the gardens of childhood.[11]

Perhaps we can detect in Anderson's conqueror who hides his marvellous corrupt face in the great purse of his soul a heroic version of Hagar Shipley's father. Here, however, he is not looking for stone angels, deliberately left behind in the museums and drawing rooms of Europe, but something more expert in a lover's trades. Looking for a mistress he has found an ingénue. The situation is awkward. He may leave her and continue his search; he may change his plans, woo her and take her in marriage; or he may simply corrupt her and use her for the time being. In the context, it is the last alternative he appears to choose.

The figure who here emerges from Island America is distinctly associated with all that is idyllic in man's vision of nature and with the humane order that might spring from its cultivation, with childhood and the garden. She might well serve as the embodiment of a conscious pastoral ideal, an ideal similar to the one which is deliberately pursued in Fréchette's poem. But when it is ignored or rejected as an ideal, as is the case here, it tends to return as an unconscious desire and to undergo a sea-change as it sinks into the subliminal world. In Philip Child's novel *The Village of Souls*, for example, the figure who emerges quite literally from the mirror of landscape (she comes out of the mist on the river) has changed her colour from white to brown. She too imposes herself in "vast intervention" before Jornay, the youthful hero of the novel.

Village of Souls is set in French Canada prior to the Conquest and takes for its theme that cultural dilemma which plagues the settler in the New World. Though Jornay has deliberately committed himself to the New World, his conscious ideal remains that of the Old, as he soon discovers when he meets Lys, a blonde and beautiful Parisienne. Lys is the representative of European culture, sophisticated in every sense of the word. Her fair appearance and polished manner are the product of an intimate if perfectly corrupt experience of aristocratic life in France. Jornay is dazzled by the surface refinement, by the controlled command of herself and her situation, that the girl possesses as the result of her father's fastidious training. What he does not see is that all her training was designed to give her an expert "monopoly in a lover's Trades," for her father lived as pander to men of wealth and position. Jornay idealizes the girl so that she can no longer recognize herself in his image of her. Lys becomes Jornay's stone angel. He falls in love with her and marries her, on the condition that he take her back to France, the last place in the world he wants to go.

The return is prevented, however, by the appearance of Anne. Dark, untutored, a half-breed girl who has come out of the heart of the continent full of vague dreams about white men and their ships with great white sails, she is everything that Lys is not. Yet when Jornay rescues the girl from a band of Iroquois, she falls in love with him and will not leave him. Infatuated with Lys, he is in the same awkward situation as Anderson's *uomo universale*; he doesn't know quite what to do with the simple young savage he has on his hands.

Later, however, when Lys, who has disappeared in an Indian raid, has been given up for dead, Jornay begins to recognize in Anne the qualities he admires and needs in his life in the New World: her practical ability, her steadfast loyalty, and her capacity as a woman to stir him with desire. Despite his continued attachment to Lys, and despite Anne's disfigurement from smallpox, he marries the girl. Yet Lys is not dead. Thus he becomes married to both, a situation which admirably symbolizes the psychological situation and the cultural dilemma from which it springs. Psychologically Jornay still suffers a split personality. The integration of his personality is effected, in Jungian terms, through a night journey into the unconscious, dramatized here by a journey through burned-over country to an Indian village that has been devastated by smallpox. This is the village of souls, and here they find Lys, the sole survivor, hardly more than a shade among shades. Only after Lys has been exorcised, only after she has stripped him of his illusions and herself expired like a wraith in a dream, does Jornay turn to embrace the girl Anne wholly and without reservation.

From some points of view, the figure presented by Anne might appear naïve, but not innocent. She is the embodiment of passion, but compared to the sensuality of the trained courtesan, Lys, Anne's is the spontaneous and creative passion of nature and animal life. That she represents the creative element in Jornay's own nature, indeed his instinctual will to live, is made evident in the course of the novel. Overwhelmed by the loss of Lys, Jornay lets himself sink into a torpor. He drinks and does nothing. One night when he is drunk and about to end his life by taking a phial of poison, the half-breed girl reappears and offers herself to him, practically forcing herself on him. Overwhelmed by exasperation as well as desire, he takes her, though he is immediately after ashamed of his own desire and furious with the girl for having seduced him into such a betrayal of Lys. Heaping insults on her in his rage, he rudely throws her out and locks the door against her. She is a mere animal. Yet her action has distracted him from suicide and roused in him once again his will to live.

The same drama of rejection is eloquently and poignantly developed in Duncan Campbell Scott's "At Gull Lake: August, 1810," though it is not followed by the same happy resolution. The story is simple enough. On the shores of Gull Lake, set in the rolling prairie, Nairne of the Orkneys has come to trade with Tabashaw, Chief of the Saulteaux. The negotiation is troubled by the fact that Keejigo, one of the Chief's wives, has taken a fancy to the trader and has come to offer herself to him. Annoyed, the Chief fires a couple of shots over Nairne's tent, whereupon the trader has the girl driven back to her master. Tabashaw in turn has her mutilated and thrown out of the camp.

Keejigo is unmistakably an image of desire which emerges from the mirror of landscape. A further development from the green tyro who appears in Anderson's "Poem on Canada," we might say that she is her daughter, the fruit of an illicit or subconscious union between the European conqueror and the North American wilderness. Like Anne, she is a half-caste, daughter of Launay, the Normandy hunter, and of Oshawan of the Saulteaux. Like Anne, her colours are no longer the white and green of childhood gardens of innocence; they are passionate, earthy, even barbaric. She sits before the trader's tents:

> Clad in the skins of antelopes
> Broidered with porcupine quills
> Coloured with vivid dyes,
> Vermilion here and there
> In the roots of her hair,
> A half-moon of powder-blue
> On her brow, her cheeks
> Scored with light ochre streaks.

Keejigo's is the wild beauty of nature, embracing its violence and its gentleness, its demonic as well as its idyllic moods. In Scott's own terms she embraces both the beauty of terror and the beauty of peace. Seen in the smoke of the campfire or in the close dark of the teepee, her vague dreams are coloured by the prairie flowers and by the lightning, by "sounds unheard – the echoes of echo," and by "voices of storm." She is Keejigo, "star of the morning," filled with "Premonitions of love and of beauty/Vague as shadows cast by a shadow."

She is inarticulate earth seeking to find expression in her lover's embrace. As the Indian girl Anne looked to Jornay for fulfillment, so Keejigo looks to Nairne.

> Now she had found her hero,
> And offered her body and spirit
> With abject unreasoning passion,
> As Earth abandons herself
> To the sun and the thrust of the lightning.

The girl's instinctive life is bound in the unconscious as her dreams are bound in the close dark of the teepee and she herself is bound in the primitive world of Tabashaw's wives. She turns to Nairne as to the sun, to find in him her release into the light of consciousness. She gives voice to this impulse in the song she repeats to herself in her own language, "the beautiful speech of the Saulteaux."

> The flower lives on the prairie,
> The wind in the sky,
> I am here my beloved;
> The wind and the flower.
>
> The crane hides in the sand-hills,
> Where does the wolverine hide?
> I am here my beloved,
> Heart's-blood on the feathers
> The foot caught in the trap.
>
> Take the flower in your hand,
> The wind in your nostrils;
> I am here my beloved;
> Release the captive
> Heal the wound under the feathers.

But Nairne is no prince come to rescue a princess, no Jungian hero who will release the anima from the grip of the Shadow. He is not here to make a marriage with the land but simply to exploit it. He is a trader. The girl is a savage, a mere animal, and when her appeals become inconvenient to the point where they may frustrate his commerce with Tabashaw, he has no hesitation in throwing her out, crying, "Drive this bitch to her master." Like other half-breeds in Scott's Indian poems, Keejigo now belongs to neither one world nor the other. She is rejected by both, and nowhere more violently than by the primitive world from which she emerged. When she returns to Tabashaw's camp the chief disfigures her face and blinds her eyes with a live brand from the fire. "Take that face to your lover," he screams. The old wives drag her away and throw her over a bank "like a dead dog."

Keejigo crawls away into the wilderness out of which she has come. And, like passions ignored and unrestrained by culture, the elemental forces of nature erupt into violence.

> Then burst the storm –
> The Indians' screams and the howls of the dogs
> Lost in the crash of hail
> That smashed the sedges and reeds,
> Stripped the poplars of leaves,
> Tore and blazed onwards,
> Wasting itself with riot and tumult –
> Supreme in the beauty of terror.

Passion exiled wastes itself in riot and tumult; the spontaneous animal energies which might be released in love and give life to human culture become destructive rather than creative. The crude violence of place remains as crude and violent as ever; the beauty of terror remains, the beauty of peace is cast out. So Keejigo is cast out, to lie like Miss Macpherson's Eve by the barren shore, while Adam wanders in the waste wood. Yet Nature's violence is spent with the storm and the beauty returns to the land:

> But Keejigo came no more to the camps of her people;
> Only the midnight moon knew where she felt her way,
> Only the leaves of autumn, the snows of winter
> Knew where she lay.[12]

Keejigo is the feminine counterpart of the drowned Adam, the sleeping shepherd, the dreaming figure who lies buried under the snow. The two figures may, in fact, be seen together in Howard O'Hagan's strange novel *Tay John*. Tay John, *tête jaune*, yellow head, is a semi-mythical figure, a half-breed born from the womb of his dead Indian mother. He comes out of the cave where she has been buried, as if out of the earth itself. A leader among the Indians, a guide to the white man, a hunter and trapper, he becomes a legend in the world of the Rocky Mountains. Yet he is at home neither in the world of the Indians nor in the world of the white man. In the end he becomes involved with a woman who, like himself, has always lived on the fringe of society. She bears the unlikely name of Ardith Aeriola. Whereas Tay John is linked with the mountain, Ardith Aeriola is linked with the plain. She was born "on the great plains of Central Europe, where the people wear forever the unchanging ring of the horizon upon their shoulders." A country girl, disturbingly attractive, extremely self-possessed, she has made her way, as a cabaret hostess and as a mistress to men of means, from Europe to America, always leaving in her wake an air of scandal. At the expense of a Canadian railroad executive, she has been brought from New York to Yellowhead Lake in the Rockies. When the highly distasteful Mr Dobble, the local entrepreneur who is intent upon creating a Canadian Lucerne at Yellowhead Lake, propositions the girl and is snubbed, Tay John comes to her aid. The whole camp turns against them. Outcasts both, they disappear into the hills, where they live together as man and wife. Later rumour has it that the girl is pregnant. They are last seen by a trapper crossing the mountains in a blinding snow storm. He meets Tay John, badly spent, pulling a toboggan. When Tay John asks him where he can find a doctor and then tells him he is going to the church, the trapper concludes he is bushed. As Tay John passes, the trapper notices that the toboggan bears the dead body of a woman. A little later, feeling guilty about leaving such a man to wander in the mountains, the trapper turns back to find him. He follows the tracks for some time, high up into the mountains, but when they fade out entirely he abandons the search. He had the feeling, he says later, "looking down at the tracks, that Tay John hadn't gone over the pass at all. He had just walked down, the toboggan behind him, under the snow and into the ground."[13] Tay John returns to the earth out of which he came. The child of the outcast culture remains stillborn. In search of an invisible church, the two figures who represent the authentic life of the spirit, as of the body, disappear from the scene. Rejected once more, male and female together, they lie sleeping under the snow.

The image of Tay John drawing his toboggan towards the invisible church evokes the story briefly told in Duncan Campbell Scott's "On the Way to the Mission." An Indian bearing the body of his wife to the local mission is trailed by two men who believe the toboggan is loaded with furs. The Indian is aware of them and of their malice, but he no longer cares. At dusk they shoot him and uncover their mistake, moving away like haunted men.

Exploited, outcast, violently rejected, the land or the figures associated with it remain to haunt the landscape. It would seem at moments to have become that savage place as holy and enchanted "As e'er beneath a waning moon was haunted/By woman wailing for her demon lover." For it is the feminine figure *par excellence* whom we find rejected and who returns to disturb the night.

There is a strangely related group of poems by Scott's contemporaries to which this pattern will provide the key. Roberts' "In the Night Watches," Carman's "Northern Vigil," and Lampman's "Midnight" are all dominated by the description of a moonlit landscape disturbed by a ghostly presence. The first two turn upon the memories of women and the tenderness, passion, gaiety which has been lost or abandoned as a result of the speaker's separation from them. The third is obsessed solely by a cry which issues from the dark landscape. It is the voice of the land, more particularly the voice of the feminine figure who embodies the land, of Eve, the "mother of all living," who lies in dejection by the barren shore. The point is more easily substantiated in another poem of Roberts', "Beside the Winter Sea." The woman who there walks by the barren shore is explicitly associated with the world of feeling, with unsatisfied and grave desire; whereas the speaker is explicitly associated with the world of reason. The bleak but potentially flourishing landscape is opposed to the speaker's "mind-worn dwelling." Were the two united, he declares, all summer's joy would lighten in her face. But he has put many miles and mountains between them and suggests no hope of his return. The other poems are likewise marked by a tone of loss and regret. What has been lost, we may suggest, is not simply a particular love, nor even the native experience of the land and of youth, as might be partially the case with Roberts, but the whole world of the spontaneous and irrational within themselves. It is that world conventionally symbolized by Eve, the world of the instinctive life, of passion, feeling, and intuition. This is the world that is feared or despised by the Rev. Mr Powelly, by Mrs Abercrombie as by Mrs Bentley, by the banker and the trader. It is the world represented by Bram and Tay John, and by Judith and Anne and Keejigo, by Ardith and by Carman's Gwendolyn, and by others not yet named. And it continues to cry out in the dark as it cries out to Lampman in "Midnight":

> No sound of man or wife or child,
> No sound of beast that groans,
> Or of the wind that whistles wild,
> Or of the tree that moans:
>
> I know not what it is I hear;
> I bend my ear and hark:
> I cannot drive it from mine ear,
> That crying in the dark.[14]

At its most profound, the drama which we have watched unfolding again and again is not peculiarly Canadian but characteristic of Western culture. It is a native variation of a theme found elsewhere in modern literature. The reference to Conrad's "Heart of Darkness" falls heavily in W. O. Mitchell's *Who Has Seen the Wind*, but is not irrelevant. The protagonist in Canadian literature is asked to accept the North American wilderness in much the same way as Conrad's Marlow is asked to accept the African jungle. The little prairie town and Conrad's Brussels, Paris, or London are equally the embodiments of a garrison culture which will remain superficial and precarious until it has recognized and accepted the wilderness, not as something alien and exterior, but as an essential element in its own life. Until it has done so, the landscape will remain haunted by voices crying out in the dark. For, as Patrick Anderson puts it, "Whatever is haunting there on the horizon/is wanting your mind."[15]

The images of the wilderness, of an Indian and other figures related to the land, provide natural symbols for the dark world of the psyche, the *yin* as opposed to the *yang*, but they are not the only symbols. Thus the same drama that we have seen enacted in terms of the land may be enacted in terms somewhat different. We may recognize in Anne Wilkinson's "The Pressure of Night" the same pattern of rejection, the same fear of the irrational, the same paralysis resulting from the refusal to accept this world of the dark powers.

> The pressure of night is on her.
> She lies stiff against her saviour sleep.
> Vicious as a scratch her cry
> "I love the light, I'll have no traffic
> With the nigger world of night."
> And her white flesh creeps.
>
> But night is, and blazed with eyes.
> Night has no shudder in
> Its whole dark hemisphere of skin
> And night replies
> "I am your shepherd lover,
> Root of daisy and the seed of clover,
> I am the poet's pasture."
>
> But she lies dumb
> Ice and fire die tepid on her tongue
> Scorched with cold, the unbeliever
> Resists her saviour.[16]

Miss Wilkinson gives us another portrait of the stone angel.

The scene may shift, but the pattern does not change. Morley Callaghan's *The Loved and the Lost* is set in present-day Montreal, but there we find the same conflict, the same feminine figure, associated in this case, not with the wilderness and the world of the Indian, but with the demi-monde of Montreal's St Antoine Street and the world of the Negro. And there we find the same pattern of rejection.

Peggy Sanderson threatens to disturb the delicate balance of the *status quo* in which various groups who make up Montreal's social world, each in itself a garrison culture, manage to co-exist. More particularly she jeopardizes the career of James McAlpine, the narrator and representative of the established society and its values. McAlpine finds himself inescapably drawn to the girl, whose courageous openness to the world around her calls in question the fundamental motives behind his present behaviour and, indeed, his whole life. Intimidated by the world since childhood, McAlpine has been engaged in a life-long search for security, which he hopes to find in material wealth, social prestige, and journalistic power. Like many others in the book, McAlpine believes that it is by the erection of barriers of race and religion, money and class, that order and security are maintained. A few, like McAlpine himself, may move from one class and one income group to another, as he has risen through the academic world to become an expert on political affairs and now prepares to move into the world of journalism as an editorial writer on a Montreal newspaper. He is on good terms with the owner; he might even marry his daughter. But the majority of people, it is implied, must stay where they belong. If order and security are to be preserved in social life, each must respect the lines of demarcation which have been drawn between groups. Peggy Sanderson does not.

Not surprisingly, Peggy Sanderson is the daughter of a small-town Methodist minister. Her mother is dead. Her childhood association with a Negro family, which, though poor in many ways, is rich in maternal affection and the real joy of family solidarity, meets with her father's opposition. She maintains her relationship with this family only at the price of defying all the social, racial, and religious barriers in which the various segments of the small community take refuge. Her childhood glimpse of a young Negro boy coming naked from the water provides her with a vision of what is most alive and beautiful. She develops a life-long sympathy for the Negroes and for the spontaneous warmth and vitality their lives exhibit.

Peggy Sanderson's approach to life is inclusive rather than exclusive. She does not fear poverty or social distance or the world of passion conventionally ascribed to the Negro. In Montreal she works in a factory and spends her evenings in a Negro nightclub on St Antoine Street. She loves the light, but she also loves "the nigger world of night."

The two poles of the irrational world which Peggy Sanderson embodies and would integrate are symbolized by the leopard and the church. She takes McAlpine to see them both. The leopard is carved in wood, crouching and ready to spring. It impresses McAlpine with a sense of "power, of lurking violence." The little church that she shows him is a mixture of Romanesque and Gothic but, above all, light and simple in proportion, as if "it could sail away lightly like a ship in the snow." He laughs at the incongruity of what he considers Peggy's enthusiasms, prompting the girl to say, "A leopard and a church. Don't they go together?"[17]

Though McAlpine replies, "From now on they do for me," he does not really understand how they go together, not at least in the girl. He cannot understand or really believe in Peggy. He cannot decide in his own mind whether she is simply a slut with perverse tastes, as his cronies around town have suggested, or an honest, unusually open and courageous individual, whose love he can accept without being made a fool of in the world's eyes. Because of his lack of faith, he leaves her on the most crucial night of her life, a night on which she has been rejected by the whole town, Negro and white alike. He leaves her when he alone might have embraced her and protected her and when, instead, she is violently raped and murdered.

At the end of the book McAlpine admits that he has lost the girl, and with her much of the potential joy in life that she embodied, through his own failure. "In a moment of jealous doubt his faith in her had weakened, he had lost his view of her, and so she had vanished."[18] She had vanished off the earth. And though he goes to look for it, the little church has vanished too. The power and lurking violence of the leopard, however, have been unleashed all around him in the fear and malice of Negro and white equally. And it has destroyed the girl as in Scott's poem "At Gull Lake" the rejected Keejigo is engulfed in a storm of violence and destroyed. Much as in Scott's poem, the beauty of peace follows after the beauty of terror. The life of the city regains its calm and the urban landscape is beautiful in the first warm hint of spring. But the beauty of the world now only stings McAlpine's eyes with a sense of pain. Everything, he tells us, "everything he saw began to hurt him: the corner store, the passing streetcar, the melting snow, the sound of the traffic, the width of St Catherine Street; it was a pain like the physical wrenching away of a part of his body."[19]

The pain is Adam's when Eve is wrenched from his side. McAlpine and the society he represents are divided against themselves. Psychologically he is torn in two. What has been lost in the separation embraces both the beauty of terror and the beauty of peace, the leopard and the church, the passion and the mystery which gave to life its intensity and its depth. Order is restored within the garrison, but what has been gained in security has been lost in joy.

Lying in the hospital, Hagar Shipley bullies a visiting minister into singing a hymn she remembers from childhood.

> "All people that on earth do dwell,
> Sing to the Lord with joyful voice.

> Him serve with mirth, His praise forth tell;
> Come ye before Him and rejoice."

The words strike Hagar with the force of revelation. Looking back on a long and essentially bitter life, she reflects:

> I would have wished it. This knowing comes upon me so forcefully, so shatteringly, and with such a bitterness as I have never felt before. I must always, always, have wanted that – simply to rejoice. How is it I never could? I know, I know. How long have I known? Or have I always known, in some far crevice of my heart, some cave too deeply buried, too concealed? Every good joy I might have held, in my man or any child of mine or even the plain light of morning, of walking the earth, all were forced to a standstill by some brake of proper appearances – oh, proper to whom? When did I ever speak the heart's truth?
>
> Pride was my wilderness, and the demon that led me there was fear. I was alone, never anything else, and never free, for I carried my chains within me, and they spread out from me and shackled all I touched.[20]

McAlpine walks in the same wilderness, and he is certainly not alone. If he is to emerge from it, as Hagar Shipley, Mrs Bentley, and others do, he must shake off the demon of fear and reject his concern for proper appearances.

Proper to whom? Hagar has asked. It is a good question. Proper, we might reply, to her father, the Manawaka merchant, or, more largely, to Anderson's Renaissance man, "captain and cousin of the Roman world,/coined in the delight of the Medici banks," that mixture of prayer and greed who represents the masculine logos of Western culture. For as we shall see, it is an exclusive, perfectionist ideal inherent in the schools and macabre churches of the traditional culture that leads to the rejection of Eve, the land or mother nature herself. And it is to the exposure of that idealism that various writers have addressed themselves.

CHAPTER THREE

The Dictatorship of Mind

The *reason* with its clear-swept halls,
Its brilliant corridors,
Where no recesses with their healing dusk
Offered asylum for a fugitive.

E. J. PRATT, "Dunkirk"

it is imperfection
the eyes see, it is
impreciseness they deserve,

but they desire so much more,
what they desire, what they hope,
what they invent,

is perfection, organizing
all things as they may not be,
it is what they strive for

unwillingly, against themselves,
to see a perfect order, ordained
reason –

and what they strive against
while they wish it, what they want
to see, closed, is what
they want, and will not be.

JOHN NEWLOVE, "In this Reed"

Anderson's *l'uomo universale* may leap on the white sands of the continent crying, "It is a joy to be alive," but he discovers in time that the very faith which assured him of his moral superiority to the wilderness and the very techniques which guaranteed him his power may drive all natural joy from his heart. The man who enters the wilderness with such triumphant joy ends by creating for himself a wilderness of pride and fear. He becomes the drab or desperate defender of the faith, for faith, as the author of *Tay John* points out, may be a heavy burden, especially if it is a faith in law, not love.

In this respect also, the world of Canadian fiction is frequently an Old Testament world, one in which man must live by the law and not by love. Were his kingdom come, he might escape from the world of the law into the world of grace. The individual protagonist may find such a personal salvation, but seldom does he escape from the problem of how to live in a world that continues to abide solely by the law. The whole body politic must be transformed, must accept the saviour sleep. Its salvation lies, not so much through the rejection of the law as through the acceptance of the wilderness.

The antagonism between nature and culture evident here is part of a larger drama involving the whole of western culture. After all, Canadian culture has been, and in many respects continues to be, a somewhat conservative extension of the culture of Europe. That culture has been more or less consistently Utopian. Rather than accept the world as it is, western man has sought to transform it, to refashion the world in the image of his ideal. Certainly he has enlarged his understanding of nature to an astonishing degree, but more often than not he has used this understanding to consolidate his power over nature rather than to extend his communion with her. He has persisted in opposing to nature the world of ideas, the world of his ideal, and in his idealism he has tended to become exclusive rather than inclusive, arrogant rather than humble, aggressively masculine rather than passively feminine. In extremes he has declared total war on the wilderness, woman, or the world of spontaneous impulse and irrational desire. At the least he has sought to subjugate these unruly elements within himself by force of will. More largely, he has sought to bind them in the body politic by force of law. And more ambitious still, with the increased confidence in his power, he has sought to control them in the world around him and even to eradicate them from the earth.

The nature of man and the human condition make it practically inevitable that some such conflict between man and nature should arise, but the proportions that such a conflict may achieve within any culture may vary considerably, as the difference in the traditional attitudes of East and West reveal.

Whether its ultimate vision is heavenly or earthly, western idealism tends to be narrowly rational. In its extreme form it tends to demand nothing less than the complete victory of mind over matter. Such a victory may require of a man that he either renounce the world or destroy it. An example of the former may be found in the religious ascetic. An example of the latter is provided by the young man who remarked to Loren Eiseley, with regard to the problem of overpopulation, "Why can't we just eventually kill off everything and live here by ourselves with more room? We'll be able to synthesize food pretty soon."[1] When man's idealism scorns all physical life or when, with what Eiseley calls "the colossal insensitivity of the new asphalt animal," it gets ready to annihilate all non-rational life, nature revolts. Life rejects the complete dictatorship of mind.

It is in this perspective that we may see behind the various representatives of established society opposed to the land or the world of night the one great figure of the European man, *l'uomo universale*. However diminished he might seem, it is he who speaks from the Rev. Mr Powelly's pulpit. It is he who, with his faith in the system of weights and measures, pauses above his accounts to look at his daughter, Hagar, applying the brake of proper appearance and impressing upon her the need to be ever vigilant in the service of his ideal.

Anderson's portrait of the European discoverer is nicely drawn, for it is frequently impossible to disentangle the three strands of *l'uomo universale*'s vision: his devotion to the Church, his devotion to the State, and his devotion to the Market. Mrs Abercrombie in *Who Has Seen the Wind* conceives it her duty as a leading citizen to serve as the conscience of the school-board, the pillar of the Church, and the voice of her husband, the banker. The Manawaka merchant is as diligent in his devotion to the Church as he is in his devotion to business. He supports all established institutions and he measures them all in much the same terms. Both he and Mrs Abercrombie keep track of the world in a system of debits and credits, the system of double entry bookkeeping that was the delight of the Medici bank and the Protestant ethic alike. Here their faith rests.

It is such a faith and just such a world that Stephen Leacock so abundantly satirizes, nowhere perhaps more pointedly than in "The Rival Churches of St Asaph and St Osoph." When the Reverend Edward Furlong, youthful rector of St Asaph's, comes to his father for help, the indulgent old man remarks, "I'm afraid you would never make an accountant, Edward."

> "I fear not," said the rector.
>
> "Your items," said his father, "are entered wrongly. Here, for example, in the general statement, you put down Distribution of Coals to the Poor to your credit. In the same way, Bibles and Prizes to the Sunday School you again mark to your credit. Why? Don't you see, my boy, that these things are debits? When you give out Bibles or distribute fuel to the poor you give out something for which you get no return. It is a debit. On the other hand, such items as Church Offer-

> tory, Scholars' Pennies, etc., are pure profit. Surely the principle is clear."
>
> "I think I see it better now," said the Reverend Edward.[2]

So do the other members of the two rival churches of St Asaph and St Osoph as they come to resolve their mutual problems in the light of the same higher vision. Mr Skinyer is the first to be enlightened, but it is Mr Furlong who again explains:

> "His idea is to form a new corporation to be known as the United Church Limited or by some similar name. All the present mortgagees will be converted into unified bondholders, the pew rents will be capitalized into preferred stock and the common stock, drawing its dividend from the offertory, will be distributed among all members in standing. Skinyer says that it is really an ideal form of church union, one that he thinks is likely to be widely adopted. It has the advantage of removing all questions of religion, which he says are practically the only remaining obstacle to a union of all the churches. In fact it puts the churches once and for all on a business basis."[3]

There has been some debate over the relative proportion of humour to satire in Leacock's work, and it has been suggested that Leacock's irony is that of a man who both loves and hates the object of his satire. No doubt that is true. No doubt Leacock had, for example, a keen appreciation of the material things in life and was yet concerned to satirize the reduction of everything to dollars and cents. More broadly, however, we may suggest that the consistent object of much of the satire is the attempt to reduce life to a system. The villain is the one who succeeds in exploiting the world by means of his system; the real fool is the man who is trapped in his own system, Mr Juggins, for example, in "The Retroactive Existence of Mr Juggins." Mr Furlong and Mr Skinyer and the other trustees of the churches of St Asaph and St Osoph are perhaps a combination of both. At any rate, though we may not feel any strong hatred for such figures, we certainly feel no sympathy for them. Those for whom we do feel sympathy are those whose very inability to comprehend or master a system prevents them from being caught in it. They retain their humanity. The hero of "My Financial Career" makes a hasty retreat from the bank; he makes no interest, but he retains his principal, and also his freedom. The barber who plays the stock-market in *Sunshine Sketches of a Little Town* makes a fortune only to lose it again; he comes back to selling eggs and cutting hair, to the warm and varied life of the little town. We sympathize with his loss, but also with his escape from an alien world.

We also sympathize with the Rev. Mr Drone. From the point of view of many in Mariposa, the Rev. Drone is a failure, not, however, because his sermons are dull or because his theology may be as weak as his Greek, but because he doesn't know how to put his church on a firm business basis. He can't raise money and he can't pay the mortgage on the Beacon on the Hill, the new church he builds. Yet his incapacity is his salvation. He remains a true man of the spirit. He loves children and model airplanes, both of which are more alive or dynamic than the matters of principal and interest or the traditional matter of sermons. The great revelation in his life is his trip across Lake Superior. His glimpse of the great lake and the wilderness stretching beyond it furnishes the material for many a sermon full of obscure parallels with the world of Galilee and the Promised Land. It is the land which again has provided the symbol for the life of the spirit, its inexhaustible power and variety. The old man is quite unequal to the task of expressing it, but he knows what it is. He is not just a ridiculous but kindly old man. The rejection of the Rev. Drone, insulted, dismissed, and pensioned off, is possibly the most poignant episode in all of Leacock's work.

Unlike the Rev. Drone, the successful churchman in Canadian fiction is opposed to the wilderness; and unlike the Beacon on the Hill, the church is usually a far more potent influence in the life of the community. In principle, if not always in practice, it has been the backbone of the garrison culture.

The faith of western man finds its most sublime expression in the spiritual idealism of Christianity. It tends to be Utopian and militantly opposed to nature. As such, it accentuates and provides the final justification for a militant secular idealism. An emphasis on faith, self-discipline, missionary zeal, a moral rigour directed against the pleasures of the flesh and the influence of the passions, these are virtues which may be prized by pioneer, businessman, and administrator alike. The Church wields a moral power equivalent to the financial power of the bank and the material power of industry and technology. And it is tempted to consolidate its power and effect its vision by means of a system, developing a body of dogma, ecclesiastical orders and laws, techniques of spiritual discipline, powers of censure and excommunication, all of which are designed to dominate and transform the savage in man.

The North American wilderness represented a spiritual challenge to the Christian idealism of Europe. It is the ardour of that idealism, stirred anew in the heart of the Old World and spreading to break like a tide on the shores of the New, that E. J. Pratt evokes in the first section of "Brébeuf and His Brethren."

> The winds of God were blowing over France,
> Kindling the hearths and altars, changing vows
> of rote into an alphabet of flame.[4]

And it is a fiery confrontation Pratt goes on to celebrate. The salvation of the savage devolves into a battle to the death between the Church and the wilderness. In fiction, if not in fact, they remain perpetual foes.

The battle is not always as pitched as it is in "Brébeuf and His Brethren." Seldom does the spiritual zeal find such heroic expression. Yet the conflict remains. It is evident in the distinctly genteel expression of Susanna Moodie's faith in the future, a mixture of the rationalism of the eighteenth century and the sentimental piety of the nineteenth. These are the weapons whereby man, even civilized man, may wean himself from the savage in his nature. A propos of the question of mental telepathy or "spiritual communication," she comments:

> The holy and mysterious nature of man is yet hidden from himself; he is still a stranger to the movements of that inner life, and knows little of its capabilities and powers. A purer religion, a higher standard of moral and intellectual training, may in time reveal all this. Man still remains a half-reclaimed savage; the leaven of Christianity is slowly and surely working its way, but it has not yet changed the whole lump, or transformed the deformed into the beauteous child of God.[5]

Mrs Moodie is right enough in some of the things she says. She could not, of course, foresee the events of the next century, in Europe and elsewhere, which would make her optimism appear a little shallow. More seriously, she could not foresee that it was precisely the things she so fervently recommends that were often to become the evil to be resisted. It is the exclusive and rather heavily rationalistic emphasis on higher intellectual and moral training that is often presented as deforming rather than transforming the human lump. It is the "purer form of religion" that frequently becomes one of the principal barriers to the fuller discovery of that holy and mysterious nature of man, and which helps to ensure that man remains a stranger to the movements of the inner life. In their rationalism, both disciplines, secular and religious, seem increasingly sterile in the fostering of love, joy, and a sense of creative adventure.

As we have seen, it is the conventional Christianity of Peggy Sanderson's father, the Methodist minister, that acts as a barrier between the girl and her fellow men in *The Loved and the Lost.* It is the conventional Christianity of the Reverend Mr Powelly, the Presbyterian minister, that seeks to expel or to bind the breath of the spirit in *Who Has Seen the Wind.* It is the conventional Christianity of the Rev. Mr Bentley, the Anglican minister, which acts as a self-imposed prison for the creative vitality of both man and wife. The Church provides the framework, if not the whole fabric, of the false front which the community erects against the winds that blow through their lives.

We are a long way from the missionary zeal of a Brébeuf or even from the still strenuous ideal of Mrs Moodie. "In return for their thousand dollars a year," Mrs Bentley tells us, the Christian congregation of the little church in Horizon expect "a genteel kind of piety, a well-bred Christianity that will serve as an example to the little sons and daughters of the town."[6] The only savages they wish to save are the children, their own. The others, like the prairie wind, are kept without. Such, Mrs Bentley explains, was her husband's experience.

> Whatever it might profess, he soon found, the Church was for only the approved and respectable part of the town. Little Main Street churches, no bigger than their Main-Street-minded members, are like that sometimes, and a little Main Street church was the only one he knew. Right or wrong, he made it the measure for all churches.[7]

Certainly the big city church in Morley Callaghan's *Such is My Beloved* bears him out. Here it is the conventional Christianity of the Catholic Church that proves exclusive and crushes the attempts of a lonely priest to enlarge his communion. The Bishop and the congregation completely frustrate the priest in his campaign to help two prostitutes, leaving the girls on the street to fend for themselves and finally driving the priest into an asylum where, in the world of the presumably insane, he can concentrate on the *Song of Solomon*, the world of love and not of the law.

However genteel the Church may become, its God is a jealous God. He is the Mosaic God who handed to man the tablets of the law and who sits in judgement on their lives. And his vengeance may be great; exile is the least the transgressor may expect. Even within the community his rule divides one from another and each from himself. It is such a God that Hugh MacLennan portrays looking down on the world of Cape Breton in the novel *Each Man's Son*.

> If God looked down on them that summer, the kind of God their ministers told them about, He must have been well pleased, for by the summer's end all of them except Alan were conscious of their sins. Longing to do their best, they had discovered there is no best in this world. Yearning for love, they had found loneliness. Eager to help one another, they had made each other wretched. Dreaming of better lives, they had become totally discontented with the lives they led.
>
> If an omnipotent and interested God looked down on them that summer, irony must have been one of His pleasures. For here in Cape Breton were these innocent ones, eager to make themselves worthy of the great world of Europe from which their ancestors had been driven long ago; and there across the sea was that great world of Europe,

> enjoying the final summer of its undisturbed arrogance. For this was the year before 1914.[8]

The stern Presbyterian God whom MacLennan portrays is the embodiment of that European idealism which rejects the world as it is; the more the men and women in MacLennan's novel strive to live up to its ideals, the more they must reject their actual lives. As Dr Ainslie, the central character in the book, comes to realize this, he rebels. In his rebellion he is finally forced to reject not only the stern Presbyterian God, but the whole logic of his life. It is only gradually, however, that Ainslie comes to realize that the ethic which stems from his father and which has informed his career has made him as ruthless towards himself and towards others as is the wrathful God he denounces.

Ainslie's marriage, like Philip Bentley's, has been barren. Like Philip Bentley, Dr Ainslie wishes for a son. And symbolically if not literally like Philip Bentley, he is given that son by another woman who is destroyed in the process. For Ainslie develops an affection for the son of a poor young woman whose husband has gone to the States and never returned. He can see no reason why he should not take the boy from his mother, since he can offer him so much more in the way of education, money, prestige. But in his callous disregard of the feelings of the boy and of his mother, Ainslie helps to drive the girl into another man's arms. In doing so, he helps to drive her to her death, for the husband, a broken-down prizefighter, returns to find his wife with the other man and he kills them both. The child becomes his, but at a price and amid a violence he had hardly anticipated.

Yet the whole tragedy was symbolically prefigured and implicit in the lives of his parents, a point brought out by his friend, Dr MacKenzie. It is during their conversation one evening that Ainslie is led to speak of his parents, saying of his father, "He was a remarkable man even though he had no education besides what he learned from the Bible and Bacon's *Essays*." It is a revealing comment. The Christianity of Ainslie's world is only one of the foundations of its faith. The other is science, whether pure or applied, whether chemistry or medicine or simply double-entry book-keeping. Behind them both stands a faith in the law and not love, in reason and not intuition, in the will and not impulse. Ainslie may have doubted the religion of his world, but up to now he has never doubted science, that world of higher intellectual training which Mrs Moodie ranked side by side with a purer religion in her campaign against the savage in man. It is a faith which in both cases serves an aggressive masculine ideal that would dominate and even destroy a more passive feminine nature.

It is frequently the fate of individual men and women in Canadian fiction to illustrate this pattern of aggression by acting it out in their personal lives. It is, for example, no accident that Hagar Shipley's mother dies in childbirth. Hagar is the spitting image of her father, and at the moment of her conception he had as good as placed the marble figure of the stone angel on his wife's grave.

Dr Ainslie's mother illustrates the pattern even more clearly. The doctor has never really valued his mother. In fact he has expressed the fear that he has inherited her weakness of character. He has admired rather his father's strength of will and single-minded devotion to the ambitious ideals he has conceived for himself and his children. A poor farmer, he refuses to borrow even when his barn burns, preferring to starve rather than jeopardize the chance of giving his sons an education. As a result, Ainslie has become a doctor and his two brothers ministers. Their mother was quite different. As Ainslie himself remarks, she always thought "it was more important for us to eat than to learn. She had none of his will-power. She died shortly after the barn was rebuilt and we were more or less on our feet again."

She died of pernicious anaemia. Dr MacKenzie knows because he attended her shortly before her death and told Ainslie's father that the woman was starving herself to death by giving her share of what little there was to her children. "You would do well," MacKenzie concludes, "to honor your father less and your mother more. She was a very loving woman."[9]

The puritanical ethic which starves the body to feed the mind has no place for love; for it demands that man love perfection, and no man is perfect. This ethic, which Ainslie has imbibed from his youth, which he has clearly inherited from his father, he associates above all with the Presbyterian God, that God who, "out of His all-wise justice, has decided that nearly all human beings are worthless and must be scourged in the hope that a few of them, through a lifetime of punishment, might become worth saving." Such a God, he decides, is nothing but the invention of "mad theologians," and has no necessary connection with Christ. Yet it is the God of the Christian Church, and it is the Church he blames for inflicting upon man such a hopelessly Utopian ideal of justice. It is the curse which has blighted their lives, his own, that of his wife, Margaret, and the lives of generations of men and women in his world.

> Underneath all his troubles, he told himself, lay this ancient curse. He thought desperately of Margaret and desperately of himself, and he knew that it was his fear of the curse which had hobbled his spirit. The fear of the curse had led directly to a fear of love itself. They were criminals, the men who had invented the curse and inflicted it upon him, but they were all dead. There was no one to strike down in pay-

> ment for generations of cramped and ruined lives. The criminals slept well, and their names were sanctified.[10]

The Utopian idealism which Ainslie discerns in the Presbyterian informs the whole spiritual vision of European man. It is enshrined in the heart of his culture, and in contrast to the situation in "Brébeuf and His Brethren," it usually enjoys a position of power. F. R. Scott reminds us of this point in his satirical reaction to Pratt's poem, itself entitled "Brébeuf and His Brethren."

> When Lalement and de Brébeuf, brave souls,
> Were dying by the slow and dreadful coals,
> Their brother Jesuits in France and Spain
> Were burning heretics with equal pain.
> For both the human torture made a feast:
> Then is priest savage, or Red Indian priest?[11]

There are few burnings in Canadian literature; yet in most of the examples we have looked at the heretic is relatively alone and defenceless against the community, which brings to bear on him all its powers, ecclesiastical, social, and financial. As a rule it prefers to isolate rather than immediately annihilate those who rebel, leaving them out on the street or out on the open prairie, placing them in an orphanage or on a reservation, locking them up in a cell or in an asylum. Yet criminal, outcast, madman, he is the hero, and whether he survives or is crushed his is the moral victory. In this respect also, the literature normally reverses the pattern of "Brébeuf and His Brethren."

Even within the context of Pratt's poem, where Brébeuf is undeniably shown as winning a moral victory over his enemies, it is hard to concede him a profoundly spiritual victory. He manifests great courage. We are impressed by the strength of his endurance, the pride of his will, the unshakeable loyalty to his faith, and the implacable defiance of his enemies which he reveals throughout. But these are the virtues of the noble soldier who dies in defence of the cause, virtues his enemy also admires and frequently possesses. One cannot help feeling that he is too exclusively the commander of the Jesuit army and that his cause is too narrowly that of a militant European culture, of the law and the prophets, Rome and Judaea.

> And sometimes the speech
> Of Brébeuf struck out, thundering reproof to his foes,
> Half-rebuke, half-defiance, giving them roar for roar.

Was it because the chancel became the arena,
Brébeuf a lion at bay, not a lamb on the altar,
As if the might of a Roman were joined to the cause
Of Judaea?

Though Pratt takes pains to deny that the strength of Brébeuf finds its source in the power of the Church or the State, it is nonetheless a rather martial image he gives us, the cross itself becoming the rude image of a naked power, cut by the straight-edge of reason and held together by the iron of Rome. Not from Richelieu's robes or Mazarin's charters was the source of his strength to be found, but rather:

in the sound of invisible trumpets blowing
Around two slabs of board, right-angled, hammered
By Roman nails and hung on a Jewish hill.[12]

In a world of grace, nature is redeemed by love, not power. The example of Christ is that of a man who gives up his life *for* the savage and not *in defiance of* the savage. His sacrifice redeems the fallen world. But in the mirror of fiction, the established church or conventional Christianity is all too often a lion at bay, not a lamb on the altar. Sometimes it only mews, but even when it roars it is doomed to defeat. For the true church, the authentic breath of the spirit, though invisible or lost in the snows, continues to exist. It is alive in the wilderness, and all the powers of night and of nature paradoxically come to its aid. Even as the priest may be savage, the Red Indian may be priest. Still, as Callaghan's true priest may appear insane, so the wilderness may emerge as the demonic parody of the Church. So it appears in Patrick Anderson's "Poem on Canada."

despite the priests, the North could beat their bible
(enormous, vague and louder than all their prayers)
where the bearded bear would prophesy like Isaiah
and the grey wolves howl – moon haloes on their hairs –
in the pulpit rocks. Or, in ikons of their lairs,
burned those red eyes unlit by any priest,
while down the Gothic glades there bellowed a moose
of agony size, with a crown of thorns like Christ.[13]

Father Rorty, the strange priest in Howard O'Hagan's *Tay John*, would understand this imagery. He is very much aware of the irrational power and violence of life. He knows that the true strength of Christianity lies in the acceptance of the destructive element and not in an exclusive idealism.

> Beauty and Truth, Truth and Beauty. But violence first. Beauty affronts the world by its violence. Its violence draws man and affrights him. Without the Cross our Saviour's life would not be beautiful. It is from His agony, not from His words, that the leaves of the poplar-tree are never still.[14]

Even so, Father Rorty's Christianity is more a matter of words than of existential passion. His Church is an essentialist Church, a garrison which opposes the letter of the law to the violence of life. More avowedly than a man like McAlpine in *The Loved and the Lost* or the Rev. Mr Bentley in *As For Me and My House*, Father Rorty is a man who fears life. The narrator tells us that he has taken refuge in the Church from a family of brawling brothers. The priest himself, in a highly personal confession to a woman he has fallen in love with, tells us of his fear of the world. "Yes," he writes, "I fear. I fear the men about me. I fear the mountains – great waves of rock, tipped with foam, waiting to break upon me who walks in their valleys. I fear this cabin where I write tonight, my hand, shadowed by the candle, moving great upon the wall." It is finally his own irrational nature, the shadow which has grown so much larger than his conscious rational self, that the young priest fears. Tay John makes the point explicit, remarking, "The woman is afraid of wind, of high country, of a wolf howling. But he is afraid – I think he is afraid – of himself."

The priest's defence is his faith. Unlike the much more unpleasant but highly enthusiastic entrepreneur, Mr Dobble, the priest behaves like a tired man, prompting the narrator to observe that faith may be a heavy burden.

> There it is distinct from belief. Dobble was a man who believed. What a man believes in, he pleasures in, and his mind assents to his pleasure. A man believes in a thing, as Dobble believed in Lucerne, but a man has faith in a principle, in a doctrine, in a rule of conduct. He trusts to his faith. He may not believe in it. He may even doubt – but a man cannot believe and doubt at one and the same time.[15]

These remarks take us to the centre of the problem, not only of Christianity, but of the whole culture as it is portrayed in Canadian literature. The evidence of our literature, and also of our history, would indicate that we are a people who have tried to live primarily on the basis of faith rather than belief. We have persistently placed our confidence in principles, doctrines, rules, rather than in ourselves or in the spontaneous processes of nature. And only too often we carry this faith, or these faiths, as a burden; we do not altogether believe in the doctrine or tradition we live by. Or, though we may believe in a principle, we may not believe in the actual cause for which the principle led us to fight. It is such a dilemma that Thomas Raddall dramatizes in his story "At the Tide's Turn," in which a Nova Scotia magistrate, with no sympathy for the government in Halifax or even the government in London, yet remains loyal to the Crown – because of his faith in law and order. Because of that faith he is led to oppose and to fire on a group of rebellious Yankee sympathizers, despite the fact that in doing so he kills fellow townsmen and even his own brother. As the narrator says of Father Rorty in *Tay John*, we may often find ourselves in the position where we live *by* our faith rather than *for* it. And our lives may give us no pleasure. Quite the contrary, whatever gives us pleasure we may come to suspect. Nevertheless, we may confess in secret, as Father Rorty confesses, our doubt in our faith and our admiration for the life of impulse, for the person who places his confidence in nature, or, quite simply, in life itself.

Ardith Aeriola, the unlikely object of Father Rorty's affection, is just such a person. She has followed her impulses to the end, till they have brought her "to the shores of this green mountain lake." It is she who makes the priest most acutely conscious of the weakness of his faith and who drives him to make a retreat in the mountains in order to come to terms with himself. And it is she who receives his confession. As Father Rorty puts it, she will understand more than most women would. But further we may say that she is his confessor, the priest of the wilderness, against whom he has sinned. And so he writes:

> Yes, you have heeded the cries of your spirit. In that way you are a more spiritual woman than I a man, for I have passed my life battling the impulses rising within me. I am a man with a faith and am bound to it, as Our Redeemer finally was nailed to His. Perhaps a man with a faith is always a material man, for he comes to prize too dearly the tangible symbols that hold him and confirm him in his way. A priest who desires and has the Love of God cannot be humble. Like all men of possessions he comes to fear the outer world. He lets the cassock, that is for his body, cloak his soul as well.[16]

Idealism leads naturally to materialism. The more of nature one succeeds in excluding, the more formidable the enemy grows. Fear follows pride and leads to a renewed emphasis on the tangible symbols of one's faith, the ritual, doctrine, system with which it may be sustained. As the wind envelops the little church in Horizon, the congregation is filled with anxiety and is more than ever concerned to see that all the forms of the service are carried out to a nicety. To little avail.

Similarly, in E. J. Pratt's "The Roosevelt and the Antinoe," the formal symbols of the Christian ritual are powerless before the savage forces of nature. The words are blown away by the wind of the storm.

This is no quiet little Main Street affair. Pratt is concerned with an immediate and actual shipwreck. During the rescue operation men die and are buried. Prayers are quite general. But the storm continues and quite explicitly disintegrates the Christian Service.

> With separated phrase and smothered word
> An immemorial psalm became a blurred
> Bulwark under erosion by the sea.
> Beneath the maddening crashes of the wind
> Crumbled the grammar of the liturgy.[17]

Earlier, in "Night Hymns on Lake Nipigon," Duncan Campbell Scott had attempted to celebrate the triumph of Christianity in leavening the lump of savage nature. There when the dark waters of the Nipigon were still, it appeared that there had been a marriage.

> Sing we the sacred ancient hymns of the churches,
> Chanted first in old-world nooks of the desert,
> While in the wild, pellucid Nipigon reaches
> Hunted the savage.
>
> Now have the ages met in the Northern midnight,
> And on the lonely, loon-haunted Nipigon reaches
> Rises the hymn of triumph and courage and comfort,
> *Adeste Fideles.*
>
> Tones that were fashioned when the faith brooded in darkness,
> Joined with sonorous vowels in the noble Latin,
> Now are married with the long-drawn Ojibwa,
> Uncouth and mournful.

Even then, however, there was some doubt that the marriage was complete, that the uncouth Ojibwa would remain an obedient and faithful spouse to the noble Latin. The poem concludes on an ambiguous note. While the waters were still, the notes of the hymn flew out in the darkness "like a dove from her shelter," returning "in circles of silver, To nest in the silence." But when the whispering waters come alive, there is some question as to the fate of the dove. The storm breaks and whelms everything in the accompanying deluge. "All wild nature stirs" with the phrases of the hymn, but there is some question as to whether it is stirred solely with sympathy.

> Back they falter as the deep storm overtakes them,
> Whelms them in splendid hollows of booming thunder,
> Wraps them in rain, that, sweeping, breaks and onrushes
> Ringing like cymbals.[18]

If there is a doubt here, there is none in Pratt's poem. The psalm is not as immemorial as the sea, and is powerless against it. Here the Dove is blown away and lost. The Christian vision and the image of the Cross cannot raise a Lycidas from the depths nor still the savage menace of the waves.

> But no Gennesaret of Galilee
> Conjured to its level by the sway
> Of a hand or a word's magic was this sea,
> Contesting with its iron-alien mood,
> Its pagan face, its own primordial way,
> The pale heroic suasion of a rood.

The only way to deal with the situation here is by:

> ... getting down again into the sea,
> And testing rowlocks in an open boat,
> Of grappling with the storm-king bodily,
> And placing Northern fingers on his throat.[19]

It is Conrad's solution: in the destructive element immerse, and by the exertion of your hands and feet, make the deep, deep sea bear you up.

It is, finally, Scott's solution as well. The one figure in his poetry who really commands the demonic irrational power of nature is the Indian shaman in "Powassan's Drum," who calls the headless and terrible figure of evil out of the lake, in the midst of the storm, and sends him back again. Scott himself was the son of a Methodist minister, and he left the Church to go, as he wrote, into the wilderness to find his religion.

It is Father Rorty's solution, going into the mountains to make his retreat. There, albeit inadvertently, he dies on the Cross in imitation of Christ. His cross is, furthermore, an actual tree. Its roots reach down in the earth, even as its branches, there on the mountain, reach out to the stars. And there on that Cross, the priest feels that the arms of the tree are his arms and that its movements in the wind are his movements. He feels his roots stir in the dark soil and he feels himself being lifted, his feet pulled from the ground.

The priest's death is not unmixed with irony. It is a foolhardy passion he enacts, and he discovers how to die rather than live. The narrator's final reflections on Father Rorty's end point up the irony. As the priest was dying, what, the narrator wonders, was before him: "the shape of the Cross, the vision of his faith, or the face of the women – pale, round, close and real as the moon that stared him down? Or up there, so high above the earth, was there only the sound of the wind blowing, and far away the sound of running water where men who thirst may drink?"[20] Father Rorty's foolhardy passion is to be compared with the foolhardy action of his brother, Red Rorty. One embodies the Catholic, the other the Protestant tradition of Christianity. One embodies a religion of faith, the other a religion of belief, but both are militant and exclusive, and both brothers are crucified on the tree of nature. And in both cases it is the Dionysian world of woman which precipitates death. One does not submit to the sea with impunity. Of the two examples, Red Rorty's excessive violence is more fruitful than his brother's excessive passivity. In taking an Indian woman, though another man's wife, he fathers Tay John, the half-breed: the man who knows the wilderness as he knows himself and is yet master of it.

Again and again, the protagonists who win a spiritual victory are those who come to terms with the savage, accepting it within themselves and yet not allowing it to destroy them. On a personal and psychological level, it is a Jungian integration of the personality that they achieve. On the cultural level, it is an integration of the Apollonian and Dionysian elements of nature. In purely Christian terms, it is the redemption of the Old Adam by the New. These protagonists have entered into a world of grace, a world whose God does not pass judgement on a fallen nature alien to his perfection, but rather enters into it and takes upon himself the burden of sin and death. He includes in his salvation the whole of suffering nature. It is the Red Indian, Anderson's medicine man with the gay moral, "whose lovely politics are only love, who says that he is responsible to these hills, in him they shall move," who is thus his authentic priest.

However, as the fate of Tay John indicates, the community refuses, as a rule, to recognize such a priest. It retains its exclusive Utopian ideal and continues to live in an Old Testament world. But as it becomes evident that the doctrine, rituals, and spiritual techniques of the Church are powerless against the forces of nature, the community shifts its emphasis from divine to natural law, from theology to science, from the power of the Church to the power of technology.

The shift in emphasis begins in the Renaissance with the birth of *l'uomo universale*. The division in knowledge and the new bias in favour of natural science is clearly announced in the work of Francis Bacon, the co-mentor of Dr Ainslie's remarkable father. It was Bacon's hope that the power of science and its applications would free man from the terrors of the universe, natural and supernatural, and by creating an order of material abundance would allow man to live more freely and fully in a kind of new Eden, an earthly paradise in which the anxieties of want and of ignorance and even, in time, the threat of physical pain would be eliminated. Yet even in Bacon, who stated the axiom that nature to be commanded must first be obeyed, we can discern the militant rational ideal of an older faith which sees it as a right and a duty to exploit the whole of irrational nature to its own ends, for the benefit and comfort of man and the greater glory of God. The ideal remains Utopian, essentialist, perfectionist. And it leads, as Lampman was one of the first to dramatize fully, not to a new heaven on earth, but to a new hell.

Lampman's "The City of the End of Things," written before Henry Ford had made his first Model-T, exposes with visionary clarity the ultimate conclusion to which this logic leads. In the City of the End of Things, as Mr Eiseley's new asphalt animal proposed, all living things have been killed off – including man himself, the last irrational surd in the system. Set in the valley of Tartarus, it is an infernal city of fire and iron, filled with the roar of machines which operate automatically in a "hideous routine." The multitudes of men that once inhabited the city are gone. Three of the master controllers, like carved idols in an iron tower, and the gigantic mindless idiot at the Gate, staring towards the lightless north, are all that remain. When they are gone all will stop:

> And over that tremendous town
> The silence of eternal night
> Shall gather close and settle down.
> All its grim grandeur, tower and hall,
> Shall be abandoned utterly,
> And into rust and dust shall fall
> From century to century;
> Nor ever living thing shall grow,
> Nor trunk of tree, nor blade of grass;
> No drop shall fall, no wind shall blow,
> Nor sound of any foot shall pass:
> Alone of its accursed state,
> One thing the hand of Time shall spare,
> For the grim Idiot at the gate
> Is deathless and eternal there.[21]

Rational man disappears from the earth; dumb nature remains.

It is precisely the power of technology that, by permitting man to realize his ideal more fully than ever before, it reveals to him the sterile and self-destructive character of that ideal. The more he succeeds in reducing life to a purely rational and mechanical system, the more surely he destroys the human spirit and life itself.

The prose parallel to Lampman's infernal city is provided by Frederick Philip Grove's novel *The Master of the Mill*, where the logic behind it is explicitly stated. Nowhere more clearly than in the work of Grove is the shift from a spiritual to a secular emphasis portrayed as simply a shift in tactics on the part of a single, exclusive, and intransigent idealism. And perhaps no purer embodiment of this idealism could be found in fiction than in Grove's Edmund in *The Master of the Mill*.

Grove himself is something of a heretic and outcast, his own life exhibiting some of the distortion and queerness we associate with such fictional outcasts as Uncle Sean or St Sammy in *Who Has Seen the Wind*. Having no faith in the Church and no faith in material progress, and living on the fringe of a society largely founded on such faith, he necessarily appears pessimistic and perverse. His voice is that of an outcast culture. "I am profoundly distrustful," he writes in his autobiographical *In Search of Myself*, "of what is called civilization. Perhaps one has to have lived – as I have done; as I am doing – on the frontier, or beyond the frontier – of a life that is reasonably secure in order to understand why I call the present civilization the consolidation of barbarism ... "[22] A large element of that barbarism which Grove attacks might simply be labelled materialism. But fundamentally, what Grove subjects to scrutiny, tests in dramatic action, and finally questions in novel after novel is the arrogant and aggressive masculine logos, the God or father figure of western culture. One suspects that he was also fighting elements of this figure in his own personality. It would appear certain that he had to contend with such a figure in dealing with his own father, an experience which no doubt sharpened his awareness of the problem.

Unquestionably, a theme which preoccupies Grove in his earliest as in his latest novels is man's will-to-power and its ultimate futility. That will-to-power may find expression in rural terms, in the desire to conquer the land, to build a large farm, house, and family and to establish over them all a patriarchal rule. It is such a dream that motivates Abe Spalding in *The Fruits of the Earth*. It is such a dream that inspires John Elliott in *Our Daily Bread*, where the story of Abraham and his sons provides the archetype of the patriarchal dynasty he dreams of establishing. The will-to-power may also find expression in more urban terms, in the desire to dominate the whole economy, to control the productive machinery of society, and to establish a patriarchal order in which the masters of the machine look after and order the lives of the masses as if they were children. Such is the dream that inspires Edmund Clark in *The Master of the Mill*. Their vision may find expression in either biblical or Baconian terms, but the impulse and rationale behind it remain the same. It is the impulse to impose upon nature, upon the life of the land as upon human life, an ideal order.

To justify his grandfather's burning down his flour mill for the insurance money to build a new one, Edmund Clark argues: "The old man had the courage to sweep a worn-out world into limbo. He had long wanted to shape the mill to man's ultimate purpose. In him he felt the power to make nature subservient to his design, to the design of man himself."[23] Men like Edmund or his grandfather are not merely demagogues or dictators; they are idealists. It is a higher law they serve and a transcendent design they seek to impose. Unlike Anderson's medicine man, they are not responsible to the hills, or to the human lives which they make subservient to their design, or to the laws of man (such as the law governing arson). Nor, ultimately, are they responsible to themselves for their own actions. For a man such as Amundsen in *The Settlers of the Marsh*, as for John Elliott in *Our Daily Bread*, the order which he would impose on the world is a divine order; it is not his will but the will of God that he serves. Similarly, for a man such as Edmund in *The Master of the Mill*, the order that he would impose on the world is the order of fate; it is not his will he serves but the future, destiny, the dialectic of history. Edmund, when asked by his father what he would do to alleviate the social injustice, the political and economic confusion and stagnation that he sees in the world around him, replies: "Nothing. I am humbly content to be the tool of evolution; or, if you prefer, to experiment."[24]

Edmund's answer means that he will fully automate the flour mill, continue his efforts to monopolize and control the economy, and generally follow the logic of the machine and of mass production to the end. His wife objects that this will only lead, as it has led in the case of the local mill, to a situation in which men will be "justified in their very existence only by the needs of the machines."[25] Edmund is unperturbed by the prospect. It is inevitable whether he wills it or not. He will therefore continue to serve history as others humbly serve the will of God. To that end he will spend his life in the creation of a state which, as he puts it, will be "based on social and economic realities instead of on political jugglings which have long since become meaningless. With only one master, one god: the machine."[26] Above all, Edmund points out, the new order will establish "a dictatorship of mind over matter."

Except for Lampman's City of the End of Things, there is no more dramatic image of the infernal end towards which Edmund's logic leads than the great flour mill which grows like Milton's Pandaemonium as if it were an exhalation from the earth itself. As one of the characters observes, "The growth had been automatic and inevitable: as if from below, from out of the still plastic igneous bedrock of the earth, new units had been pressed up like intrusive dykes, hardening on exposure to the air, and cooling."[27] So it grows until at last, bathed in floodlights, gleaming white and in full production, it seemed to those who looked at it "as if no human will could stop it; as if, even though the whole population of the earth perished, it would go on producing flour till it had smothered the globe."[28]

The flour that was to sustain life ends by destroying it. Hannah Arendt in *The Human Condition* has pointed out the paradox that a society which devotes itself wholly to the production of consumer goods in order to free man from his bondage to the natural cycle, ends by enslaving him to it: everything becomes a consumer good; it is consumed and must be produced again. According to Jay Macpherson, the principal spectre which haunts the Canadian imagination is that of a life that "takes its interest and directions only from the natural struggle – staggers around the white circle and dies without the possibility of renewal." Such a spectre haunts much of Grove's work, but it is not simply the result of a belief that we can live by bread alone. The paradox of the great flour mill is part of the paradoxical character of Edmund's idealism. The world Edmund envisages is a Brave New World in which the majority of mankind, largely unemployed, will be supported by the state, "held in subjection by the life of ease they will live," by "mental and emotional suggestion," and by "material welfare."[29] It is Edmund's father who points out the paradox that though Edmund's new order may represent a dictatorship of mind over matter, as far as the mass of mankind are concerned, "Matter will rule over mind." The mass of mankind will become the grim Idiot who sits by the gate in Lampman's City of the End of Things.

Edmund staggers around the white circle of his ideal and dies. (He is shot on the outer ramparts of the mill trying to defend it during a strike.) He dies young, childless, the last of the Clarks. His sister, who would prefer to blow the house, the mill, and the town to kingdom come, wanders around the world to escape from herself and wants no perpetuation of herself or her family.

Neither Edmund nor his father married the woman he loved. Musing on father and son and that unrealized possibility, Edmund's wife Maud asks herself, "What would have been the course of events if each of them had been able to obey his heart instead of his reason?"[30]

The fate of the women in Grove's novels again illustrates the aggressively rational and masculine character of the ideal which dominates the lives of the men and all those who live with them. When Abe Spalding, in *The Fruits of the Earth*, succeeds in conquering the spirit of the prairie, builds a great house and barn, all completely mechanized, his wife becomes lost in it. She is simply the manager in a machine for living, empty of love, joy, or spontaneous enthusiasm. He loses touch with the land; he loses his best-loved son; he loses the love of his wife. The novel ends more happily than some because Abe realizes that he "had started a vast machinery going which he had controlled at the outset but which had begun to control him instead." He realizes that though the machine "might 'pay' in a money sense; it did not pay in terms of human life."[31] It requires an eruption of irrational forces, however, to change Abe's ways. Specifically, he has to face and accept the fact that his daughter has conceived an illegitimate child.

Mrs Elliott in *Our Daily Bread* makes no complaints; but after bearing a large family in the service of her husband's dream of abundance, she develops cancer of the womb. Where she had been grossly fat, she becomes alarmingly thin. Her end is grotesquely ironic. After an apparently successful operation, she goes to a Thanksgiving dance, dressed in her old clothes with pillows stuffed into the bosom and around the waist, and there terrifies the crowd, asking one after the other to dance with her. And when she returns, having opened the incisions and ensured her death, she exclaims, "For once in my life I've had a good time."[32]

Amundsen's wife, in *The Settlers of the Marsh*, is forced to abandon two of her children in Europe when her husband emigrates to Canada. She works like an ox in the field and is generally given the same respect as the livestock. Though her husband insists he wants no more children, he also insists that his wife satisfy his sexual desires. In a scene objected to by nearly all the hostile readers of 1925, Mrs Amundsen's daughter, Ellen, overhears her father forcing his attentions on his wife, "that skeleton and ghost of a woman." When his wife protests that it will mean another child and that she has been a murderess enough times already, he only replies, "God has been good to us ... he took them." And so, the girl says, "the struggle began again, to end with the defeat of the woman."[33] It is not God who gets rid of the unwanted children, but Mrs Amundsen herself. She discovers that by doing extra heavy work she can bring on a miscarriage. It is the third such miscarriage that causes her death.

Here the sins of the father are clearly visited upon the next generation. Ellen vows she will never be the slave of any man, rejects her role as a woman, and refuses to marry the young man who loves her and has even built her a house before asking for her hand. As a result, the young man ends up married to her demonic opposite. Naïve and lonely, he is seduced by a local prostitute one night while in town. Waking to find her in bed, he proposes, not out of love, but out of a sense of duty. She accepts and he takes her home to begin a long nightmarish existence. There is no love between them; yet even when Niels discovers that she is a whore, he refuses to let her leave. He eventually moves out to live in a little shack nearby, taking her wood and other supplies each day. The woman haunts the house; her presence is proclaimed at first only by the drop in the level of the water pail, the disappearance of an egg, the diminishing supply of wood. Later, however, she begins to haunt Niels more directly, descending to the kitchen, no matter how late he comes to the house. She confronts him in silence, dressed in her most revealing silks and laces, but without make-up, "yellow, lined with sharp wrinkles and black hollows under the eyes, the lips pale like the face."[34] A spectre indeed.

The elements which Ellen Amundsen, and Niels too, have spurned and denied in themselves have split off to lead an autonomous existence in the person of Niels' wife. Insistently sexual, yet perversely sterile, they mock and torment him. The body of sensual joy and the feminine side of life become a leering mara, a painted death's head, which leads a danse macabre through the lamplit rooms, finally turning the house he had built as a home for his wife and children into a brothel for midnight visitors and their lascivious laughter. Niels is surrounded by the largely invisible presence of lust. It follows him even into the fields. One day he is approached by the libidinous young wife of a German settler who is helping with the harvest. When he rejects her advances, she charges him with hypocrisy. Who is he to pretend to such moral righteousness, she cries, the man who has married the district whore? He leaves the field, wandering in a daze until morning, when he takes his gun, enters the house, and, scattering the midnight visitors, shoots his wife. He then goes out and shoots the gelding in the barn.

Niels goes to jail, and in the description of the prison itself there is a sombre evocation of man's attempt to control the irrational passions of life by law rather than by love. The story, however, goes on to a happy conclusion. Niels is released and returns to discover Ellen has changed. She now wants marriage and children. Referring to her earlier rejection of him and her statement that she could never marry, she says: "I have been to blame ... I should not have said at the time, what you wish can never be. I should have said, what you wish cannot be so long as I live under the shadow of my mother's life."[35] Or, as she might have said, so long as she continues to live in the shadow of her father's world.

That shadow has not diminished since Grove wrote *The Settlers of the Marsh*. There may be fewer actual fathers like Amundsen, but there are more daughters like Ellen. The masculine idealism with its systematic aggression against the impulsive and irrational in life continues to provide the official rationale of an increasingly secular culture, and its puritanical character is all the more difficult to discern in a society which enjoys a sexual freedom unthinkable in Grove's day. But the point is that sexuality has itself been caught up in the machine. Making love, like making bread, can be reduced to a series of mechanical and increasingly routine techniques. Like everything else, sex can be exploited, producing what Leonard Cohen in *Beautiful Losers* calls "Montreal's desire apparatus."* Like everything else, sex can be perfected, producing what Cohen calls, with a diabolical pun on Charles Atlas, "the ideal Charles Axis lover."

*From *Beautiful Losers* by Leonard Cohen.

Beautiful Losers is a satirical fantasy which cries out against a desire for perfection that would reduce the whole of life to a system. It is a protest on behalf of irrational nature, which includes both the life of the body and the life of the spirit. It is fundamentally a spiritual book. It is superficially an extremely obscene book, much more obscene in language and in imagery than anything Grove's readers took such violent exception to in 1925. But the obscenity is deliberate and significant. As if Uncle Sean and Bram Shipley and other outcasts could no longer contain themselves but must burst out in the most defiant language they know, so Cohen's characters burst out in a steady stream of obscenity. It is the language of irrational man, of inarticulate nature, of the body which revolts against a world that would "prettify, dress up, deodorize, embellish, primp" until the body looks like a corpse or a neo-classical stone angel.

That is exactly what happens to the two women in *Beautiful Losers*. One is Catherine Tekakwitha, an actual seventeenth-century Indian girl who died in Ville Marie on the Island of Montreal and was afterwards proclaimed a saint. The other is Edith, the wife of the narrator, who is also an Indian, of the same tribe as Catherine Tekakwitha. The narrator, a student of Indian history, mourns for them both, for both are dead when the book opens. Though worlds apart in time and in the manner of their lives, the two are identical in the fate they illustrate. Both imbibe the spirit of *l'uomo universale*, turn against nature and themselves, and, in effect, commit suicide.

Catherine Tekakwitha is clearly associated with the wilderness and the world of the savage in which she was born. But after coming in contact with the missionaries, she turns her back on her savage inheritance. Wishing to make herself worthy of the white man's God, she denies her body and her role as a woman, takes the vow of virginity, and after convincing the authorities of the absoluteness of her intentions, scourges her flesh, lashes her body, sleeps naked on a bed of thorns, and finally dies, fully prepared to meet the bridegroom, Christ Jesus. And upon her death the wished-for miracle occurs. She turns white. Père Cholenec records it:

> "From the age of four years, Catherine's face had been branded by the Plague; her sickness and her mortifications had further contributed to the disfigurement. But this face, so battered and so very swarthy, underwent a sudden change, about a quarter of an hour after her death. And in a moment she became so beautiful and so white ..."[36]

As Cohen puts it, Catherine Tekakwitha has been caught up in the *eternal machinery* of the Church.

The contempory Edith, we learn, also began life as a poor, outcast Indian girl, disfigured by acne. Edith, however, did not have to die to achieve her transformation into the smooth-skinned, luscious, long-limbed beauty she becomes. The many techniques of modern science have managed that. Edith, unlike Catherine, does not deny sex; on the contrary, she explores it thoroughly. But each in her fashion has rejected her original and imperfect self, each has spurned and exploited nature in the attempt to make herself perfect and worthy of union with an ideal lover.

For a long time Edith despairs of ever achieving that complete and ideal union. She even wishes she might return to her original condition, to the primitive world of the savage and imperfect nature. At one point she paints her whole body red. Finally, however, during an orgiastic weekend in Argentina, she finds the appropriate consummation of her dream. It begins in frustration with her friend F. She too must use the scourge if she is to awaken the least glimmer of desire. F. proposes that a tale of torture might stimulate her a little, an account of the persecution of the Jews, perhaps. Too foreign, says Edith. Whereupon F. proceeds to give a fairly horrific account of the martyrdom of Brébeuf and Lalement. It helps, but is hardly sufficient to transform F. into the ideal lover or to provide the satisfaction she seeks. But just as she is ready to give up hope of ever attaining orgasm, the saviour arrives. The machine, called a Danish Vibrator, is as elaborate as the machine Kafka creates in his story "In the Penal Colony." But unlike that machine, which executes criminals while tattooing their sentences on their naked flesh, this is a machine for making love. The apparatus makes love to them both with equal success. Caught up in the machine, Edith finds complete satisfaction in its embrace, again and again, before it finally crawls out of the window, down the wall, and at last disappears in the sea.

The episode concludes with a more ordinary sadomasochistic romp conducted with the help of a third figure who arrives on the scene and who appears to be a compound of Hitler and Mephistopheles, perhaps Satan himself. The gentleman asks his devotees to kiss the whip with which he will flagellate them. They end cleanly, sudsing themselves in the bath with soap derived from melted human flesh.

Here as elsewhere in the book, Cohen underlines the aggressive and sadomasochistic character of the perfectionist cultural ideal by which both Catherine and Edith have been seduced. He makes a bold, and what would normally be unthinkable, equation between the savagery of the Iroquois, the savagery of the Church, the savagery of Nazi Germany, and the savagery inherent in the modern urban and technological world, its culture and its physical machinery.

After her experience with the Danish Vibrator, there is nothing left for Edith to live for. She has become one more victim of the masculine logos of *l'uomo universale*. Appropriately, she stands beneath the elevator in which the delivery boy from Chicken Bar-B-Q descends and is found lying crushed at the bottom of the elevator shaft.

The whole society is caught up in the illusion of the System Theatre. The world of appearance is the world of the movie, and the tendency to live with reference to external order is symbolized by the vicarious life of the movie audience. At one point the character F. remarks, "We are now in the heart of the last feature in the System Theatre."[37] Engrossed in the projection of western man's dream of order, we are unaware of ourselves and the others around us, sitting in the dark theatre. We cannot see our actual lives, except briefly when the newsreel projects its *actualités* on the screen. What will happen, Cohen asks, when the newsreel has escaped into the feature? If the dream of order is large enough and vital enough, we may reply, it will simply digest the raw stuff of the newsreel. But if it is not, the feature will disintegrate and the illusion will fade, leaving us suddenly aware of ourselves and the world around us.

This is what happens towards the end of the book. As F., presumed terrorist leader and madman, merges with Edith's husband, stinking hermit and pervert who has spent the last years in a tree house meditating on their past lives, the narrator becomes the embodiment of all that the feature excludes from its dream of order. Sitting in the System Theatre, he discovers he cannot see anything on the screen. He offers the fantastic explanation that his eyes are blinking at the same rate as the shutter in the projector, but the point is that he has escaped from the world of appearance projected on the screen. The feature no longer conveys the illusion of reality. Looking around him, the dirty old man sees rows of eyes shifting back and forth mechanically, mouths that now and again make the same noise in unison, a noise called laughter. But for him, there is nothing to laugh at. Unlike the others he is wholly aware of himself, of the people and things around him. "For the first time in his life," we are told, "the old man relaxed totally."[38]

He wanders out of the theatre into St Catherine Street, walking through the broken-down machinery of the Main Shooting and Game Alley, the disintegrating world of "Montreal's desire apparatus," to St Lawrence Main. It is spring. And a real miracle occurs. Something happens.

We may recall that in Cohen's first novel, *The Favourite Game*, Montreal was described as a place where nothing happened. It was a city, he said, designed to preserve the past, a past that happened somewhere else. Here, however, something is happening right now. As the rumour of it spreads, all the theatres empty out and people start pouring down St Catherine Street to converge on the Main.

What happens is that, just as the mob is about to attack the old man, seeing in him the escaped pervert or the escaped madman and terrorist leader, he begins to fade and to reform before their eyes.

"His presence was like the shape of an hourglass, strongest where it was smallest. And that point where he was most absent, that's when the gasps started, because the future streams through that point, going both ways." Reforming, he becomes a movie of Ray Charles:

> The moon occupied one lens of his sunglasses, and he laid out his piano keys across a shelf of the sky, and he leaned over them as though they were truly the row of giant fishes to feed a hungry multitude.

"Thank God it's only a movie," cries someone with relief. But it is not *only* another movie. Besides the image of Ray Charles as the authentic man, the New Testament figure who relives the parable of the loaves and the fishes, the point is that the man is his own movie, is making it out of himself.

> Hey! cried a New Jew, laboring on the lever of the broken Strength Test. Hey. Somebody's making it![39]

Beautiful Losers celebrates the triumph of the outcast irrational world against an overly exclusive and overly mechanical rationalism. The latter, though apparently all-powerful, is sterile and leads to death. It is *then*, says F., that we must listen to the Savage Priest. As in the Huron story of the journey that the soul must make if it would find salvation after death, we must take the dangerous and difficult path that goes by the hut of Oscotarach, the Head-Piercer, who removes the brains from the skulls of all who pass.

It is F. who most explicitly and bluntly reaffirms the two poles of the irrational, the world of the flesh and the world of the spirit. He sits in the asylum for the presumably insane, one hand between the nurse's thighs to give her pleasure, the other writing a passionate proclamation that God is alive.

> Though his shrouds were hoisted the naked God did live. This I mean to whisper to my mind. This I mean to laugh with in my mind. This I mean my mind to serve till service is but Magic moving through the world, and mind itself is Magic coursing through the flesh, and flesh itself is Magic dancing on a clock, and time itself is the Magic Length of God.[40]

Mind remains, but as an aspect of a larger and more mysterious order an order in which it must speak through the flesh, or with the flesh, and not against it.

The masculine will which began, whether in pride or in fear, by ignoring or exploiting feminine nature, ends by confessing its need, and by humbly invoking her return. Thus the narrator in *Beautiful*

Losers confesses his love and his need for the composite Catherine Tekakwitha-Edith figure, destroyed by the system or excluded from the public life of society. He would find her, not in heaven but on earth, not in church on Sundays only but everywhere in his daily life. He would ask her for the most ordinary everyday things. "Phrase-book on my knees, I beseech the Virgin everywhere."[41] He writes out little dialogues, like those in a Berlitz language course, in which he would ask her for all the little things he needs. He would beseech her in the Wash House, in the Tobacconist's, in the Barber Shop, in the Post Office, at the Bookseller's. "O God, O God," he concludes, "I have asked for too much, I have asked for everything! I hear myself asking for everything in every sound I make. I did not know, in my coldest terror, I did not know how much I needed. O God, I grow silent as I hear myself begin to pray."[42] The final prayer is a list of phrases in Greek and in imperfect English of the type that might be used by a man asking for things at the druggist's.

L'uomo universale, it would seem, has discovered that he is not self-sufficient, that his ideal itself is inadequate, that Creation is too large to be contained in his laws, or in the laws of the Creator he conceived and served. He discovers that he must learn from the medicine man a new language of prayer.

CHAPTER FOUR

The Problem of Job

I wish I had been born beside a river
Instead of this round pond
Where the geese white as pillows float
In continual circles
And never get out.
JAMES REANEY, "The Upper Canadian"

Beside us frocked and righteous men
Proclaimed their absolutes as laws.
They kept their purity of creed
By twisting facts that showed the flaws.
F. R. SCOTT, "Eclipses"

And this planet dancing about Apollo,
the blood drying and shining in the sun ...
IRVING LAYTON, "Seven O'Clock Lecture"

When Edmund Clark in Grove's *The Master of the Mill* opposes his father in a scheme to automate the great flour mill and monopolize the economy, he justifies himself by saying:

> "It was the Victorian attitude, and it was yours and your generation's, to mistrust the future as you mistrusted me. So they fought the coming of that future with laws and guns; and finally, seeing that they could not shoot holes into a tide, they fought it with concessions to the rabble designed to retard the coming of the tide. They were intent on saving their skins. They did save them, for the moment. But what was their answer to the question asked by the centuries, the question asking for justice? Their answer was the *status quo*. But, hold on to the *status quo*, and you strangle life."[1]

In the same way Daniel Ainslie in Hugh MacLennan's *The Return of the Sphinx* accuses his father of indecision, political cowardice, and conniving with those whose only interest is in preserving the *status quo*. Daniel joins an extreme separatist movement in Quebec, publicly attacks the government his father represents, and effectively ruins his father's political career. Like Edmund, Daniel is a frustrated idealist acting in the name of justice. Like Edmund, he is prepared to further his ideas at the expense of family ties and all values based on personal affection. Like Edmund, he is prepared to use violence to effect his vision without compromise and without delay.

Both young men are ironic or false heroes. In their rebellion against the passivity or indecision of their fathers they do no more than assert in extreme form ideals that their fathers have come to doubt. Alan Ainslie is profoundly skeptical of the narrowly nationalistic society his son would establish. Senator Clark is profoundly skeptical of the narrowly technocratic society his son Edmund would create. That skepticism is at the root of their indecision and apparent reaction. We may sympathize with the young men's frustration, their need to act, and their zeal for justice, but not with their ideals and the kind of puritanical justice they inspire.

The puritanical element is particularly evident in MacLennan's portrait of Daniel, since his political frustration is linked to his sexual frustration and both are related to his early Jesuit schooling. However, the Oedipus story which provides the basic structural motif for *The Return of the Sphinx* serves to dramatize a more general conflict between the generations. It is indicative of the failure of the older cultural logic and the consequent disappearance of the strong father-figure. The omnipresent but invisible sphinx may be associated with what Grove vaguely calls the *tide* and with the inchoate and largely irrational impulses which have emerged to threaten the old order everywhere in modern society. It is against that threat that the older generation holds on to the *status quo*, but paradoxically it is against the same threat that the sons advance their more aggressive ideals.

The old order was too narrow. But, as the fathers themselves are aware, the new order that Daniel or Edmund would impose is narrower still. Each is inspired by a vision of logical purity which has its roots in the older culture and which each now asserts in an even more intolerant, exclusive, and intellectualized form. Ironically, then, the order that Daniel and more especially Edmund would create is designed to strangle life more effectively than the *status quo* against which they have rebelled.

Obviously, to escape from this dilemma both parties must look to a more open and inclusive ideal. Instead of maintaining or fortifying the garrison of the old order they must open it up to the wilderness that lies beyond its walls. Yet neither is willing to do this, for the wilderness fills them with fear or contempt. In this dilemma, the sons who act grow ever more desperate, the fathers who hold on to the *status quo* become ever more impotent.

Nowhere, perhaps, is the paralysis arising from a fear of life more starkly explored than in Sheila Watson's novel *The Double Hook*. Here there are no real father-figures. The community is dominated by old women, particularly the fiercely possessive and devouring Mrs Potter. As John Grube writes in his introduction to the New Canadian Library edition, "She becomes a symbol of death, and is always associated with the chilling sound of the coyote which has been a symbol of fear from time immemorial both to the settler and to the native Indian who preceded him."[2] The shadow of fear and of death is cast on William, James, and Greta, the old woman's children, and on everyone else in the little drought-ridden community. Even when she is killed at the beginning of the novel, her presence remains. William's wife Ara sees her jealously and maliciously fishing all the pools of the stream that runs through the settlement. She fishes them dry. To Ara, who has second sight, the very water appears to undergo a demonic transformation under the old woman's influence, becoming the waters of death. Ara sees her, with branches wrapped about her head like weeds, drawing the water out of the ground.

Greta remains briefly under her mother's spell. She too is associated with Coyote, and the weedy design on her housecoat relates her to her mother. Left alone in the house with the old woman's body, she locks the door against the outside world. When people twist the knob to get in, she feels: "hands twisting her ribs. Plucking the flowers on her housecoat and bruising them. Stripping off the leaves until her branch lay naked as a bone on the dusty floor." As she prepares to set fire to the house in a final gesture of withdrawal, she strips off the housecoat and burns it: "The flowers in the stove-box were breathing out fragrance which filled the whole room. They were raising purple faces and lifting green arms into the air above the stove."[3] Coyote cries from the hills that he has taken her to himself.

Both mother and daughter appear in the guise of Ondine, the Lorelei or destructive water-nymph, who provides one of the archetypes for the spectre of life turned in upon itself, narcissistic, frozen in its own reflection or caught in the grip of its own past.

As long as the members of the community remain under the old woman's spell they cannot act, they cannot love, they remain frustrated, isolated, divided one from the other. As Mr Grube notes, it is another wise fool named Kip who puts his finger on the problem. "People," he says, "go shutting their doors. Tying things up. Fencing them in. Shutting out what they never rightly know." Theophil embodies the traditional order. He still remembers some fragments of the Catholic ritual. As a result, Felix Prosper's wife Angel has gone to live with him. Yet Kip remarks of Theophil, "A man can't peg himself in so tight that nothing can creep through the cracks." Kip, says Mr Grube, "diagnoses fear as the malady that is infecting, not only Theophil, but most of the settlers: 'Angel can see but Theophil has let fear grow like fur on his eyes.' "[4]

It is fear that motivates the Widow Wagner. Having lost her husband, she too withdraws from life in the hope of preserving herself and her children from the pain and loss that living and loving entail. Like her husband's watch, which she has kept packed in a trunk with the dead man's clothes, time has stood still in the Widow's house. The boy is infected by his mother's fear. When he looks at Kip's horse standing in the yard in a blaze of sunlight, the boy, we are told, "Stood thinking of sweat and heat and the pain of living, the pain of fire in the middle of a haystack. Stood thinking of light burning free on the hills and flashing like the glory against the hides of things." The boy himself would like to be free to catch the glory, but, he confesses, "I'm afraid ... and even the light won't tell me what to do."[5]

The fire in the haystack, the free light burning and flashing on the hills, is associated with the Widow's daughter Gretchen, with her blonde hair, her youthful beauty and sexuality. And it is this glory that James Potter, the youngest of the old woman's two sons and central male character in the story, would like to catch. He has met the girl in secret; he has made love to her in the folds of the hills, under cover of darkness and the thick branches of the trees, but never openly. He too is afraid and, until the moment when he rebels and strikes the old woman down, has been intimidated by his mother. According to Kip, his problem was the same as that of the old woman: he did not know that "when you fish for the glory you catch the darkness too. That if you hook twice the glory you hook twice the fear."[6]

This lesson James learns in the course of the action, which began with his killing of the old woman and continues to unfold in the midst of a storm and the razing of his house by fire. It is one that all the characters learn as James gathers the courage to act. The flame contains the glory and the darkness both; it is at once creative and destructive.

Unlike Edmund and Daniel, James has no intellectual program. He acts instinctively. And though his action is immediately more violent, it is also more fruitful. He knocks down the walls of a static, defensive order, not in the hope of erecting a new order whose walls will more effectively exclude the undesirable and preserve only the desirable elements in life, but in order to let in life itself in all its ambiguity. He lets in death and fire, but he also lets in love and the waters of life. It is life, not justice, especially an abstract justice, he seeks. The only hope that the new order will be more just lies in the promise of greater fulfilment for himself and others. The only hope that the future will have an order lies in James's intuitive awareness of the double-edged character of all action and his faith in the ordering power of nature and of love itself. Despite the violence that attends his action, his faith seems justified by the over-all transformation that occurs in the life of the community. Ara registers the change. Looking at the smoking doorsill of the Potters' house, she has a vision parallel and opposite to her earlier vision of the old woman.

> The door of the house had opened into the east wind. Into drought. She remembered how she'd thought of water as a death which might seep through the dry shell of the world. Now her tired eyes saw water issuing from under the burned threshold. Welling up and flowing down to fill the dry creek. Until dry lips drank. Until the trees stood knee deep in water.
>
> Everything shall live where the river comes, she said out loud. And she saw a great multitude of fish, each fish springing arched through the slanting light.[7]

The new order emerges as the Widow's daughter Gretchen, heavy with child, is taken to Felix Prosper's house. Felix makes the delivery, his wife Angel returns, and James arrives to acknowledge his newborn son. The story that began with a death ends with a birth, though Coyote may still have the last word. Ara hears him crying down through the boulders from a cleft in the rock:

> I have set his feet on the soft ground;
> I have set his feet on the sloping shoulders
> of the world.[8]

Every birth implies a death and breeds simultaneously new joy and new sorrow. Love, sex, the affirmation of life is a double hook that hauls in both the glory and the darkness. Instinctively, James has found the courage to accept the dual consequences of all such affirmation and thereby escapes from the dilemma that continues to plague Daniel and Edmund and the world of their fathers.

This dilemma is not peculiar to the three novels we have looked at. We can see it emerging in the work of Charles G. D. Roberts and his generation, and it continues to occupy both poets and novelists down to the present. Characteristic, perhaps, of any transitional period in a culture, in its fundamental challenge it here lays bare the essential difficulty in the way of any attempt to formulate a more open and inclusive view of life. It is the problem of how, not only to tolerate but in some measure affirm the darkness as well as the glory, the apparently negative element in nature. It is the inability to do this that creates and perpetuates a culture garrisoned against nature. It is essentially the problem of evil, or, as its frequent formulation in Canadian writing might suggest, the problem of Job. What shall we make of Leviathan?

Politically, the problem was posed by the American Revolution, when the Loyalist refusal to liberate a Hobbesian Leviathan revealed a basically conservative and exclusive element in Canadian culture. Yet the problem was posed by wilderness America itself and was not to be resolved by any single political frontier. If anything impressed the early explorers and settlers more than the fertility and variety of the New World it was its violence and savagery, especially in the north. As the romantic Lefroy in Charles Mair's *Tecumseh* contemplates the vastness of the West and the abundance of its animal life, he is led to exclaim:

> Yes, life was there! inexplicable life,
> Still wasted by inexorable death.[9]

The illustrations that follow might have been drawn from the animal stories of Charles G. D. Roberts or a poem by Irving Layton. The two terms of Lefroy's vision of nature continue to engage Canadian writers from Roberts to the present. For with every attempt to step out of the established social order, in the name of a more inclusive or vital order to be discovered in nature, the protagonist finds himself confronted by the destructive element, by inexorable death.

As for Job, the problem is one of affirming a creator or, more simply, a creation, whose only morality would seem to be a morality of power, or of creative exuberance. Job cries out for justice only to be answered by the thunder and lightning of the universe. Unfolding the variety and vastness of his power, Jehovah fails to distinguish the lion from the lamb, the young roe and the patient ox from Behemoth and Leviathan. For the traditional western man, whom Aldous Huxley has characterized somewhat bluntly as a Manichee who would "perpetuate only the 'yes' in every pair of opposites,"[10] it has been particularly difficult to affirm such a universe. His sense of the meaning, worth, or justice of life depended upon his faith that sooner or later the serpent would be destroyed and the dove preserved, that the dark would be separated from the light and finally banished from the universe. He had assumed that the will of man, or ultimately the will of God working through man, would bring the powers of darkness under control and in some millennium, secular or divine, would eradicate them from the earth. But the experience of modern man has repeatedly shaken all his assumptions. The more he has looked closely at nature, the less assured he has become. The science that promised to give him greater power over nature also removed the foundations for his simple faith that he and his world were the special creations of God and that man had a privileged role to play in the great debate between dark and light. Man and his world came to be seen as evolutionary accidents in a universe that as it was vastly expanded in time and space was resolutely swept clean of spiritual intelligence and any sign of divine purpose. No longer the fixed stage of a spiritual drama, it evolved with its creatures towards the final stagnation implied by the law of entropy. More immediate historical events appeared to offer existential proof of the implacable irrationality and indiscriminate destructiveness as well as creativeness of life. The justice of God, the inevitability of progress, and the authority of reason could no longer be taken for granted in a world increasingly dominated by the experience of two world wars, the extermination of the Jews, the destruction of Hiroshima, and the continuous dislocation of familiar and often immemorial patterns of life. Life became violent and unpredictable, whether in the stars or in the street or in the world of microscopic particles no man had ever seen.

A number of these ideas and events are relatively recent, and most have had a more immediate impact on the life and literature of other countries. Yet we may say that they have only magnified the face of Leviathan Canadians glimpsed in the wilderness around them and that even before the turn of the century their impact was felt in Canadian life and in Canadian literature. As Grove's Edmund suggests, however conservative and apparently secure, the established society with its traditional ideas of justice and order felt threatened by the changing climate of opinion, and they often reacted by holding more tightly to the *status quo*. Yet the old patterns of thought and action continued to break down; the traditional response to the problem of Job no longer appeared adequate. In the new climate, the events capable of shaking an individual's faith in the traditional values, and thus his general confidence in life, did not need to be sensational or apocalyptic. As in Grove's *The Fruits of the Earth*, they might be no more than the barrenness that Abe Spalding discovers in a life wholly devoted to the operation of a large and increasingly successful farm, the perversity of his fellow settlers who knowingly elect to public office a man less able and less honest than Abe himself, the accidental death of his favourite son, and the humiliating discovery that his own daughter will give birth to a bastard.

At the death of his son Abe cries out that there is no justice – perhaps no God. Abe is a man in whom will and reason must dominate life. He sees the world clearly in black and white, and he expects his fellow men – above all, he expects God – to be equally discriminating. At one point Abe declares that if a daughter of his were to conceive an illegitimate child he would kill her. His justice is prepared to destroy the fruit of irrational desire root and branch. However, the above series of events forces Abe to modify his views, humbling his will and forcing upon him an acceptance of the imperfection and irrationality of the world. He is changed in the process from a righteous to a loving man. He who had withdrawn from the life of the community because of its human imperfection finally resolves to enter and to serve it once again.

Abe Spalding's conduct is exemplary. For many, the reaction to such events may be bitterness or confusion, a stiffening of old attitudes or their still more extreme assertion with the aid of more powerful technological weapons. Yet, as the example of Abe Spalding implies, the required response is a more understanding and even loving attitude towards the imperfect nature that poses the threat.

Roberts, Carman, Lampman, and Scott are conventionally regarded as the poets of nature. They were clearly influenced by the nineteenth-century Romantics. But they also reflect an authentic desire to get out of a garrison culture that was becoming increasingly oppressive. The Romantic movement was itself a reaction to the increasingly exclusive and aggressively rational culture of Europe. From the turn of the century on it makes itself felt in Canadian literature as a personal conviction and not only as a literary convention. Roberts' generation of poets are the first to really explore this reaction. Dissatisfied with the established culture, they clearly look to nature in the hope of discovering a larger and more vital conception of life. In the rest of this chapter we shall take a close look at the precise terms of their reaction and at some of the problems they encountered.

Like some of the later fictional characters we have looked at, these poets gradually found themselves faced with a dilemma. Within society they could choose between the conventional Christian idealism and the newer secular idealism inspired by technology. One was increasingly moribund, the other increasingly dynamic, but each tended to do violence to human nature and to eliminate all spontaneous joy in life. They therefore looked outside the walls of the city, hoping to find in nature the medicine that would restore their vitality. But outside lay the wilderness with its threat of disorder, irrational passion and violence, the crude, the mortal, and the absurd. In order to abandon the garrison they would be forced to reconcile themselves to the various threats against which the walls were initially built. It is not surprising that Roberts, for one, should hesitate.

In the title poem of his first volume, *Orion*, Roberts concludes his portrait of the great hunter on a highly affirmative note: cured of his blindness, Orion opens his eyes on a fresh and dynamic world and proceeds to give his heart up "straightway unto love." Six years later, with the volume *In Divers Tones*, Roberts' youthful optimism is gone. Here the story of Acteon, in which the hunter turned hunted is pursued by his own hounds, seems more prophetic. Roberts' personal disillusionment, something of his dismay arising from his experience of life during the intervening years, is evident in the well-known "Tantramar Revisited," which appeared in the same volume.

The poem celebrates the speaker's return to the land of his boyhood and is largely descriptive; yet, despite the grandeur and tranquillity of the landscape, the poem is elegiac in tone. The speaker's mood is a mixture of relief and anxiety. Since he left the scene of his childhood, he tells us, the "Hands of chance and change have marred, or moulded, or broken,/Busy with spirit or flesh, all I have most adored."[11] There is nothing to suggest that his experience will be any different in the future. Only the immediate moment offers him some sort of haven from the pressure of time. The world of his youth appears untouched by the erosion of the years; yet, even here, it may be no more than a "darling illusion" of distance, and he resolves not to test it by a nearer view. Meanwhile, as he moves back and forth in his mind between childhood memories of a sustaining activity and the hushed inactivity of the present, the landscape before him mirrors his own situation. Just as the speaker has arrived at a pause in his struggle with life, so has the world of the fishing villages. The boats are pulled up on the beaches; the nets have been hung up to dry; the hay waves golden on the hillsides; the sea sparkles in the distance, giving no hint of its potential menace. The speaker is nonetheless aware of the ever-present destructive power of the sea. For the moment, it is contained. The "green-rampired" point and the "long clay dikes" fencing the fields from the turbid "surge and flow of the tides vexing the Westmoreland shores" protect the land and the ordered life of the villagers. While the world is washed with wind and light and the grey hawk wheels above the haystack, the moment seems poised between the forces of creation and destruction, precarious but still.

Beginning with this volume, Roberts' poetry reveals a gradual withdrawal: an increasing inability to affirm the immediate moment, to celebrate action, or to look with confidence towards the future. It is the mutability and irrationality of life which he cannot account for and which continually take him by surprise. Roberts was aware of a division between culture and nature, and, as we have seen in "Beside the Winter Sea," his separation from the woman is also a separation from the land. Yet it is the land and the world of woman that alone seem capable of comprehending and healing the injuries of life. In "At the Tide Water" he appeals to the land to illumine the experience he brings: "Love, and the ashes of desire, and anguish,/Strange laughter, and the unhealing wound of death." These, he confesses, "in the world, all these have come upon me,/Leaving me mute and shaken with surprise."[12]

It is in his animal stories that Roberts celebrates life with the greatest confidence. There his characters move in a Darwinian world – more broadly, in a world of Job. Writing of Roberts' animal stories,

Joseph Gold maintains that the "strong sense of the infinite scale of size in the universe, from the minute forces of energy to the unconquerable seasons, is characteristic of Roberts' awareness."[13] Often, as in the opening pages of "The Last Barrier," the story of a salmon, Roberts creates through a series of sharply observed details the picture of a universe everywhere dependent on the dynamic interplay of forces in conflict. Again and again in his stories, creature preys upon creature, the snake on the mouse, the hawk on the snake, in a continual struggle to survive. Yet, though the eagle preys on the lamb, as in "The Young Ravens that Call Upon Him," Roberts obviously delights in the eagle as much as the lamb. As long as he is dealing with animals alone, he tends to rejoice in the energy and variety of life despite its indiscriminate violence. "Roberts' animal world," writes Mr Gold, "amounts to an affirmative vision in which the conditions of a wilderness struggle for survival are accepted and confirmed." What this acceptance may mean in terms of a purely human order is another and more complex question, one which Roberts does not appear to have worked out very clearly.

Mr Gold sees Roberts confronted with the problem of "man's apparent lonely helplessness" in an indifferent universe. For the solution of this problem, Mr Gold contends, "The terms of his clerical background were not acceptable, the raw materials of a New Brunswick wilderness were to hand, and so Roberts brought his imagination to bear on nature and animals and produced his own Canadian mythology. The principal feature of this myth is that, while individual creatures constantly lose the struggle for survival, life itself persists. In the long run death itself has no sting and is ironically defeated by the uses nature makes of its processes."[14]

It is true that Roberts introduces this "myth" or evolutionary idealism into his poetry, but the poems in which it appears are not among his best work, precisely because, in the context, the baldly stated idealism is frequently not convincing. In the poem "As Down the Woodland Ways," for example, after observing the crumbling stumps of trees, crushed beetles, mangled grubs, Roberts goes on to conclude:

> Through weed and world, through worm and star,
> The sequence ran the same –
> Death but the travail-pang of life,
> Destruction but a name.[15]

In leaping from the particular concrete situation to a more distant abstraction, the poet manages to lose sight of the grubs and beetles and the actuality of their quite individual destruction. Death ceases to exist. That "darling illusion" is achieved by a logical distance or sleight-of-hand. The assertion fails to meet the questions posed by the preceding stanzas because it shifts to another level of discourse. A number of the later poems are weakened by just such a lack of integrity, by vagueness, or by an overly facile optimism.

To recognize that the life of the species continues at the expense of the individual is, in any case, cold comfort. The survival of the species is in itself an obscure good. It hardly answers the queries that grow out of Roberts' personal anxiety, the bewilderment so central to various of the poems. Roberts seems loath to accept the conditions of a wilderness struggle for survival as applicable in the realm of human affairs. Even in the animal stories, whenever the human point of view is introduced, the picture becomes troubled by conventional moral distinctions between just and unjust, guilty and innocent. Witness the following passage from "The Moonlight Trails":

> Then the boy's sharp eyes marked a trail very slender and precise – small, clear dots one after the other; and he had a feeling of protective tenderness to the maker of that innocent little trail, till Andy told him that he of the dainty foot prints was the bloodthirsty and indomitable weasel ...[16]

It is the human point of view which prevails in the most personal of the poems, "Tantramar Revisited" (1886), "Beside the Winter Sea" (1896), "In the Night Watches" (1927), "Westcock Hill" (1934), which are all elegiac poems characterized by a poignant sense of loss, division, and death, the sense of the speaker's dismay. Typically Roberts escapes by withdrawing to a distance. In many of the sonnets, for example, he becomes the impersonal, passive observer. Even so, the picture of life which he presents is frequently sombre. Even in the gayest, "The Pea-Fields," for instance, we encounter a certain frustration, a final check on the immediate enjoyment of life. Certain of the later lyrics are images of life's variety and potential vitality locked and frozen in ice. In "Kinship" the speaker withdraws to what he terms rather vaguely "the borderland of birth." In one of the best and most ambitious of the late poems, "The Iceberg," the speaker's point of view is identified with the berg; and though he may celebrate the vast forces and teeming life of the world through which he moves, his own role is passive and resigned. It is a ruinous career in which the speaker is reduced to a "little glancing globe of cold," content, he tells us, to merge "forever in the all-solvent sea."[17]

Roberts' poetry is informed by a stoic courage, that is, by a courage to suffer rather than a courage to act. In the animal stories, on the other hand, we are often impressed by the characters' capacity, not simply to endure, but to rejoice in life, however precarious or bitterly fought. There too Roberts tends to keep his eye much more steadily on the individual and the reality of the individual creature's suffering or joy. And the emphasis on the positive significance of struggle and suffering is there more convincing. Mr Gold makes the observation that the animals in these stories lead more dignified and meaningful lives than do the characters in the novels of such contemporaries of Roberts as Zola and Dreiser. He argues:

> It is precisely because the contest is always finally lost that the struggle is meaningful. Roberts' animal world, like ours, is a fallen world and the best that can be achieved in it is a persistent denial of death, hunger and fear. Every moment wrenched from time is a major victory and every meal is a conquest over an indifferent universe. Roberts would agree with Blake that "everything that lives is holy" but he would add, I suspect, "And holy because it lives."[18]

Such a philosophy has its dangers. Stated baldly, it may still seem little more than a stoic pessimism or the justification of a morality of power. It needs to be amplified before we can tell how significant or palatable it might be. Particularly we should like to know what its implications might be for life in human society. How does it bear on the individual human being? Is sheer survival to be his principal aim? Is survival in itself the supreme virtue and justification of the individual existence? Roberts never seemed to have answered these questions clearly, with the result that his poetic energies were sapped by indecision and anxiety. The stories may be his best work. After the promise of the early volumes, his later poetry emerges as a diminished thing.

None of Roberts' contemporaries – Archibald Lampman, Bliss Carman, or Duncan Campbell Scott – seems to have suffered quite the same fate. Though seldom any more prepared than Roberts to analyse and resolve the problems presented by the age, each in his own way arrived at an intuitive if sometimes vague answer to the questions that plagued Roberts and, as a consequence, found a continued release for his vital energies within his poetry. In some cases the poetry reveals a continued growth in vigour, penetration, and power. Each of these poets turned his back to some extent on the traditional piety and conventional morality of their day and, like Roberts, looked to nature or the wilderness to discover a larger and more vital vision of life.

Carman, it is true, in poems such as the early and well known "Low Tide on Grand Pré," exhibits a nostalgic regret and disillusionment reminiscent of Roberts. Both his occasional melancholy and the frequent jubilant celebration of the joys of the open road owe a good deal to the conventions of the period. The gusto with which he sings of the vagabond life is frequently forced. His delight in nature and his optimistic conception of man's relationship to her can be superficial in expression or intolerably vague. He wrote too much and often too glibly. Ultimately, however, Carman's outlook rests upon a vision of nature as realistic as any we can find in Roberts.

Carman's poetry does not exhibit the violence or the variety of life that we find in Roberts' animal stories; nevertheless, Carman was aware of the darkness as well as the light, of the lethal as well as the vital implications of all life, love, or action. And he accepted them both without the reservations that troubled Roberts. For this reason, it would seem, he escaped the sort of paralysis that overtook Roberts, going blithely if naïvely on his way. Carman's image of the individual life, of his own life, is characteristically modest, delicate, even fragile. It is the image of the snowflake in "The Great Return," of the moth in "Pulvis et Umbra," of the wind-flower in the poem of the same name.

> Between the roadside and the wood,
> Between the dawning and the dew,
> A tiny flower before the sun,
> Ephemeral in time, I grew.

The wind-flower opens its petals, rejoicing in the sun, only to be overwhelmed by a storm.

> Tonight can bring no healing now;
> The calm of yesternight is gone;
> Surely the wind is but the wind,
> And I a broken waif thereon.[19]

The flower may live but a day; yet it delights in that day nonetheless.

The hands of chance and change do not dismay Carman, do not take him by surprise, as they did Roberts. He is prepared to accept the mortal and ephemeral nature of all things and still affirm the glory and value of the individual life. His conception of nature was not so much childish as childlike. More than any other Canadian writer he had the kind of faith in the goodness or justice of life that is implied in Christ's parable of the lilies of the field, which neither toil nor spin and yet are clothed in a glory greater than Solomon's. It is in the spirit of this faith that he addresses nature in the opening stanza of "The Great Return":

> O mother, I have loved thee without fear
> And looked upon the mystery of change,
> Since first, a child, upon the closing year,
> I saw the snowflakes fall and whispered, "Strange!"[20]

Carman is the only poet of his immediate generation who could fairly be called a love poet – a distinction which seems ordinary enough within the context of the whole history of lyric poetry, but a significant one within the context of his own generation and in the perspective of our present discussion. Unlike Roberts, Carman continued to give his heart up straightaway unto love. However it might hurt him, his initial impulse was not to defend himself from the world, to order and control it, but to love it. Thus, though his writing was marred by a lack of critical insight and by much that was conventional in thought and expression, throughout his career he was able to write poems in which we glimpse an authentic sense of the joy and poignancy of being alive – of what it means to love a woman or the world.

For Archibald Lampman, it was not the violence of the wilderness that was disturbing, but rather the violence of the city. His problem was to escape from the garrison of a culture that was itself becoming a wilderness, a desert of boredom on the one hand and a jungle of violence on the other. Even in Ottawa Lampman could glimpse the infernal outlines of Baudelaire's Paris or Eliot's London, the spectre of the wasteland. He attempts to evoke it in such poems as "The Railway Station" and "Reality." These are not his best poems. Except in "The City of the End of Things," Lampman never found very adequate expression for this infernal vision of the city and of modern life. As a lesser poet living on the periphery of contemporary culture, he lacked the resources of a Baudelaire or an Eliot, but he also lacked their consuming interest in the spectre that threatened from within, and was drawn towards a promise that beckoned from without. Beyond the city limits lay another reality, inarticulate but compelling.

It was not only the sterility of a highly aggressive urban, commercial, and technological world that Lampman wished to escape, but the sterility of the *status quo*. Lampman suffered personally from the boredom and aridity of his position as a civil servant in the postal department of a provincial city, but he was also aware of the increasingly moribund character of the ideals which theoretically ordered and inspired the society in which he lived. Engineers, businessmen, politicians, the man in the street, paid less and less attention to the moral and spiritual formulae of a Christian humanist culture. Or else, as Lampman states in "The Modern Politician," they manipulated them to blind the "multitude with specious words."[21] The language which had served to express the spiritual vitality of traditional culture was worn out. Those who continued to employ that language were either blind or hypocritical.

Lampman's attempt to escape from boredom and sterility led him to a search for the vital in nature and in language. The cultural confusion of the time is reflected in the mixed diction of his poetry. Various poems that deal with man's relationship to nature keep up a mimic strain that is a direct echo of Wordsworth. Many poems critical of the time or concerned with proclaiming Lampman's own moral fervour and sense of integrity simply reiterate traditional pieties in conventional rhetoric. Elsewhere, however, we see him struggling to replace the conventional word or image with those that will carry more weight and conviction. Sometimes, as in "The Uplifting," the attempt to wipe the "moonshine" from the heavens may have rather odd results. In this sonnet he tells us how, after a depressing evening in a house filled with domestic strife, he is relieved to walk out into the night where he beholds:

> The holy round of heaven – all its rime
> Of suns and planets and its nebulous rust –
> Sable and glittering like a mythic shield,
> Sown with the gold of giants and of time,
> The worlds and all their systems but as dust.[22]

The holy round of dust!

The language of science and technology carried increasingly more weight than that of traditional theology and morality and Lampman's awareness of the fact is evident in a variety of poems in which he attempts to replace conventional expressions with more technical sounding words. These attempts, although sometimes resulting in grotesque examples of mixed diction, are nonetheless highly instructive, as we shall see in a moment. Still, though Lampman might wish to avail himself of the language of science and technology, he could not subscribe to the cultural logic with which they were most closely associated. However much he might wish to escape the stagnation of the *status quo*, he could not, like Grove's Edmund, embrace the ideal of the technocrat who would submit nature to the domination of a wholly economic and technological order. The conclusion to which that cultural logic leads is exposed with visionary clarity in "The City of the End of Things." It is the very opposite of the humane Arcadian city Jay Macpherson speaks of as a perennial ideal. It is an order not unlike that proposed by Loren Eiseley's new asphalt animal, in which all living things have been killed off – no animal, no plant survives.

Lampman knew that the life of the spirit arose from an inner vitality, not from an external order. And whereas the passive attempt to preserve the traditional moral and religious ideals starved the life of the spirit, the active impulse to dominate nature threatened to annihilate it. As he says of man in "The City of the End of Things":

> caught by the terrific spell,
> Each thread of memory snapt and cut,
> His soul would shrivel and its shell
> Go rattling like an empty nut.[23]

The alternative to this situation was to go outside the social or cultural order and to embrace the wilderness of nature, "not as they/ That labour without seeing, that employ/Her unloved forces, blindly without joy," but "with the fond lover's zest."[24] Here he was led and, at times, misled by Wordsworth, echoing both his diction and his ideas, an excessively benevolent conception of nature and an excessively passive conception of man's relationship to her. Nevertheless, Lampman was convinced that the vitality he sought was to be found only in nature's embrace, and in a number of poems he expresses his conviction in terms that are distinctively his own. These poems embody a conception of the individual life and of its relationship to the life of nature as a whole which is perfectly definite and which, more than anything else, determines the unique character of Lampman's work. It answers some of the questions Roberts' poetry left unanswered, and it constitutes Lampman's reformulation of what is commonly called the life of the spirit. Here, Lampman's own peculiar emphasis is reflected in the use of the word "energy" and in images which are the embodiment of energy. Energy is all – at least that "primal energy" he speaks of in the following passage.

> Nature hath fixed in each man's life for dower
> One root-like gift, one primal energy,
> Wherefrom the soul takes growth, as grows a tree,
> With sap and fibre, branch and leaf and flower;
> But if this seed in its creative hour
> Be crushed and stifled, only then the shell
> Lifts like a phantom falsely visible,
> Wherein is neither growth, nor joy, nor power.

This primal energy is not unlike Wordsworth's "a motion and a spirit" that impels all things. It is closer, perhaps, to Dylan Thomas' "force that through the green fuse drives the flower." But the one thing that Lampman emphasizes here is that this energy is individualized in each creature. The passage, especially as it unfolds, sounds oddly like one of D. H. Lawrence's characters lecturing another to the effect that he must stop looking for a God or a goal outside himself but must simply develop his own soul as a dandelion develops into a dandelion and not into a stick of celery. The soul is energy; the life of the spirit, like the life of the body, is rooted in the irrational vitality of nature and not in the rational activity of the intellect. It takes its reference from an internal, not an external power. The soul becomes, it does not conform.

When Lampman maintains that the growth of the soul consists in each creature's following its own bent, he diametrically opposes the central impulse of his culture, which would change or transform life to make it fit some ideal pattern – which would impose an order upon life. Thus, though he may not be fully aware of it, he becomes a spokesman for the God of Job, who recommends all his creatures as equally good. Like an earlier romantic poet, Lampman is led inevitably to an affirmation of every form of life, from the tiger to the lamb. In the sonnet from which we have just quoted, and which Lampman calls "Salvation," he goes on to say:

> Find thou this germ, and find thou thus thyself,
> This one clear meaning of the deathless I,
> This bent, this work, this duty – for thereby
> God numbers thee, and marks thee for His own:
> Careless of hurt, or threat, or praise, or pelf,
> Find it and follow it, this, and this alone![25]

Lampman can sound like the conventional Victorian moralist bitten by the bug of spiritual progress. In "The Clearer Self," for example, he exhorts us "to know, to seek, to find," to make that strenuous effort whereby the soul shall be freed from the "folds of thwarting matter." Yet his most authentic poems, such as "Heat" or "Solitude," hardly suggest Tennyson's Ulysses; if anything, they are closer to Wordsworth's wise passiveness. Still, it is energy that occupies Lampman's attention. Indeed, in the above-mentioned poem "The Clearer Self," it is the use of the word "energy" where we might have expected "the Power of God" or "the Divine Spirit" that betrays Lampman's particular emphasis. There he says that:

> ... through the ancient layers of night,
> In gradual victory secure,
> Grows ever with increasing light
> The Energy serene and pure.[26]

It is as if Lampman conceived the progress of the spirit as a steady transformation of matter into energy.

It is the reverse process, however, that seems to interest Lampman most: the transformation of energy into matter. More accurately, it is the embodiment of a kind of undifferentiated energy within the unique creature – the sense that it at once draws in, to use Lawrence's phrase, the great wandering vitalities of the world and, at the same time, gives them unique definition. This is what really captures Lampman's imagination. At the centre of his poetry we find a celebration of the abundant well of universal energy and of its embodiment or epiphany in the manifold variety of life.

No more naturalistic and rudimentary image of man's relationship to the vital power of the universe could be found than in the poem "Among the Timothy," where we are presented with the direct physical experience of living creatures absorbing into themselves the vital energy of the sun.

> ... hour by hour, the ever-journeying sun,
> In gold and shadow spun,
> Into mine eyes and blood, and through the dim
> Green glimmering forest of the grass shines down,
> Till flower and blade, and every cranny brown,
> And I are soaked with him.[27]

The association of the sun and its energy with the divine is evident in "The Sun Cup," in which Lampman likens the earth to a cup which the sun fills every morning, thereby making it divine.

It is this conception which lies at the heart of Lampman's best known poem, "Heat," and which gives to it the otherwise puzzling religious dimension indicated within the poem itself solely by the remark, "I think some blessèd power/Hath brought me wandering idly here." The experience of the heat itself is an experience of the superabundant well of power, the divine energy of the universe that feeds and informs all things. And there in the solitude, at the height of noon, in the absence of all external pressures that might distract one or stifle the "primal germ," each creature manifests that energy fully and uniquely, with the particularity of the buttercups or the marguerites which the speaker counts one by one. Each thing emerges under these conditions with complete clarity and distinctness, just as, in the concluding lines, the speaker says, "In the full furnace of this hour/My thoughts grow keen and clear."[28]

A. J. M. Smith has said that Lampman became dull and unoriginal when he attempted to philosophize and that he was best at pure landscape where his painter's eye for significant detail produced impressive results. Though this is true on the surface, the fact is that many of Lampman's most sharply realized and convincing poems are the result, not of some happy gift for painterly description, but of a fundamental, essentially philosophical conviction. Poems like "Heat" and "Solitude" are not pure landscape but the most convincing poetic statements of Lampman's view of life.

It is Lampman's conviction that each individual must realize his full and distinct definition that gives him his eye for particulars. In that self-realization and in that alone does God "mark thee for His own." As the spoken word registers itself best against a background of silence, so in solitude does each particular creature register itself clearly. Only there does Lampman apprehend most vividly what he calls "the clearer self" of all things. In the sonnet "Solitude," even the air finds palpable definition; it hangs "quiet as spaces in a marble frieze." Above all, in the stillness of that solitude, each distinct sound makes itself heard, the scream of a hawk, the tap of a woodpecker. The poem concludes:

> Sometimes I hear
> The dreamy white-throat from some far-off tree
> Pipe slowly on the listening solitude,
> His five pure notes succeeding pensively.[29]

In the same way, another well-known poem, "The Woodcutter's Hut," derives much of its appeal from the gradual, effortless display of the various concrete and particular phenomena of the winter woods as they reveal themselves in the surrounding solitude. There they are displayed in the same fashion that the small birds, the siskins, are said to "scatter the dimpled sheet of the snow with the shells of the cedar-seed." The final image of the woodcutter is itself an image of the individual who has found a certain completeness of definition.

> He is gone with his corded arms, and his
> ruddy face, and his moccasined feet,
> The animal man in his warmth and
> vigor, sound, and hard, and complete.[30]

"The Woodcutter's Hut" is one of the few poems of this type which also mentions "a sense of a struggling life in the waste." Despite the fact that energy and its embodiment in every creature implies its release in action in a dynamic world, Lampman was not much concerned with the problem of action or with what Mr Gold terms the conditions of a wilderness struggle for survival. As "The City of the End of Things" suggests, he was more concerned about the destructive element in culture than in nature. In turning his back on the city and looking to nature, Lampman in effect was turning his back on a society increasingly concentrated on the manipulation of an external or mechanical power in order himself to concentrate on the husbanding of an internal or spiritual power. Relatively, the wilderness had become more propitious to spiritual life than the human community. It is not, however, the ideal human environment. As Lampman wandered through the waste fields, the dream that wrapped him like a cloak against the falling snow was undoubtedly one which, though inspired by his experience in nature, saw its fulfilment in a human order – an order that would concentrate on the cultivation of the inner or spiritual vitality of man, that would be primarily concerned with making possible the fullest development of each individual in his own, peculiarly human way. It is the dream of a humane Arcadian city, beautiful, not simply as a façade transfigured by the sunset on the distant horizon, but beautiful within, in the spirit that informs its human culture. Only then will man find relief from "a sense of a struggling life in the waste."

Perhaps if Lampman had lived longer he might have been led to explore more thoroughly some of the problems of action implicit in his poetry. D. C. Scott's comments upon Lampman's lively mind and the growing boldness of his thought towards the end of his life give some basis to such speculation. On the other hand, he might never have become primarily interested in such problems. He appears to have been essentially a contemplative man, as much of his best poetry is of a contemplative kind.

By contrast, the work of Duncan Campbell Scott is primarily narrative and dramatic, even when it is concerned with the inability to act. And even more obviously than for Lampman, the universe for Scott is dynamic; life is energy; and energy implies action. Where Lampman emphasizes the white-throat and the calm of windless days, Scott fastens on the hawk and on the hours of storm. But, more than Lampman, he is aware of both, of the two poles of human experience which characterize the world of Job. And he is more clearly preoccupied with the problem of Job, with the destructive violence of such a world, particularly as it is exacerbated by the activity of man.

Desmond Pacey has characterized Scott's view of the world as essentially "a vision of a battleground where nature is in conflict with itself, man in conflict with nature, and man in conflict with man." Of Scott's reaction to this world, Mr Pacey goes on to say:

> Out of the conflict emerges, whether sooner or later, peace and beauty. He has faith in the ultimate rightness of things, in a presiding spirit which in the long run has a beneficent purpose, and in man's capacity to endure. The final note of Scott's work is not that of the storm but of the silence which follows the storm, is not despair but serenity. But it is not an easy nor a complacent serenity; it is a serenity achieved after much effort.[31]

Such serenity may be the final note in Scott's work; it is not that of many poems. The beneficent purpose upon which Scott speculates in "The Height of Land" remains pretty obscure. As a rule, the major poems do not formulate any clear-cut purpose, which would account for the often harsh and tragic activities of man and nature that these poems dramatize. The load of passion, violence, and sheer terror which many of these poems carry is considerable. Like the fictional Abe Spalding and like his author Frederick Philip Grove, Scott himself had to digest the irrational or inexplicable loss of his only child, a twelve-year-old girl whom he had seen alive and healthy only a few days before receiving the telegram announcing her death. The effort which Scott's poetry implies is first of all the effort required to recognize and accept such events, the effort required to hold the destructive and creative elements of life, the calm and the storm, simultaneously before him. And then, perhaps as Mr Pacey wishes to suggest, it is the effort to see them both against the background of a cosmic power which, whatever its purpose, has the characteristic air of an imperturbable creator and destroyer, the serenity of neither calm nor storm but of that out of which both arise and into which both subside. Such is the nature of the peace or serenity which Scott evokes in the sonnet "In Snow-time." The octave is concerned with the ordinary tranquillity of nature, the peace that comes with "Calm after storm, wherein the storm seems blessed." The sestet is concerned with another, less ordinary peace that he glimpses in the snow-covered earth.

> But here a peace deeper than peace is furled,
> Enshrined and chaliced from the changeful hour;
> The snow is still, yet lives in its own light.
> Here is the peace which brooded day and night,
> Before the heart of man with its wild power
> Had ever spurned or trampled the great world.[32]

One of Scott's earliest and best poems, "The Piper of Arll," ends with a similarly serene vision of a power which lives in its own light. Not unlike Lampman's sense of an undifferentiated, superabundant energy, it is a vision of the potentiality of life, not of actual life. "The Piper of Arll" is first of all a poem which dramatizes the withdrawal from the forces of actual life. The quiet piper is wooed by the world of passion and action, represented by the sea and the pines and the violent colours of the sunset, and more especially by the strange ship that enters the bay. Yet he cannot act. As much as he would like to, he has not the courage to join the sailors and set sail on a voyage of struggle and adventure. After singing out his longing, he expires. The serenity which the piper himself discovers is the serenity of death. The serenity with which the poem as a whole ends is that of the rich but unrealized potential for life. Sunk beneath the sea, the piper lies surrounded by the ship and all its crew, like a lost diadem or symbol of a power which lives in its own light.

A number of the Indian poems written about the same time, notably "Watkwenies," "The Onondaga Madonna," and "The Half-Breed Girl," are similarly concerned with the failure or inability to act. They explicitly dramatize the paralysis that results from cultural confusion. These contemporary Indians, culturally disinherited, have no clear or acceptable view of life and so remain uncertain about how to deal with it. Their vitality remains stifled within them. The conflict in these poems can never issue in serenity.

In "Watkwenies," we are told in the octave of a woman who fought against the white soldiers in her youth. In the sestet we see her standing idle, wrinkled "like an apple kept till May," waiting for her government pension.

> She weighs the interest-money in her palm,
> And when the Agent calls her valiant name,
> Hears, like the war-whoops of her perished day,
> The lads playing snow-snake in the stinging cold.[33]

We infer the frustration, the sense of humiliation and impotence in this Indian woman.

In "The Onondaga Madonna," the contrast is drawn between the full-throated beauty of the Indian mother, in whose face "all her pagan passion burns and glows," and the pallor and restlessness of her half-breed child.

> The latest promise of her nation's doom,
> Paler than she her baby clings and lies,
> The primal warrior gleaming from his eyes;
> He sulks, and burdened with his infant gloom,
> He draws his heavy brows and will not rest.[34]

It is a rather sardonic portrait of a madonna and child since the child, and the Indian nation and its culture embodied in the child, is here being crucified on the cross of western culture, a Christian culture at that.

The baby's infant gloom has matured in the half-breed girl of the third poem to an extreme unrest, even despair. Psychologically divided between the incomprehensible inheritance of her Scottish father and the no longer relevant inheritance of her Indian mother, she is paralyzed in her capacity to act. She cannot live in terms of either inheritance, and her vital energies are dissipated in frustration.

> Her dreams are undiscovered,
> Shadows trouble her breast,
> When the time for resting cometh
> Then least is she at rest.

In this dilemma, her existence becomes a living death.

She covers her face with her blanket,
Her fierce soul hates her breath,
As it cries with a sudden passion
For life or death.[35]

One may doubt that these poems on the contemporary Indian arose from a purely professional interest or were solely the result of a disinterested sympathy on the writer's part. The condition of the Indians is but a specific and notable instance of a condition which preoccupies Scott in a number of poems. "The Piper of Arll" has no connection with Indians nor, in its pastoral form, with any particular group in actual society; yet it dramatizes much the same theme: the suppression of passion leading to a consequent stagnation or paralysis of life. Another poem, "Thoughts," reveals that Scott himself was perfectly familiar with the state of mind of such figures as the half-breed girl. He writes:

These thoughts of mine
Oh! would they were away.
Thoughts that have progress
Give me stay
And eagerness for life;
But these dead thoughts
Hang like burned forests
By a northern lake,
Whose waters take
The bone-grey skeletons
And mirror the grey bones;
Both dead, the trees and the reflections.

Compare these thoughts
To anything that nothing tells, –
To toads alive for centuries in stone cells,
To a styleless dial on a fiery lawn,
To the trapped bride within the oaken chest,
Or to the dull, intolerable bells
That beat the dawn
And will not let us rest[36]

We have no way of knowing, on the basis of the poem alone, precisely what thoughts have produced this state of mind. The dead trees which here represent his dead thoughts do, however, find an echo in "The Height of Land," and it may be interesting to follow up the association. It is an association with thoughts of mortality, the contemplation of the destructive element in life. Alone beside the campfire on the height of land above Superior, the speaker has felt a presence in the universe around him, a presence he identifies as "the ancient disturber of solitude." Meditating on this presence, he at first conceives life and all its struggles as proceeding towards some ideal resolution. But at the height of that vision he is suddenly reminded of another which is equally associated with "the ancient disturber of solitude." As that presence "Stirs his ancestral potion in the gloom," the speaker notes that "the dark wood/Is stifled with the pungent fume/Of charred earth burnt to the bone/That takes the place of air." He proceeds to describe a previous encounter with this disturbing ancient presence. After paddling through a fetid swamp, he had come to the portage, where "a bushfire, smouldering, with sudden roar/Leaped on a cedar and smothered it with light/And terror." It is an image that E. K. Brown cites as one of several in the poem of "an almost ferocious energy."[37] The fire leaves the portage a tangle of burnt trees and smoking resin that "even then began to thin and lessen/Into the gloom and glimmer of ruin."[38]

Whether these thoughts in "The Height of Land" are of the same variety as those in the previous poem we cannot say with any certainty. Certainly they have something of the same effect, providing in "The Height of Land" a momentary check on Scott's fervent if intuitive affirmation of the beauty, purpose, or meaning of life's struggle. Certainly Scott is aware of the darkness as well as the glory, of the potential violence as well as the sweetness of nature's ferocious energy, of the difficulty of comprehending such a world as Jehovah unfolds before Job and, more especially, of man's frequent failure to comprehend such a world so that its vitality may flow harmoniously into the forms of human life. As we shall see, the violence which attends such a failure is the subject of the poem "At Gull Lake: August, 1810." Yet the way must be found, for the frustration which attends man's attempts to shut out nature's ferocious energy is equally grave. As we have seen, the inability to act, whether out of fear or confusion, is equally the subject of Scott's poem. Its stifling effect is reflected in poems one might consider purely descriptive. "A Night in June" will illustrate the point. It begins:

> The world is heated seven times,
> The sky is close above the lawn,
> An oven when the coals are drawn.

The image suggests enormous energy cut off from its source. The source has been withdrawn. It creates at once an impression of power and of impotence, an impression sustained by many of the images that follow. The lightning flashes only to let the darkness settle more intensely. A bird calls only to have the silence return more completely. The thunder rolls through the heavens, but no rain falls. Instead:

> A fountain plashing in the dark
> Keeps up a mimic dropping strain;
> Ah! God, if it were really rain!

The mood evoked in the poem is one of frustration. Vast energies hang in the air and flicker about the speaker, but they are not available to immediate life. The storm refuses to break and release these energies in a life-giving rain, clearing the air, stimulating action. One image in particular vividly evokes the kind of frustration we have noted in the other poems: we have a glimpse of a ferocious energy struggling to find release in the stifling atmosphere.

> A hawk lies panting in the grass,
> Or plunges upward through the air,
> The lightning shows him whirling there.[39]

Few, if any, of these poems could be said to issue in serenity. Each in its own way dramatizes a failure or inability to draw in the great wandering vitalities of the world and to release them effectively in the immediate social or individual life.

One of the poems that does end in serenity is "The Forsaken," which Mr Pacey admires as being, along with "The Piper of Arll," Scott's best work. This is also a poem about Indian life, but not that of the contemporary Indian on the reservation. "The Forsaken" is a narrative poem in two parts, both of which dramatize the courage and endurance of an Indian woman in the face of great hardship. In the first part we see her as a young mother.

> Once in the winter
> Out on a lake
> In the heart of the north-land,
> Far from the Fort
> And far from the hunters,
> A Chippewa woman
> With her sick baby,
> Crouched in the last hours
> Of a great storm.
> Frozen and hungry,
> She fished through the ice
> With a line of the twisted
> Bark of the cedar;
> And a rabbit-bone hook

Polished and barbed;
Fished with the bare hook
All through the wild day,
Fished and caught nothing;
While the young chieftain
Tugged at her breasts,
Or slept in the lacings
Of the warm *tikanagan.*[40]

Finally the woman baits the hook with her own flesh, catches the fish she needs to go on feeding her baby, and through three days of storm makes her way back to the Fort.

In the second part we see her as an old woman left on an island to die according to the ways of her tribe. Again she endures three days of hardship, this time by waiting patiently as the storm gradually covers her over with snow, only her breath revealing her presence, until death finally comes.

Both the first and the second parts of the poem end with the line: Then she had rest. In both instances the struggles of this Indian woman issue in serenity because in both instances she was able to act appropriately. Whether faced with the question of her son's survival or with the survival of the tribe, she has been prepared by her culture to meet the harsh necessities of life. Moreover, as her behaviour reveals, it is a culture that accepts death and the destructive element as an inevitable and necessary part of life. As a result, the whole action, barbaric as it might first appear, has an unexpected simplicity and quietness, a notable lack of violence. She does not oppose the harsh world in which she lives as if it were an unjust world. She does not become bitter or defiant. She sacrifices herself to life in the interests of life: slightly in the first instance, wholly in the second instance, appropriately in each. She behaves in each instance without violence, without rancour, and without any sense of guilt. She acts serenely.

"At Gull Lake: August, 1810" proceeds to a quite different conclusion. The action in this poem is at the opposite pole to the dreamlike inactivity of the shepherd and the ship's crew who are finally immobilized in "The Piper of Arll." It is quite different from the restless frustration that characterizes the Indians on the reserve in "Watkwenies," "The Onondaga Madonna," and "The Half-Breed Girl." Nairne, the trader in this poem, acts without hesitation. Keejigo is no girl haunted by shadows, her dreams undiscovered, who takes to her bed and covers her face with a blanket. Keejigo also acts without hesitation. Yet, quite unlike the action in "The Forsaken," the result here is tragic. As far as the human actors are concerned, the poem does not end in serenity, but in waste and violence.

Where the failure to find a formula that would release the vital energies of nature within the forms of social life led in earlier poems to a kind of death through inactivity, the same kind of failure here leads to death through conflicting and violent action. The Indian girl, Keejigo, embodies the beauty and vitality of nature. She is capable of both passion and tenderness. She is both the hawk and the dove. The beauty of peace and the beauty of terror are equally attributed to her. She has belonged to the primitive man, Tabashaw, Chief of the Saulteaux, but he has no large appreciation of her. She offers herself to the civilized white man, but he also fails to appreciate her. Both end by driving her away. Available to both, comprehended by neither, between them she is destroyed.

Nairne, the rational man, refuses to have his commercial activities disrupted by passion. Tabashaw, the irrational man, indulges his passion. Neither catches the glory of life; both increase the darkness around them. They are antithetical but equally destructive. Such, we may say, is the fate of Eros in a culture which cannot embrace and integrate the irrational within the rational order, which excludes or ignores or degrades passion: passion or the irrational energies of life continue to go their own way, uncontrolled and furious.

The cultural attitudes that inform the action in this poem tend to be largely commercial; primitive and civilized man meet in a common concern to exploit nature – in the pursuit of the world's goods, material wealth and power. Its formulae release men to act with all the violence of the material world itself, a world of things and possessions. The girl is but one such possession: to be owned, to be traded, to be driven to her master, or to be beaten and thrown over the bank like a dead dog. Here there is no communion, but only opposition. Each maintains himself against the other, never accepting, as the woman in "The Forsaken" accepts, the possibility of self-sacrifice. Essentially divisive, the formulae of this commercial culture blindly perpetuate and extend the basic violence and destructiveness of life. Certainly the serenity with which this poem ends is quite different from that of "The Forsaken." It is the serenity of the God of Job, of nature as a whole, perhaps, not the serenity of the human actors. It is the serenity of the battlefield the morning after the battle.

Nairne is a reasonable man. He would like to act in a world of light and rational order. The commercial world he represents appears to assume that it can avoid the darkness if it is willing to forego the glory. But one cannot act without releasing the darkness, and the only way to control it is by comprehending it and by ordering or dominating it on its own irrational terms – if not by love, then by some other art. That would seem to be the implication of "Powassan's Drum," in which we are presented with one of the strangest and most naked visions of the demonic face of nature in all Scott's poetry. In this poem the shaman, through his irrational ritual, calls into view a headless warrior who rises out of the death-like water and is then brought under control and sent back into its depth, as if by the forces of the storm called up by the shaman himself. It is not the sun but the storm that "crushes the dark world."

Leonard Cohen's character F. in *Beautiful Losers* remarks:

> Now what about this silence we are so desperate to clear in the wilderness? Have we laboured, ploughed, muzzled, fenced so that we might hear a Voice? Fat chance. The Voice comes out of the whirlwind, and long ago we hushed the whirlwind.[41]

Yet, has not the desperate attempt to silence the wilderness not only failed to make available a Voice, but failed absolutely? We may think we have hushed the whirlwind, but it erupts from our own hands in a mushroom cloud. It is the Chippewa woman in the midst of the whirlwind who truly finds silence. Accepting the darkness, she hooks the glory. And where we find terror she finds peace.

The picture of a universe increasingly at odds with the assumptions of conventional piety has created a certain cultural confusion. One reaction is to fall back on the *status quo*, another to assert even more vigorously certain traditional assumptions, to impose an order on a disorderly world. But, as the writers we have discussed here have indicated, neither of these tactics is successful. One leads to paralysis, the other to violence. To escape this dilemma, the poets like Lampman have moved out of the traditional cultural order to find a more vital order in the wilderness of nature. There, especially when they come to consider the implications of all action, of life's self-assertion, they confront the one fundamental problem, Job's problem of how to affirm an ambiguous and seemingly hostile creation.

Whatever the answer to the problem of Job, if it does not lie in abject acceptance of Jehovah's universe, neither does it lie in outright defiance. However terrifying Behemoth and Leviathan, we must neither cower before them nor try to annihilate them. We must somehow learn to delight in them. E. J. Pratt, of the poets who follow in the generation after Scott, was one who did. Earle Birney, on the other hand, has found the task much more difficult. Each in his fashion might be said to have taken up the theme where Scott left off, for it is a theme that remains central to twentieth-century poetry.

CHAPTER FIVE

The Courage to Be

> Let me swallow it whole and be strong,
> accept it whole and be strong!
> Let me take it whole and be strong!
>
> JOHN NEWLOVE, "Resources, Certain Earths"

> Where others enter
> Where no one enters
> There is courage.
>
> RALPH GUSTAFSON, "The Silence"

With E. J. Pratt's "The Cachalot," Leviathan heaves into view, and he remains a presence in much of twentieth-century Canadian poetry. For Pratt, he rides triumphant, aureoled with light on the Atlantic seas. For Earle Birney he is Cetegrande, who swims the sea of time and like that sea itself devours all things. Fathoms down in the world of Phyllis Webb, between a mermaid's thighs, he sleeps. And in the universal flood that inundates the world of Jay Macpherson, man, with candles at his head and feet, lies cradled in his belly as in Noah's ark. Lately in "The Sperm King," Gwen MacEwen hails him and exclaims:

> O ocean, boil in his throat!
> from his terrible mouth his millions spill;
> Sperm burns in the wake of the fragrant whale,
> massive as of seas is the throw and the thrash of it.[1]

The present chapter traces the reaction of a later generation than that of Roberts or Scott to the problem Leviathan poses. Particularly it looks at the work of E. J. Pratt, A. J. M. Smith, Earle Birney, and Irving Layton to determine how they reconcile themselves to nature's prodigal powers, its threat of violence and death. Generally speaking, each in his fashion moves towards a more inclusive attitude than that of the existing social order, and each tends to reconcile himself to the order of nature along the lines already implied in the work of Duncan Campbell Scott: by accepting rather than defying Leviathan and by recommending the seemingly old-fashioned virtue of courage as fundamental to any attempt to both affirm and delight in the world he inhabits. Even Earle Birney, who in many of his poems would seem to be an exception to the rule, arrives at a statement of this kind in "The Damnation of Vancouver," where the attempt to justify life before man's more exclusive rational or moral laws is abandoned in favour of a more inclusive view. It is only through a courageous acceptance of life for better and for worse that one can justify or rejoice in life. But let us look more closely at the way in which each of these writers approaches the problem posed by Leviathan.

In E. J. Pratt's "The Cachalot," the whale destroys the giant squid and rises from the deep to steam like one divinely favoured on the surface of the sea. He is attacked by whalers and destroyed, but in his death grows violent, scattering the ship and crew over his grave. Pratt looks on as might the God of Job, displaying no more sympathy for the men than for the whale. Clearly Pratt's initial impulse is to delight in nature and her powers, however prodigious or violent. In his essay "E. J. Pratt's Four-Ton Gulliver," Paul West accuses Pratt of a propensity to betray his fellow men and openly or secretly to identify himself with the Leviathans or Titans of Jehovah's world. "Pratt," he writes, "displays an almost Jewish complicity with cosmic forces ... " He runs the risk, therefore, of throwing in his lot with Jehovah, of becoming the spokesman for a deity who is no more than a god of power, a bully, morally inferior to the physically quite helpless but morally quite formidable Job. Though his alliance with the cosmic powers is often quite flattering, it runs the risk, says Mr West, of turning us against ourselves and of "making *thanatos* out of *eros*."[2]

Pratt in "The Truant" disavows any allegiance to a mere god of power whose chief or most intimidating feature is "the power to kill." There Pratt seems to defy Jehovah, to scorn his universe and so to take up arms against the sea, against all nature's powers. But the Great Panjandrum he defies is a nineteenth-century rationalist's parody of the God of Job, entirely lacking in the latter's unpredictable creative exuberance. It is not the natural universe that Pratt rejects in this poem, but merely a conception of it.

Fundamentally Pratt looks on nature and finds it good. His poetry implies that life, especially human life, finds its fulfilment in a partnership with the elemental forces of nature. He is determined from the outset to accept the influx of the sea. Where the protagonist in

Duncan Campbell Scott's early poem "The Piper of Arll" was overwhelmed by the tidings from the sea, the speaker in Pratt's "Newfoundland," an equally early poem, celebrates precisely that intercourse of sea and land. As the elemental energies of wind and tide flow into human life they may find a new and richer release.

> Here the tides flow,
> And here they ebb;
> Not with that dull, unsinewed tread of waters
> Held under bonds to move
> Around unpeopled shores –
> Moon-driven through a timeless circuit
> Of invasion and retreat;
> But with a lusty stroke of life
> Pounding at stubborn gates,
> That they might run
> Within the sluices of men's hearts,
> Leap under throb of pulse and nerve,
> And teach the sea's strong voice
> To learn the harmonies of new floods.[3]

Pratt is perfectly aware that the new floods may sound a tragic harmony or even discord. At the end of his first volume, *Newfoundland*, he takes up this theme at a point not too far removed from Scott's "At Gull Lake." The action of "The Ice Floes" takes place in a world of incarnate energies, beautiful, conflicting, and finally tragic in their violence. It is the story of a seal hunt in which man destroys seal, storm destroys man, and the slaughter is general on both sides. Again, for man and seal if not for nature at large, the beauty of terror overwhelms the beauty of peace.

> And the rest is as a story told,
>   Or a dream that belonged to a dim, mad past,
> Of a March night and a north wind's cold,
>   Of a voyage home with a flag half-mast;
> Of twenty thousand seals that were killed
>   To help to lower the price of bread;
> Of the muffled beat ... of a drum ... that filled
>   A nave ... at our count of sixty dead.[4]

There is an ambiguity in the poem. In saying that the seals were killed to help to lower the price of bread Pratt might appear to be saying that the sixty men also died in a necessary struggle for existence. Pratt accepts the destructiveness of life as radical in the sense that all life feeds on other life and man cannot escape from this condition. Yet here man has added needlessly to the basic violence of life, and the sixty dead are the victims of their own excessive or wanton behaviour. For the sealers were so engrossed in making a record kill and so caught up in the excitement, greed, or lust for slaughter that they did not notice the storm coming up nor the signals that called them back to the ship. When they did it was too late and, left exposed on the pans of ice amid the carnage of the hunt, they died needlessly.

These men are as moon-driven as the tides. Yet they are simple men and Pratt does not go out of his way to criticize them. But neither does he withhold his general affirmation of life.

Here the world of E. J. Pratt is much like that of Roberts' animal stories, except that Pratt regards these men with the same objectivity as Roberts regards the salmon or the lynx, the eagle or the mouse. The anxiety we note in Roberts whenever man appears on the scene is absent in Pratt. Failing to realize the degree of consciousness or self-awareness that as men they might have realized, the sealers act as impulsively or unconsciously as animals, and like the seals they are caught up in the blind struggle for existence. They die, and Pratt extends to them almost the same impersonal sympathy he extends to the seal. He seems to look on such events with a large and almost passionless irony.

Often, though not always, the same large irony controls Pratt's pictures of more lavish waste, of men more dangerous and less easily excusable, as in the case of "The Titanic" or "Dunkirk." These poems reiterate our point that the attempt to proclaim man wholly superior to nature, to defy her and to shut her out, is folly and only adds to the destructiveness of life.

The men of the *Titanic* or Dunkirk are not merely simple seamen. They are men who have attained a high degree of consciousness, who act with much deliberation, and who have assumed the right to act for other men and to direct their lives. The fate of whole societies is in their hands.

The men who have created the *Titanic* claim to be the equals of Leviathan, equals in power. They assume that man is able to defy, exploit, and utterly shut out the teeming but devouring waves of the sea, and that he can create within the human order of his ship a world quite free of nature's irrational or destructive elements. But this is an arrogant piece of folly. The menus on the spotless tablecloths proclaim, to begin with, that man cannot escape putting his own foot in the slaughter-house of nature. And the course of events attests that despite his considerable technical power he is no match in the long run for the destructive power of the natural universe. And more to the point, these events reveal that he cannot shut out, much less in this instance control, the irrational and destructive elements of nature which he carries in his own veins. It is that sea within which actually delivers them into the sea without. In the end these men behave with the same blindness as the simple sealer.

The iceberg and the ship are notoriously alike in Pratt's presentation of the matter, and Pratt notoriously displays no greater sympathy for the ship than for the berg. Yet this is not so puzzling. Of the resemblances between the iceberg and the ship, the most apparent are that each is the product of a long period of development; that both are large, complex, and even beautiful in the intricacy of their superstructure; and that both, when stripped to their foundations, emerge as crude instruments of power. And here we approach the most significant resemblance, the point in which they find a common identity. Both are the instruments of chance, driven by the blind currents of the sea, whether within or without, towards a conjunction which can only be described in the language of the insurance adjuster as an act of God.

Though the poem celebrates the courage and self-sacrifice of certain men during the last hours of the *Titanic*, the narrative is focussed on the ship as a symbolic whole, and the type of man embodied in that ship can command no more sympathy from Pratt than can the berg. For both, as we have seen, have the same character. The ship becomes one more embodiment of force in a world of forces in conflict. And the drama on this level proves nothing more significant than the final insignificance of man and all his ships before the destructive processes of the universe at large. "The grey shape with the paleolithic face," remains, as it will ever remain, "the master of the longitudes."[5]

Bacon's dictum that nature to be commanded must first be obeyed seems often to be forgotten – except in a superficial sense. Yet every time man assumes that he is superior to nature and that he can command her without obeisance, he ends by proving Bacon's law, by being himself commanded, and by enlarging the field of nature's violence.

"Dunkirk" is a further illustration of this point. The attempt by Hitler's armies to conquer the world and to impose upon it the more perfect order of the superman is only a little more obviously mad than most. The more impersonal their military machine becomes the more it acts as blindly as the stars. That is, the more it claims to be completely rational and self-controlled, the more it is in fact controlled by the irrational and quite unconscious currents of the sea. And in the end it fails before the spontaneous and logically absurd activities of motley groups of men with a ridiculous flotilla of small boats.

As Mr West observes, a little puzzled, it is the retreat and not the resistance which Pratt celebrates. The retreat is the real victory, the triumph of life over the machine. To celebrate resistance or attack would, in this context, be to celebrate no more than force, a contest of machines or of destructive power. Here, as in "The Titanic," Pratt proclaims what Mr West has termed "the futility of regimen and system,"[6] and of all attempts to dominate the apparent disorder of the world by force.

Generally, Pratt's poetry implies that whenever man attempts to improve the world or add to his own stature by means of force, he fails. His efforts to annihilate nature's imperfection, whether in the name of reason or in the name of morality, always end in irony and in a holocaust of destruction. To oppose Leviathan and harrow the sea is finally insane and suicide. That would seem to be the moral of "The Great Feud."

"The Great Feud" can be read as a parody of man's attempt to assert a spiritual reality by attacking the natural world, more specifically by declaring total war upon his original nature. In this instance it becomes an all-out war against the sea. A mother ape, the "most thoroughbred pedestrian" of all the creatures of the land, having seen a crocodile devour one of her young only to be itself struck down by a falling coconut, concludes that she has seen a revelation of the universal moral law. She calls together all the creatures of the land and, proclaiming that they must not kill their kind, counsels them to become vegetarians and to organize for an attack upon the creatures of the sea. They, the "ignorant, inarticulate/cold-blood barbarians of the sea," are proclaimed the source of evil. By annihilating these devouring devils of the sea, the land animals will presumably eradicate all evil from the world and the earth will then become a kind of paradise or Eden. A ferocious battle ensues. But the result is not the peace and plenty of a paradise regained. It is a most amazing slaughter. At first the death toll on both sea and land seems equal. Then Tyrannosaurus Rex becomes confused and kills without discrimination as to sides. With night, the land beasts revert to their habitual ways and begin to prey upon each other. Finally the earth itself becomes distempered and erupts in a volcanic explosion. Pouring lava down the hills, it drives the last surviving forces of the land into "the drowning mercies of the sea" or seals them in a tomb of living rock. The ape alone survives, escaping in the nick of time into more distant hills.[7]

Man is an even more thoroughbred pedestrian. His capacity for reflection releases him from the bondage of the winds and tides, of a purely instinctual behaviour. He is free, at least potentially, to create new harmonies – or new discord. Often enough, Pratt seems to say, he does not avail himself of this capacity for reflection and behaves like an erratic or imperfect animal. Worse, he may reflect, but not profoundly. He may use his freedom only to increase his strength; he may conceive himself the equal of the God of Job and try to match him, power for power. Or, like the female anthropoidal ape, he may grow grander still, conceive, or misconceive, his own peculiar role to be both judge and executioner of the unconscious world. Yet, however noble this conception might at first appear, it drags him into a futile trial of strength within a universe where might is right, and where, if he does not execute himself and all his followers, he will be executed nonetheless with time and death, whose patience can frustrate and cut short all his efforts.

On the level of mere power, death always wins. Pratt's truant may challenge the great Panjandrum's power to kill, but he cannot do so without absurdity unless he shifts his point of view. This he does, challenging him on the purely human level, the level of value. Though there is also a sense in which he here catches out this shrunken version of Jehovah on his own ground. The embodiment of regimen and system, no more creative than the analytical mind that conceived him, this master of the universe is little more than a machine, which like all machines is subject to the second law of thermodynamics. Not only man, but the great Panjandrum and all his works are doomed to end in the final heat-death of the universe.

No matter on what level man may choose to live, he must accept the common fate:

> The road goes up, the road goes down –
> Let Java or Geneva be –
> But whether to the cross or crown,
> The path lies through Gethsemane.[8]

The fully meditated acceptance of death, which the image of Gethsemane implies, leads neither to the withdrawal of the piper of Arll nor to the resistance of the anthropoidal ape. One runs neither towards death nor away from it. Rather, one takes precisely the attitude of D. C. Scott's Indian woman in "The Forsaken," which is that there is a season for all things and a time to live and a time to die. Early in life the woman struggles against death, later in life she surrenders to it willingly; in both cases she behaves in a spirit of self-sacrifice. Pratt's poetry recommends the same approach to life. As Jay Macpherson has remarked in an unpublished thesis, Pratt implies that "the highest human virtue is self-sacrifice, and the blindest and crudest evil is the urge to sacrifice others."

Much of Pratt's work is a Rabelaisian satire on the human follies just described, and many of the major poems conclude in irony. One of the most straightforward and most pure in its mode is "The Roosevelt and the Antinoe," in which men become aware that neither the magic of words nor the power of technology can save them from the naked encounter with the destructive forces of the sea; they get down into the sea itself and struggle with it. Because they act with strength, with courage, and in a spirit of self-sacrifice, they succeed not only in making the rescue but in rising above the terms whereby the waves could claim a victory. They may die; yet they set out prepared to make that sacrifice.

Only in this spirit can man oppose nature without adding to her destructive violence. Only in this spirit can he claim a superiority to the forces of nature or to a mere God of power. And when he has arrived at this reflection he does not defy the world of Behemoth and Leviathan, but rather he comprehends it. In a more truly godlike gesture he would become responsible to it and seek to nurture it.

Rarely does Pratt preach this lesson directly or explicitly. Many of his poems are satirical or ironic accounts of the reverse kind of behaviour. But the lesson is implied. And the tone of these ironic narrations is seldom bitter, because Pratt looks upon the folly of mankind from that more comprehensive view in which man is but one creature in the cosmic whole. Job is but another creature of Jehovah. Yet now Job may contain his creator, seen simply as a demiurge, within a larger view.

Mr West says much the same thing when he declares that Pratt has chosen to affirm an alliance with nature. Enlarging on this theme, he writes:

> Man is a conscious participant in a process from which he cannot divide himself, and all his interpretations, like the omega-point or whatever it is that Creation moves towards, are guesswork. But even guesswork is human, is brave; it's more inventive than being a vegetable. And Pratt's notion of martyrdom, covering what both Nature and Man do to men, begins with the decision to accept and develops with the impulse to justify.[9]

It is hard to say precisely how Pratt would "justify God's ways to man," most especially to the single individual, the lonely Job faced with his own suffering and death. He might seem to say (and here we anticipate a later argument) that the necessity of facing death and the spirit of self-sacrifice, which springs from the acceptance of this necessity, gives birth to a nobility that would not otherwise exist. Frequently he appears to celebrate the spirit of struggle, the adventure of creation as such, which inevitably depends upon change and death. It is a celebration of life in general. Pratt's vision, says Mr West, tends to be generic rather than individual; perhaps in the end "All he declares is the power of the spirit and his conviction of spirit's constant availability."[10] Such a general affirmation may be of little comfort to the individual man, and it is surely true that, as a rule, Pratt does not explore the problem of Job from a very private, personal, or uniquely individual perspective. Yet this very bias might imply that, for Pratt, the solution to the individual's problem lies precisely in the escape from himself which the acceptance of death, on the one hand, and the enlargement of his world-view, on the other, provide. Through his identification with the whole of mankind, indeed the whole of creation, he escapes from his isolation and from the threat of absolute negation which death brings.

Pratt's often technical interest in the instruments of communication, stressed by Northrop Frye in his introduction to the *Collected Poems*, points towards the same conclusion. It is the power of the word which brings men together (though it may also divide), and the word is a token of that power of the imagination whereby man may comprehend the cosmos and may see his life as one with the creation.

If there is a poem in which we do detect a sense of terror before the hostile and devouring sea, it is in Pratt's "Silences." The hatred and ferocity of this underwater world is intensified by the silence and the darkness. Isolation and hostility emerge as the natural consequences of a world in which communication is almost nil. On the other hand, in "The Cachalot" we may see the whale's victory over the giant squid and his triumphant return to the surface as a movement away from the self-enclosed isolation of the deep towards the liberation of the light and air, which make possible a greater degree of communication.

"Towards the Last Spike" is supremely occupied with this theme: the struggle to link, not simply provinces, but men "from sea to sea." It is an epic in the struggle for communication and community. The project of building a transcontinental railway is conceived in the imagination and executed only by virtue of the courage which the imagination and the vision of community provide.

At first glance, the realization of that transcontinental project would seem to call for a defiant assault on nature. But as A. J. M. Smith notes, "The ironic solution to the conflict is that man triumphs over his antagonist, the Laurentian Shield and the Rocky Mountains, by a fusion with it or a merging into it."[11]

Which brings us back to the dialogue of wind and wave, man and nature, that provides the central image in Pratt's vision of life. It is the intercourse, the dialectic of the two, that gives to life its drama and its definition. It is not merely a communication but an interpenetration, a merging and a fusion that gives to forms and features that developed *character* we most admire and then, paradoxically and finally, proclaims the oneness of the world by destroying the original forms or features altogether. We come back to one of the earliest, shortest, and best known of Pratt's poems, "Erosion."

It took the sea a thousand years,
A thousand years to trace
The granite features of this cliff,
In crag and scarp and base.

It took the sea an hour one night,
An hour of storm to place
The sculpture of these granite seams
Upon a woman's face.[12]

Here Pratt's vision of life coincides with A. J. M. Smith's vision of "The Lonely Land," whose beauty is "the beauty/of strength/broken by strength/and still strong."[13] Smith, while sharing something of Pratt's general view of life, approaches the threat of death and the justification of a world that includes death in a much more intimate or individual fashion.

Like Pratt, Smith welcomes the influx of the sea. He has a bone to pick with "the Christian doctors" or anyone who would send "the innocent heart to find/In civil tears denials of the blood." Man's vitality depends upon the animal vitality of nature, and we must welcome and cultivate that vitality or remain spiritless and without character. For we are by "Holiness designed/to swell the vein with a secular flood/In pure ferocious joy, efficient and good,/Like the tiger's spring or the leap of the wind." Our flame is like theirs in origin if not in end:

though in its human mode
Like theirs in force, it is unlike in kind,
Whose end it is to burn sensation's lode,
With animal intensity, to Mind.[14]

It is not a narrowly rationalistic Mind preoccupied with reducing life to a safe and abundant order. Many of Smith's satirical poems are aimed at the superficiality and futility of a life organized around the elaboration of a technological and productive machinery with the sole aim of creating a perfectly safe and comfortable surrogate world, a world whose techniques would "Scuttle the crank hulk, of witless night." To eliminate the darker side of life, were it possible, would only be to cheat oneself. Smith rejects this "war cry" in the irony of "Noctambule."

The great black innocent Othello of a thing
Is undone by the nice clean pockethandkerchief
Of 6 a.m., and though the moon is only an old
Wetwash snotrag – horsemeat for good rosbif –

Perhaps to utilize substitutes is what
The age has to teach us,
        wherefore let the loud
Unmeaning warcry of treacherous daytime
Issue like whispers of love in the moonlight,
– Poxy old cheat![15]

The attack on night can never be really successful, and as often as not breeds its own dark threat. Smith is aware that "Business as Usual" leads to "Fear as Normal," here associated with the production of the Hydrogen Bomb. He is aware that as long as such attitudes prevail the Panic vitalities he celebrates so joyfully at one moment may become Panic violence the next, enormously enhanced by human reason.

It is in our own life and our own death that the problem of Job may touch us most acutely. And it is here that Smith is often most impressive. Again and again, he has approached this theme. How should he, he asks, in "On Knowing *Nothing*," with his little experience of dying know the horror of death:

        the horror
That breaks the dream,
Hateful yet clung to
As the image hugs the mirror
With such a silver shiver
As chills and almost kills?

Whatever the answer, he does know this horror. And it brings up directly the question of Job, the individual's demand for justice:

        What have I done
To bring the Angel round my head
That I can smell his pinion
(Bond or wing?)
Whom I must hate and love?[16]

He will resist it, yes. But he will not rage forever against the dying of the light. The flesh itself appears so forcefully to repudiate the bone, he must conclude:

That all this energy and poise
        Were but designed to cast
A richer flower from the earth
        Surrounding its decay,

And like a child whose fretful mirth
Can find no constant play,
Bring one more transient form to birth
And fling the old away.[17]

And so he accepts the destructive element as an inevitable and even desirable part of the process, a part which:

enlivens my darkness,
Progressively illuminating
What I know for the first time, yes,
Is what I've been always wanting.[18]

This is not the capitulation of despair. In an attempt to make this point Smith borrows the language of the seventeenth century in his poem "To Henry Vaughan," where it is made obliquely in an exclamation:

Yet art thou Homesick! to be gone
From all this brave Distraction
Wouldst seal thine ear, nail down thine eye;
To be one perfect Member, die;
And anxious to exchange in death
Thy foul, for thy Lord's precious, breath,
Thou art content to beg a pall,
Glad to be Nothing, to be All.[19]

Even before death, the acceptance of it brings, not resignation and despair, but enthusiasm, joy. It opens the way to communication or communion now. It is in fact what gives life worth. Thus, with something still of Vaughan's perspective but with a distinctly more modern accent, he would praise "The Wisdom of Old Jelly Roll." He would not praise death falsely, try to dignify and disguise Nothing as if it were Something, but:

'Nothing' depends on 'Thing', which is or was:
So death makes life or makes life's worth, a worth
Beyond all highfalutin' woes or shows
To publish and confess. 'Cry at the birth,
Rejoice at the death,' old Jelly Roll said,
Being on whisky, ragtime, chicken, and the scriptures fed.[20]

In the elementary or primitive conditions that often prevail in E. J. Pratt's poetry it takes courage merely to survive. It takes courage to survive in the urban world also, but not, as the advertising slogans might lead us to believe, to prosecute a war on cancer, a war on insects, a war on nature generally. Fear and pleasure will sustain these exploits. Where courage is required is in the acceptance of some of these aspects of life as irremediable, above all, one's own death. Such courage, not cowardice, Smith exhibits in these poems. And it leads, not to a withdrawal from, not to a defiance of life, but to its celebration.

Similarly, it is this brand of courage that E. J. Pratt extols, not only the courage to contend with the destructive forces of the world, but the courage to accept destruction for oneself, especially in those situations where one may choose death deliberately to save another or to contain the violence of life by trying to absorb it within oneself. It provides the foundation for his philosophy of self-sacrifice, and his large affirmation of the world.

Earle Birney is also a poet who would single out courage as a chief virtue. Yet in Birney's case it is frequently if not finally of a different stamp. It tends to be a stoic or a pagan variety, as opposed to Pratt or Smith's distinctly more Christian courage. In all this argument Birney presents an illuminating, if at times ambiguous, example.

From "David" to "ARRIVALS Wolfville," Birney is preoccupied with the problem posed by death, with the meaning or justice of a world that moves with such power and such magnificence towards obscure destinations, indifferent in its progress to the carnage left behind in its wake. In both the above poems, the hand of the dead or dying, whether the victim has been smashed on the mountain's rock or on a locomotive's steel, hooks into Birney's conscience like the hand of Job. However we may forget the details of the accident, surely, he says in the latter poem, we must remember:

> the longfingered hand
> stretched in some arresting habit of eloquence
> to the last irrational judgement
> roaring in from the storm
> Or is it only in me that the hand hooked
> and I who must manage it now like a third?[21]

It is the lawyer's hand, here, which appeals for justice before the "last irrational judgement" of the God of Job.

When Birney looks at nature he is struck by "the cobra sea and the mongoose wind," and by the great flint of the mountain which comes singing into the heart. The human situation is imaged in "Mappemounde" as that of a man voyaging in a frail ark through a hostile sea, a sea hardly distinguishable from the devouring Leviathan who swims there. At best, life is an exploration and adventure. But, like Captain Cook, each man sinks to explore his last reef with the spear in his back. The awareness of final annihilation permeates Birney's poetry.

"November Walk Near False Creek Mouth" is one of the longest of the meditations on the human condition, and it is focussed precisely on the nothingness that lies behind the whole vast process and that appears to await all things. As in Roberts' "Tantramar Revisited," the moment is poised between winter and summer, day and night; it is a period of inactivity and relaxation. During the lull in the perpetual struggle to defend and create, the speaker pauses to contemplate, in a larger perspective than usual, the process in which he and the city, here between the mountains and the sea, are inevitably caught. What strikes him most is that even in this moment of quiet there is no security; no final victory over the forces of time can be hoped for. Even now the tide is slipping "its long soft fingers into the tense/joints of the trapped seawall." The last leaves of the alders have turned the lawns into "a battlefield bright with their bodies." The city apartments may be "aseptic penthouse hillforts," but nothing can stop the dissolving sea. On the highest ledge of all, beyond the apartment antennae, the pylons marching over the peaks, the jetstream of planes and the farthest galaxies, "lies the unreached unreachable nothing/whose winds wash down to the human shores," where they slip, shoving into each of his thoughts, nudging his footsteps, driving him back to his own "brief night's ledge."[22]

Before this final oblivion, Birney here adopts a tone of quiet acceptance, and upon his fellow man, who wittingly or unwittingly must share this fate, he appears to look with an ironic or wry compassion. But Birney's attitude towards a destructive or hostile universe, as expressed throughout much of his work, is neither the withdrawal of Roberts nor the affirmation of Pratt; it is rather a vigorous defiance. When Desmond Pacey declared that the principal virtues celebrated in the poems of E. J. Pratt were courage, courtesy, and compassion, Birney cried no. They were courage, loyalty and defiance. Or perhaps, they were the Anglo-Saxon virtues of loyalty, initiative, and endurance. For the world of Birney's poems is an Anglo-Saxon world, in spirit and not only in diction and rhythmic device. Akin to the world of "The Wanderer" or "The Seafarer," it is grim, full of menace, where life is the flight of a sparrow through the hall – but where nonetheless one endures and fights to the last, though the end is certain. "Come then," he says, in "Pacific Door":

Come then on the waves of desire that well forever
and think no more than you must
of the simple unhuman truth of this emptiness
that down deep below the lowest pulsing of primal cell
tar-dark and still
lie the bleak and forever capacious tombs of the sea[23]

With courage and initiative man may even tackle Jehovah on his own terms. At one point Birney allies himself with Promethean man and throws his defiance in the face of a malevolent universe. Know, he proclaims in "Vancouver Lights":

> These rays were ours
> we made and unmade them   Not the shudder of continents
> doused us   the moon's passion   nor crash of comets
> In the fathomless heat of our dwarfdom   our dream's combustion
> we contrived the power   the blast that snuffed us
> No one bound Prometheus   Himself he chained
> and consumed his own bright liver   O stranger
> Plutonian   descendant   or beast in the stretching night –
> there was light[24]

Yet to have outwitted Leviathan by destroying oneself is a dubious virtue indeed, though one consistent with Birney's frequently sardonic view of man. That view emerges in "Hands," as he remarks on man's obvious superiority to the rest of nature. The hands of the cedar are cold and unskilled and shall neither focus on a bombsight nor sew up a bayoneted bowel. "We are not of these woods." No, we are worse, "our roots are in autumn and store for no spring."[25] Nature may be hostile but "Man is a snow that cracks/the trees' red resinous arches/and winters the cabined heart ... till frost like ferns of the world that is lost/unfurls on the darkening window."[26] No more to be trusted than the cobra sea, he is more to be feared. The iron rain of the bombs in "Vancouver Dusk" moves with the inevitability of natural forces towards the sleeping city, but with a directness and purpose that is human alone.

Birney cannot, in the end, ally himself with the aggressive Promethean man any more than with the encroaching sea. Even if he doesn't destroy himself, the Promethean man creates an infernal city, the Sudbury of "Way to the West." In the "skull of a hill," the "dumps of cans," the Pandaemonium and "20 miles of deserted battlefield" that the city presents to the travellers we find a real-life version of Lampman's City of the End of Things. Like Satan's kingdom it is a miserable imitation of heaven. The wilderness, by contrast, is a welcome relief. There in the dark woods, the travellers suddenly realize the river still flows. After Air Canada's night jet passes, "we begin to realize/we'd been hearing the river too."[27]

It is Vancouver with its many lights that is put on trial in a later drama and very nearly doomed or damned. Its promoter, the aggressive Mr Legion, is charged with misrepresentation and dematerialized by Birney's spokesman, Mrs A. With him Birney rejects the Promethean "Advance."

Still, distrustful of man and distrustful of nature, Birney tends to walk with vigilance through a world of strangers, where courage and ingenuity are primarily defensive. "Meeting of Strangers" is the epic in miniature of a world of every man for himself. When a black figure approaches him in a deserted street, with a knife in his hand, saying, "Nice jacket you got dere, man," the speaker makes a spectacular leap into the intersection, where he is lucky enough to encounter a taxi. He even wins the admiration of his would-be attacker, who calls out, "dat a nice jump you got too."[28]

As long as his world is one in which men go armed against nature and against each other, Birney can truly say:

> men are isled in ocean or in ice
> and only joined by long endeavour to be joined.[29]

Real communion is rare in Birney's poetry. In the poem "For George Lamming," he is surprised, for example, to discover that he has temporarily lost his identity as a white man, and with it his isolation; he has become one with a dark circle of friends whose goodwill or acceptance has allowed him for a time to forget himself. It is only later, when he looks in the mirror, that he remembers his difference and realizes their generosity, their charity or love.

As often as not, the courage displayed in Birney's poems is a stoic courage which defies death rather than a Christian courage which accepts it. It is not, except in a few poems, the courage of Gethsemane. "El Greco: Espolio" is instructive. It is not accidental that in looking at this crucifixion scene, Birney found his eye drawn to the carpenter preparing the cross, rather than to the carpenter's son who is to hang there. Concentrating on the job, on doing it well, the carpenter does not take sides in the issue in which he is involved. As a result he will live long.

> To construct with hands   knee-weight   braced thigh
> keeps the back turned from death.

He is not ready to explore his last reef. Yet, though he may observe with truth that it is too late for the other carpenter's boy to avoid death, he cannot say with anything but a superficial truth that it is too late for Him "to return to this peace before the nails are hammered."[30] For having accepted His death and further forgiven His executioners, He presumably carries His peace within Him. The words are those of the carpenter, and Birney attributes the whole emphasis of the painting to El Greco; yet the tone cannot be wholly ironic for the man who advised us to think no more than we must of the simple unhuman truth of the emptiness that presumably attends us all.

Indeed, the man who sails so warily through Birney's mappemounde invites the question posed by Jay Macpherson's "Ark Astonished."

> Why did your spirit
> Strive so long with me?
> Will you wring love from deserts,
> Comfort from the sea?
>
> Your dove and raven speed,
> The carrion and the kind.
> Man, I know your need,
> But not your mind.[31]

As long as his defiance is radical, man shall remain an isolated voyager, a moving point on the map, surrounded by the threatening waves. Only when he is prepared to accept his final, if not immediate engulfment, shall he find comfort, love, communion. To escape from his defensive position in his frail ark he must embrace the sea. This is the burden of Miss Macpherson's "Ark Overwhelmed."

> When the four quarters shall
> Turn in and make one whole,
> Then I who wall your body,
> Which is to me a soul,
> Shall swim circled by you
> And cradled on your tide,
> Who was not even, not ever,
> Taken from your side.[32]

Leviathan, the sea, all nature, and all time become one in Eve, in Adam's rib. It is more a question of attitude than fact. In the decision to embrace her, man would recognize that he has always embraced her. And in doing so he would discover that he embraced himself.

The solution lies in a feminine inclusiveness. A masculine exclusiveness leads only to despair. In Birney's trial of a city the masculine witnesses whom Mr Legion calls on for the prosecution all serve to ensure the damnation of Vancouver. Neither explorer, geologist, nor Indian chief, not even the tavern-keeper, can justify the city's continued existence. Before the law it is doomed. Of William Langland, perhaps the most exclusive because the most righteous of the witnesses, Mrs A. remarks, "His eyes were on the sins he loved to hate." It is Mrs A. who succeeds where the others failed, and it is her feminine inclusiveness that underlies her argument and gives her case its strength.

> For all mankind is matted so within me
> Despair can find no earth-room tall to grow.

Her argument proceeds from love, not law. She can affirm the life of the city, as she says she had affirmed it that very morning, "However my world had sinned."[33]

We may recall that in the nineteenth century Isabella Valancy Crawford also affirmed life against the threat of inexorable death in the name of love, her pioneer hero proclaiming that love had its own peculiar sky, "All one great daffodil, on which do lie/The sun, the moon, the stars, all seen at once,/And never setting ... ."[34] Yet between Bliss Carman and Irving Layton, Canadian verse is not remarkable for its love poetry. There is little of love or woman in E. J. Pratt, or even in Earle Birney. Still, it is in the experience of love that man has most readily abandoned his separate identity in favour of a larger whole, exchanging his isolated existence for that communion with the human race embodied in Mrs A. or with the whole of creation embodied in Miss Macpherson's Eve.

Something of this theme is evident in Earle Birney's "This Page My Pigeon." And in another war poem, "The Road to Nijmégen," he writes:

> December my dear on the road to Nijmégen
> between the stones and the bitten sky was your face
>
> ...
>
> I thought that only the living of others assures us
> the gentle and true we remember as trees walking
> Their arms reach down from the light of kindness
> into this Lazarus tomb.[35]

In the context, however, it is not the memory of love that primarily serves to persuade us to go on with the struggle. More convincingly, it is the spectacle of the old man hacking at roots, of the children groping for knobs of coal, of the women "wheeling into the wind on the tireless rims of their cycles/like tattered sailboats tossing over the cobbles" that argues a further affirmation of life. It is the living of others here in the blasted landscape rather than the memories of those far away, however beloved, that really inspires us.

Romantic love, the hyacinth girl in the garden, the personal relationship of two lovers – as a justification of life this type of thing has lost much of its force in the twentieth century, with its mass destruction and mass dislocation of people. But a more diffused love, a general solidarity and, above all, the courage of those who in the midst of devastation continue to show an affirming flame – these have become more pronounced and more important, in Birney's work as in others. There is a real question whether such courage is not prior to love as the ground of our continued affirmation.

In "The Fertile Muck," Irving Layton writes: "How to dominate reality? Love is one way;/imagination another."[36] There are different kinds of love, and in Layton's poems love, like woman, has different roles to play: as menace, as distraction, as a form of salvation. Again, we would argue that courage underlies the latter, that it is the ground of love and of imagination alike.

With Smith, Pratt, and Birney, Layton is vividly aware of the lethal character of Jehovah's universe and the equally lethal character of Promethean man. "Knowing that the blade dies," he remarks in "Saratoga Beach," "makes our kind unkind or wise."[37] Rarely does the knowledge of mortality make man wise. More often it makes him cruel, or it spurs him on towards the creation of a Brave New World, the cultivation of faces "washed clean of Death and Agony."[38] Much of Layton's work is devoted to the castigation of man's inhumanity to man and to all living creatures. But it is equally concerned about condemning this "well-lit fluorescent age" with its "chromium gods," the sterile asylum that Henry Miller dubbed "the air-conditioned nightmare." Still, beyond the menace of man's own invention lies the menace of nature itself, the world of winter and of death. How is man to contend with that? What righteous man, he asks in "First Snow: Lake Achigan," can claim to understand God's justice in the face of that general condemnation?

> Lonely and fleshed with hates, who here
> Would be God's angry man, a thundering Paul,
> When December, a toga'd Cato, slow to anger,
> At last speaks the word that condemns us all.[39]

It is the harsh God of such a wintry world that Layton characterizes in "Orpheus," where he also describes the love of woman as a needed distraction. Like the waves of desire that well forever in Birney's world, the "sexual dream" leads us to think no more than we must of our final dissolution, life's violence, and pain.

> God was not Love nor Law,
> God was the blood I saw,
> The ever-flowing blood
> Staining water and sod.
>
> Woman I loved. Enough
> She made me dream of love
> And in that sexual dream
> Forget the whitethroat's scream.

Finally, however, it is the power of the imagination that the speaker here claims makes possible an unblinking celebration of a world characterized by both love and death. More precisely, it is the power of the poet's heart. That heart, he says, has nowhere counterpart:

> Which can celebrate
> Love equally with Death
> Yet by its pulsing bring
>   A music into everything.[40]

"Heart" suggests both love and courage, and Layton's conception of the imagination might be defined as "that dream of courage by which we live" referred to in the poem "Parting." Elsewhere Layton celebrates the poet for his capacity to bring together "nature's divided things." His role is to praise the world; the act of composing is an act of communion. But clearly this act depends upon his courage to celebrate life *and* death; otherwise he would himself be one of nature's divided things. It is this capacity to affirm both at once that distinguishes Layton's imagination in such a poem as "The Birth of Tragedy," with its strange conclusion that is simultaneously elegiac and joyous. There, the poet himself lies "like a slain thing":

>   noting how seasonably
>   leaf and blossom uncurl
> and living things arrange their death,
> while someone from afar off
> blows birthday candles for the world.[41]

There are two poems that will suggest how Layton was forced to contend with the problem of Job. In the earlier "Vexata Quaestio," he did not know how to resolve it. The poem begins with a celebration of the poet and his power to praise. Able to make articulate a dumb nature, he walks like a god among the insects biting and dying on his arm, among the dwarfed stalks of summer, the prayerful birds. The very blades of the grass proclaim his greatness and seem to say:

> "Give your stripped body to the sun
> Your sex to any skilled
>   And pretty damsel;
> From the bonfire
> Of your guilts make
>   A blazing Greek sun."

But he is neither a Greek god not the Maccabean hero who would deliver nature from its bondage, from division into communion, himself free from division. No sooner has the grass inspired him to abandon his anxiety than the wind recalls him to it with a reminder of his mortality.

> Then the wind which all day
> Had run regattas through the fields
> Grew chill, became
> A tree-dismantling wind;
>
> The sun went down
> And called my brown skin in.[42]

In "A Tall Man Executes a Jig," Layton returns to the field, determined to explore the problem more thoroughly and to arrive at some more satisfactory resolution. The poem begins with the same situation, though with an added sense of menace.

> So the man spread his blanket on the field
> And watched the shafts of light between the tufts
> And felt the sun push the grass towards him;
> The noise he heard was that of whizzing flies,
> The whistlings of small imprudent birds,
> And the ambiguous rumbles of cars
> That made him look up at the sky, aware
> Of the gnats that tilted against the wind
> And in the sunlight turned to jigging motes.
> Fruitflies he'd call them except there was no fruit
> About, spoiling to hatch these glitterings,
> These nervous dots for which the mind supplied
> The closing sentences from Thucydides,
> Or from Euclid having a savage nightmare.

To the threat of guilt and death there has been added the threat of meaninglessness (problems that Lampman, lying in the grass and soaking up the sun, had never broached). All life becomes identified with the random jigging of the gnats. "The grass,/Even the wildflowers became black hairs/And himself a maddened speck among them." For a moment the struggle of the flies enmeshed in the hair of his arm gives their jigging a meaning, a purpose that it did not have in the "unrestraining air." Restriction, the struggle to survive, gives life direction. Once again, the poet rises like a god in the insect world, only to be deflated again by a realization that the most successful life is nevertheless ephemeral and that survival may have little point in a universe which is itself doomed to final extinction. No longer deified in the eyes of nature, a bee sees in him only a tall man and leaves him for a marigold. So he drops his "aureole of gnats" and identifies instead with the sinking sun, "a dying god upon the blood-red hills." As the embodiment of "Ambition, pride, the ecstasy of sex,/And all circumstance of delight and grief," the setting sun should reveal in its final splendour the ultimate purpose or meaning of these things. But nothing happens; no apotheosis takes place:

> He thought the dying god had gone to sleep:
> An Indian fakir on his mat of nails.

And so he must doff the halo of the mountains also. He is reduced to his human dimension and made to contemplate mortality in the form of a "violated grass snake that lugged/Its intestine like a small red valise." If Behemoth has been depreciated in the modern technological world and become merely the bull calf, to be killed because there is "no market for bull calves," Leviathan similarly, it would seem, has shrunk to the proportions of the miserable grass snake:

> A cold-eyed skinflint it now was, and not
> The manifest of that joyful wisdom,
> The mirth and arrogant green flame of life;
> Or earth's vivid tongue that flicked in praise of earth.

And just as Layton wept for the bull calf, so here "the man wept because pity was useless."

> "Your jig's up; the flies come like kites," he said
> And watched the grass snake crawl towards the hedge,
> Convulsing and dragging into the dark
> The satchel filled with curses for the earth,
> For the odours of warm sedge, and the sun,
> A blood-red organ in the dying sky.

Once more the sun goes down and calls all brown skin in. But the man's reaction is neither defensive nor defiant. Though the snake:

> opened its thin mouth to scream
> A last silent scream that shook the black sky,
> Adamant and fierce, the tall man did not curse.

Rather, the man's attitude is one of acceptance. He embraces the grass snake in all its mortal inconsequences, discovering in "the fellowship of death" a communion more profound than that provided by the more immediate fellowship of life. And at that point the revelation he had despaired of occurs. The grass snake is transformed, becomes the cosmic serpent, the ambiguous symbol of the universal power which is both dark and light, the speaker's identification with a cosmic power that comprehends both life and death. He attains the wisdom of the serpent and the aureole or bright crown he had too hastily or too easily assumed before.

Beside the rigid snake the man stretched out
In fellowship of death; he lay silent
And stiff in the heavy grass with eyes shut,
Inhaling the moist odours of the night
Through which his mind tunnelled with flicking tongue
Backwards to caves, mounds, and sunken ledges
And desolate cliffs where come only kites,
And where of perished badgers and raccoons
The claws alone remain, gripping the earth.
Meanwhile the green snake crept upon the sky,
Huge, his mailed coat glittering with stars that made
The night bright, and blowing thin wreaths of cloud
Athwart the moon; and as the weary man
Stood up, coiled about his head, transforming all.[43]

The problem posed in "Vexata Quaestio" is here resolved by accepting the threat of death and identifying with a cosmic power that contains both creation and destruction, the darkness and the light. It is not unlike Paul Tillich's conception of a cosmic power that contains its own negation, of being which contains non-being. And the gesture that the tall man makes, the quality of the imagination Layton displays here and in other poems, resembles Tillich's conception of the courage-to-be, which he defines as the courage of the unique individual to affirm himself and his world despite the threats of guilt, meaninglessness, and death that are inherent in life itself. Since the cosmic power, Being-itself, continually maintains itself against non-Being, he concludes that the "*courage to be is rooted in the God who appears when God has disappeared in the anxiety of doubt.*"[44]

Tillich's book, *The Courage to Be*, seems almost to have been designed to provide an analytical comment on many of the problems explored dramatically or poetically by the writers we have been looking at. This is partly because he too begins with the difficulty of affirming life in the face of various forms of negation.

For example, Tillich's lament for the loss of the older concept of *areté* or *virtu*, in which the ideas of vitality and intentionality were united, illuminates Lampman's concern to emphasize the unique particularity of each creature and the energy with which it affirms that unique self. Lampman's desire to avoid the division of man's spiritual life into either a bloodless intellect or a meaningless vitality was a desire to recover such a conception of *virtu*.

Similarly, Tillich's observation that when faced with the threat of guilt, meaninglessness, or death man frequently loses the courage to affirm himself as an individual and seeks to affirm himself solely as a part, illuminates the tendency to create, in one form or another, what we have called a garrison culture. It is the tendency to identify with some collectivity, the church or state, which is larger than the individual but less than cosmic, and which also fails to represent the individual's unique or authentic life. Even if his identification is one that makes him subject to the God of traditional theistic religion, his affirmation will lack authenticity; he will have abandoned himself to an abstraction. For such a God, says Tillich, is conceived, not as being-in-itself but as *a* being, all-powerful and all-knowing, and as such he becomes the type of the tyrant, the bully who emerges from Jung's portrait of the God of Job or in Pratt's great Panjandrum. He is a projection of the collectivity, the vengeful justice of the Presbyterian spiritual order that MacLennan speaks of in *Each Man's Son*, or the embodiment of that tyranny of mind that Edmund serves in Grove's *The Master of the Mill*. "This is the God," writes Tillich, "Nietzsche said had to be killed because nobody can tolerate being made into a mere object of absolute knowledge and absolute control."[45] He is the God who in Cohen's *Beautiful Losers* demands the complete renunciation of one's original nature, rather than its affirmation.

To identify with such a God or such a collectivity may be to escape the threat of mortality or absurdity; yet it also leads to the loss of self and may only increase the burden of guilt. On the other hand, to affirm oneself against the world is a barren defiance, since the individual can realize himself only in participation with the whole. One must accept oneself and the universal nature of which one is a part, affirming both – as Birney's characters along the road to Nijmégen appear to do, as Layton's tall man, as he lies down in the fellowship of death, breathing the odour of night, most clearly does. And nothing serves to make this affirmation possible but courage, of the kind that Tillich terms the courage to be. It precedes even love. For, says Tillich, "as long as there is an *object* of fear, love in the sense of participation can conquer fear," but the ultimate threat of non-being or absurdity has no objectivity; that anxiety cannot be removed. Thus, until the courage to accept what cannot be helped is found, one will not be able to participate in, to love or affirm the "other" or the world.[46] What is needed is precisely what Layton calls the poet's heart, which can celebrate both love and death, "yet by its pulsing bring/a music into everything."

Just such a heart informs Isabella Valancy Crawford's much earlier affirmation of life. For her world was clearly a world of extremes, of "moss, a soft and gentle breeder/Of dreams and rest" and equally "of icebergs bellowing in the throes of death." It was a world of "slaughtered deer" and slaughtered fish, in which again and again the hawk or falcon with his iron beak fell upon the gentle dove, where trees had souls and men axes with which to fell them. It was a world of violent conflicts, of love and death, yet beautiful. And the cosmic power that sustained the reality she so vigorously affirmed was clearly one that contained both the glory and the darkness, the creative and the destructive element. When, in her poem "Gisli, the Chieftain," the young man who has lost both his love and his life journeys down the Hellway to confront the god of the underworld with his demand for justice, he is met by the following reply:

> Said the voice of Evil to the ear of Good,
> "Clasp thou my strong right hand,
> Nor shall our clasp be known or understood
> By any in the land.
>
> "I, the dark giant, rule strongly on the earth;
> Yet thou, bright one, and I
> Sprang from the one great mystery – at one birth
> We looked upon the sky.[47]

Good and evil, dark and light, Satan and Jehovah are but two aspects of the one great mystery. Though men may see them as two opposed powers, which they must keep separate and with which they must take sides, one way or the other, Miss Crawford insists that they are inseparable and that, despite the fact that man may turn the dark powers against himself, both are necessary and both must be affirmed. Miss Crawford is not disturbed by the tree-dismantling wind. She can praise the world and celebrate the power of love because she has the courage to celebrate love equally with death.

In "The Damnation of Vancouver" Mrs A. remarks, "How could I know, without the threat of death, I lived?"[48] We may also recall the lines of A. J. M. Smith. "'Nothing' depends on 'Thing', which is or was:/So death makes life or makes life's worth." Similarly, for Tillich it is death or non-Being at the heart of reality that makes the world a dynamic world and God a living God: "non-being drives being out of its seclusion, it forces it to affirm itself dynamically."[49] And that affirmation can only be made through individual beings in all their uniqueness. It is on this point that Birney ends his "Damnation of Vancouver."

Ultimately Birney's defiance becomes less bitter, more in fact that necessary self-affirmation against death and doubt we have called the courage to be. No longer an absolute defiance, it is characterized by that complicity a player shows when in a game he must assume a role, as hero or as villain, and maintain it to the end, for otherwise the game could not exist, could not be played at all. All this is made explicit in the final dialogue between Mrs A. and Mr Powers, who is the embodiment of fate and of the inevitable doom the future will pronounce on Mrs A. and her world. Mr Powers reminds her that she has won only a brief reprieve, her doom is still pending. She replies:

> Mrs A.: How could I know, without the threat of
> death, I lived?
> Powers: But do you know why you defy me?
> Mrs A.: (*Looking up almost tenderly at him.*)
> That you might also be.
> Without my longer will, my stubborn boon,
> You'd have no mate to check with but
> the cornered moon.
> (*Slowly*) It's my defiant fear keeps
> green this whirling world.[50]

Mr Powers congratulates the lady on her insight and, shaking hands, reminds her that they will meet or mate again, on Judgement Day. Mrs A. is content, but insists that meanwhile she will keep the key. To which Mr Powers punningly replies: he shall have the skeleton. The important thing for both, however, as Mrs A. points out in the final line, is that she will have had *a life*.

To the question, What shall we do with Leviathan? the answer would appear to be, Swallow him. Or, as John Newlove says of death in "Resources, Certain Earths," "Let me swallow it whole and be strong."[51] Among these poets, from Isabella Crawford through D. C. Scott, E. J. Pratt, A. J. M. Smith, Earle Birney, and Irving Layton to such younger writers as Jay Macpherson or John Newlove, there is a very real unanimity in their awareness and in the resolution of the problem of Job. All, in their fashion, abandon the garrison of an exclusive culture and go into the wilderness, where they experience, not a greater sense of alienation, but a greater sense of vitality and community. Implicitly or explicitly, each may be said to accept the fellowship of death, to lie down with the grass snake among all the other skeletons of badgers and raccoons and men, only to discover that the one great serpent has crept out upon the sky and coiled about his head like a crown of power. The night is transfigured, and a menacing world takes on the beauty of strength broken by strength and still strong.

Death may be viewed here as a positive good, as revelatory, as driving life to manifest itself, its worth. But there is no attempt to gloss over its essential reality and individuality, to say that because life in general continues, death in effect does not exist. It is life in general that does not exist. It is the individual life, and individual death, that are immediately real. Though such a view may "justify" death, it does not justify the taking of life beyond that necessary for each creature's authentic self-affirmation. It does not justify the destruction of anything in the universe on the ground that it is by nature evil. Rather, it suggests that man, with his peculiar human awareness, ought to conserve as much of the varied individual life of the universe as possible.

The view of life that tends to emerge, though ultimately optimistic, is nonetheless a harsh one. It is an essentially sacrificial view of life, in which, as Pratt maintained, whatever the beginning or end, the path lies through Gethsemane.

Though not necessarily Christian, this view is frequently expressed in Christian terms. Thus, caught in a sphere of natural violence and preoccupied with the "meaning of the moth, even the smashed moth," Margaret Avison in "The Butterfly" was tempted to look to a Christian analogy: "The Voice that stilled the sea of Galilee."[52] She has since become an explicitly Christian poet. She would agree with Tillich when he says that any Church that would be adequate to his conception of life must be a Church under the Cross, "the Church which preaches the Crucified who cried to God who remained his God after the God of confidence had left him in the darkness of doubt and meaninglessness."[53] Miss Avison speaks for such a Church in her latest book *The Dumbfounding*, where she writes in "The Word":

"*Forsaking all*" – Your voice
never falters, and yet,
unsealing day out of a
darkness none ever knew
in full but you,
you spoke that word, closing on it forever:
"Why hast Thou forsaken ... ?"

This measure of your being all-out, and
meaning it, made you
put it all on the line
we, humanly, wanted to draw – at
having you teacher only, or
popular spokesman only, or
doctor or simply a source of sanity.[54]

Yet one need not be a Christian or draw on Christian terms to express something of this view of life. Layton's sense of the fragile but triumphant affirmation of life and his equal insistence on the reality and individuality of death is expressed in quite natural imagery in "Butterfly on Rock," where its terrible ambiguity is perhaps even more poignant.

> The large yellow wings, black-fringed,
> were motionless
>
> They say the soul of a dead person
> will settle like that on the still face
>
> But I thought: the rock has borne this;
> this butterfly is the rock's grace,
> its most obstinate and secret desire
> to be a thing alive made manifest
>
> Forgot were the two shattered porcupines
> I had seen die in the bleak forest:
> Pain is unreal; death an illusion:
> There is no death in all the land,
> I heard my voice cry;
> And I brought my hand down on the butterfly
> And felt the rock move beneath my hand.[55]

To fish for the glory is to catch the darkness too. Yet once the essentially sacrificial character of life has been recognized and accepted, with courage one may then affirm the whole world. It is from this perspective that Jay Macpherson in "Leviathan" recommends that we rejoice.

> Now show thy joy, frolic in Angels' sight
> Like Adam's elephant in fields of light.
> There lamb and lion slumber in the shade,
> Splendour and innocence together laid.
>
> The Lord that made Leviathan made thee
> Not good, not great, not beautiful, not free,
> Not whole in love, nor able to forget
> The coming war, the battle still unmet.
>
> But look: Creation shines, as that first day
> When God's Leviathan went forth to play
> Delightful from his hand. The brute flesh sleeps,
> And speechless mercy all that sleeping keeps.[56]

CHAPTER SIX

The Sacrificial Embrace

... having learned to sing when there is really no reason at all, when there is no excuse for a single song, Souster is surprised on occasion with the gift of inexplicable joy. Renunciation and acceptance of inevitable tragedy set the stage for a burst of song such as could only be equalled or surpassed by the first promise with which life began.

LOUIS DUDEK, "Groundhog among the Stars"

See,
I'll unravel it: to plant a root
You have to bury it. He who loses
His life shall find it, etc., or,
In rusted terms: we have to love.

There's a grief to it. Then, you have
Your miracle.

RALPH GUSTAFSON, "The Exhortation"

Despite the smashed moth, shipwreck, or the prospect of their own death, the poets recommend that we rejoice. Pratt and Birney, Smith and Layton, Avison and Macpherson, each in his fashion affirms the world, putting forward an essentially sacrificial view of life. Similarly, the novelists whose work we will consider in this chapter share the same preoccupations and the same ultimate convictions.

The novels we shall look at are Colin McDougall's *Execution*, Gabrielle Roy's *The Cashier* and *The Hidden Mountain*, Adele Wiseman's *The Sacrifice*, Douglas LePan's *The Deserter*, and Hugh MacLennan's *The Watch that Ends the Night*. The characters in each of these novels are led to a view of life that not only comprehends suffering and death but sees in them the conditions that make possible the highest human values. Without those conditions life would lack all inwardness and depth. It might attain to the delights of Olympus or to the comfort and stability of Brave New World and yet lack significance. For value does not lie in such perfection. For these writers also, it lies in the beauty of strength broken by strength and still strong. Both our uniqueness and our oneness with the world, the twofold root of our identity, depends upon death. And our capacity to love, our compassion and communion with the world depend upon our recognition and acceptance of these facts. Those who would give meaning to their lives by identifying with some collective enterprise designed to eliminate suffering and death are doubly deceived. Man and his world are mortal and value does not lie in either an individual or a generalized immortality.

Like the poets, the novelists here insist on the radically individual character of all existence, and on the fact that sooner or later every separate existence is destroyed. Outwardly we are faced with a picture of absurdity: a world of conflict and suffering doomed to dissolution. Yet they persist in asking us to rejoice.

It is Hugh MacLennan's central character who announces towards the conclusion of *The Watch that Ends the Night*, "Here, I found at last, is the nature of the final human struggle. Within, not without. Without there is nothing to be done."[1] It is by virtue of a shift in perspective that the picture of futility is transformed. What was a menace may become a promise; the invasion of the world becomes the condition not of our defeat but of our release. To vary Donne, what we endure is not a breach but an expansion.

It is probably no coincidence that two of the more profound literary critics in Canada have both expressed their conviction that life is ultimately both individual and one. In his conclusion to the discussion of Milton in *The Return of Eden*, Northrop Frye contends that "the central myth of mankind is the myth of lost identity: the goal of all reason, courage and vision is the regaining of identity." He further explains that "The recovery of identity is not the feeling that I am myself and not another, but the realization that there is only one man, one mind, and one world, and that all walls of partition have been broken down forever."[2] Similarly, George Whalley has declared his belief that all poetry arises "from our knowledge 'that every Thing has a Life of it's (*sic*) own, & that we are all *one life*' " and further, from our sense that "in this one life anything can become identical with anything else."[3]

Just such an identity is affirmed in the novels we shall look at. And they make it quite clear that it is not a matter of a purely logical identity of the individual with the species or of a more or less imperfect reality with an ideal world of Platonic forms. It is an existential identity of the individual with the world, a conviction experienced in time. The individuality of each creature is the result of his interaction with others, of his participation in the life of the whole. Whatever one's role in life, one cannot avoid a certain complicity, even with one's opposite. The hunter is also the hunted, an unmistakable implication of Gabrielle Roy's *The Hidden Mountain*. The burden of this, as of other works, would appear to be that the knowledge of our simultaneous oneness and uniqueness can be existential, can be personal, substantial and real, only in the context of a world where creatures conflict, each sustaining the invasion of the "other" as a kind of precious damage, that is, in a world of suffering and death. It is thus that we become aware that we are not independent, isolated identities. Only in such a world may it be possible for everything to have a life of its own and yet be one life. Absurd as it might seem, our death is the condition of our larger life.

In *Execution*, Colin McDougall places his characters in the context of the Second World War, where the indiscriminate violence, pointless suffering, and often quite unjustifiable death of human beings poignantly argues the absurdity of life. As the evidence mounts, Major Adam and Padre Doorn find themselves increasingly unable to deal with it. Padre Doorn is shaken to the point where he may lose his faith, and even his wits: he goes berserk on the battlefield, and in one bizarrely comic episode he conceives a naked man perched in a tree to be an angel. Major Adam is driven to withdraw mindlessly before the problem; he continues to function, coldly and quite cynically, like a machine. The general doom, the execution that all men must face sooner or later, in war or in peace, guilty or not guilty, is then given a sharply individual definition in the case of Jones, an ordinary soldier who, towards the end of the book, is condemned to face the firing squad. A simple and likeable young man, Jonesy has been under the protective eye of Doorn and Adam throughout the campaign. But now they cannot protect him; they are helpless before the injustice and absurdity of the action of the military court. For Jonesy has been found in the company of blackmarketeers, and since the American forces have executed one of their men who was caught in the illegal operations, the British and American forces feel compelled to exhibit the same severity to satisfy public opinion and, more especially, to maintain a certain goodwill between the allied forces. Jones, in the eyes of anyone who knows him at all, is obviously innocent of any crime except that of association with the criminals. Yet, despite the efforts of the Padre, of Major Adam, and of others besides, Jones is executed, largely or entirely for political reasons. The accumulated evidence of the viciousness and absurdity of life is focussed in that event. Yet, because of the example set by Jones himself, the reaction Doorn and Adam actually experience is the reverse of what they might have expected.

When Jones discovers what his sentence is, he does not protest its injustice, he does not cry out in fear or anger or self-pity; he accepts.

When Doorn and Adam come to comfort him, Jones makes a special effort to appear unafraid, even gay. As Adam comments, it was almost as if Jonesy were trying to comfort *them*. The young soldier's attitude persists right up to the end. We read:

> Adam had filled with astonishment and wonder – which remained with him now as they walked together toward the place of execution. Jonesy was trying to make it easier for them; and he had produced a dignity of his own which was stronger than the terror and the brute degradation of the coming moment.[4]

The example of Jones produces unexpected results. When the Padre and Adam return to the front after the execution, they discover that they have been released from the prison of their own minds and the insoluble problems that the war has raised. Driving through the autumn countryside, noting the clarity and freshness of the day, the farms and the fields spread out in the afternoon sunlight, a mare among a grove of trees frisking with her colt, each is puzzled by his mood. "I feel all right now," Adam says, whereas earlier he had believed that "when the execution was over everything would be over."[5] Both of them feel that they have been "restored to whatever they had been before Sicily," before the real slaughter had begun. Later, as Adam lies in the grass quietly waiting for the moment to begin a new attack, he reflects:

> Today he possessed a slow, sad certainty of knowledge. The mystery of man and his plight lay revealed before him. He knew man because he *was* man. Today he felt himself to exist at the central suffering core of all humanity. He was filled with a huge compassion and love and understanding for every man who had ever lived.[6]

Adam's reaction follows, without explicit explanation, from Jonesy's example. Ronald Sutherland has argued in *Canadian Literature* (Winter 1966) that the theme of *Execution* is that life can be lived only on the basis of a "vital pretense." That might well be another phrase for Tillich's "courage to be." McDougall argues that we must have the courage to affirm life in the face of its absurdity, that we must have the courage to say I love you to a girl whom we have met only minutes before and to whom we may make love partly because her parents need the money, that we must have the courage to fire our machine-guns at our fellow men while conjugating the Latin verb *amo*, *amas*, *amat*, that we must have the courage to die, as Jones did, while saying I love you to the world. When we do have that courage, McDougall implies, we shall find that the world is restored to us in all its freshness once again, and that we are restored to a communion with all mankind, exist "at the central suffering core of all humanity."

If *Execution* lacks a certain force, it may be because we do not see into the mind of the condemned man himself. He is, perhaps, a somewhat too simple version of the Christ figure, viewed as the ordinary man, to be entirely convincing.

In *The Cashier*, Gabrielle Roy takes us inside the mind of such a man. Alexandre Chenevert, second teller in a Montreal bank, is the average man with a vengeance. Preoccupied with the trivial details of his domestic world, plagued by the anxieties of the daily news, the threat of the Bomb, the more distant threat of overpopulation and of universal famine, Alexandre has nothing much to distinguish him. His life is without adventure; nothing that he does is either glamorous or sensational. He is neither rebel nor hero. He lives obscurely, unmolested in his little world by courts or armies or society at large. Yet he too is condemned, nor will his execution be as swift as that of Jones, for Alexandre is sentenced to die from cancer.

The problem of the justice, goodness, meaningfulness of life is raised once more by Alexandre himself. He has often considered the problem as he looked about him at his fellow men, noting the narrowness and meanness of their lives, much like his own. When he discovers he has cancer, at the point when his own life seems to open into nature and a brighter future, the problem becomes personal and deeply poignant. Yet it is precisely his experience during the long illness that takes him to his death that convinces Alexandre, as Jonesy's example had convinced Doorn and Adam, that the question of life's justice has been somehow misconceived and that, more patently than ever, life appears as good.

During his illness Alexandre becomes more profoundly aware of the paradox of human life. He is impressed on the one hand by the fact that "We kill others – all the people we know – a little bit."[7] He is impressed on the other hand by the extraordinary kindness of men. He is even led to proclaim rather blasphemously to the priest that "If God had as much heart as a man, that would already be a fine thing ... " And when the priest attempts to be agreeable by saying that it might be so in the case of the saints, Alexandre replies that he wasn't thinking of saints at all: "For indeed his heart marvelled only at men, ordinary men."[8] He is struck by the irony of the fact that both he and his wife, who have never been very affectionate, suddenly realize that they love one another, now that it is too late to do much about it. He is made more conscious of his own helplessness and insignificance, and, at the same time, of his own inexplicable worth – because a handful of casual acquaintances remember him and make the effort to come to see him, because the doctors, nurses, and technicians to whom he is practically unknown, devote such time, energy, and skill to his last days on earth. "To the very end, now one person, now another defended this poor life as though it had been precious, unique, and in some sort beyond replacing." From Alexandre's illness there has sprung up a profound appreciation of his own uniqueness and equally of his communion with all men.

> During the last moments, so great a gentleness had touched his face that those who saw it might have persuaded themselves, with this dying man, that the only assurance on earth comes from that tenderness for human beings which goes furthest beyond the bounds of reason.[9]

Clearly this is not the conventional holy death. The look on Alexandre's face is not the result either of an easy death or of a heavenly faith, of trust in a merciful or loving God. Early in his illness Alexandre remarked of God that He too must be touched with the love and pity of men. But as the cancer enters the bone and Alexandre is racked with pain, he comes to a different conclusion. God is not gentle. God, in fact, surpasses man in his capacity to inflict pain or suffering. He tells the priest:

> "God goes deeper than we. He it was Who invented making people suffer. ... He knows far more about it than we. ... No one has yet gone as far as He. ... It's strange! Strange! ... Even the Nazis ..."[10]

The association might evoke a comparison with Leonard Cohen's equation in *Beautiful Losers* between the sado-masochistic asceticism of certain Christian disciplines and the behaviour of the Nazis. But the comparison is superficial. The implications here are wholly different. Alexandre is not torturing himself and neither he nor the God who tortures him is here concerned about disciplining the will in order to control or to reject the natural world. It is just the opposite. The suffering which God is seen to inflict on Alexandre forces him to abandon his will, to give up his concern about many of the details of his life, to realize that he cannot control the destiny of others, nor even his own. Alexandre is forced more clearly to accept his body, the irrational imperfect world of nature. His suffering leads precisely to a greater love for the world he is about to leave. It is that love which, we are told, gives his expression such a gentleness and such assurance. As in *Execution*, we are presented with the picture of a man who dies affirming life.

In both novels the conventional Christianity of the Padre and the priest is tested and found wanting in the face of death and suffering. For the priest in *The Cashier* is also driven by the evidence of God's cruelty, and of its paradoxical fruit in Alexandre, to re-examine his own life and to reassess his own conventional assumptions. He admits his ignorance before the mystery which the conventional religious formulas do not prepare him to explain. Nonetheless, both these novels have been cast in largely Christian terms. Jones, especially, in *Execution*, is presented as a type of Christ. However, as Gabrielle Roy goes on to show in a later novel, *The Hidden Mountain*, the same drama can be cast in quite other terms.

The experience of Pierre, whom we have already encountered earlier in this study, finds expression in terms more akin to the myths of the early hunters than to the Christian religion. It goes back to a vision of the world conceived in the image of the hunt, in terms of killing and being killed, where the life of one most nakedly entailed the death of another. Yet the recognition of this fact led, within that vision, not to further enmity and division between man and nature, or between the hunter and his prey, but rather to a greater fellow feeling, to a recognition of the sacredness of every individual life and to a sense that life is one. Life became a sacramental hunt. That is how it appears to Pierre.

The mountain that Pierre discovers in Ungava, which he spends the summer season trying to capture with his brush, is clearly a symbolic mountain, an embodiment of the divine or cosmic power. Radiant at first, it changes with the changing season, becomes grim and awful wrapped in cloud and in the swirls of the first snow. And it is then that Pierre is led into the secret of the mountain itself. From the darker of the two hands of God he is given a harrowing revelation of the sacrificial character of all life.

The revelation springs from his encounter with an old buck caribou. As Pierre stands debating whether to hunt for provisions before setting out for the coast or to trust to luck along the way, the caribou appears, as if from out of the mountain and as if deliberately inviting his own death. Pierre gives chase, wounds him, and is led further and further into the maze of the rock, without provision, without any more ammunition, amid the gathering dark. "In what strange corner of creation was he?" he asks. "What could be the meaning of such a monstrous tangle of tormented, almost suffering, stone? You might have thought it a forest of rocky arms, half broken, yet which strove to rise straight in the air."[11] Here the distinction between animate and inanimate disappears. When the caribou crashes to the ground to rest for a moment he takes on the look of a "glacial boulder," indistinguishable from his surroundings except by the shadow his antlers cast in the moonlight.

When the animal rises and forces the already weary Pierre into further pursuit, he stirs in Pierre "something like hatred for this animal that took so long in dying."[12] But, at the same time, the chase has stirred in the man a sense of kinship. At the start Pierre had felt "a queer emotion, as though this were a man he was tracking, in order to slaughter him."[13] The identification is reinforced by the description. Running side by side, "their shadows in the moonlight were again strangely mingled, like that of a single, exhausted being."[14] The duality of Pierre's attitude is fully revealed when, after pausing to let the wounded animal drink, he brings his hatchet down on the animal's bent neck, for the last time.

> The prostrate animal's eyes turned toward him, stared at him in a still living distress, infinitely resigned, then clouded over. Pierced with cold, Pierre let himself slip down next to the dead caribou, which gradually began to give him its warmth. In the endless stretches of the tundra they formed a tiny, motionless, almost fraternal patch of shadow. The dawn came. The keenness of Pierre's hunger awakened him. Now, having warmed him, the caribou was to become for him flesh, blood, and his very thought.[15]

It is Pierre's identification with his prey which establishes his communion with all living things – and we may note that the whole action is said to occur beneath the *living* moon, amid the *living* rock. It awakens in Pierre an intense compassion for all of life, which he has glimpsed as a continuous process of killing and being killed.

> The suffering of animals seemed to him limitless, horrible, forever beyond acceptance. He saw mink gnawing at their legs crushed in some trap, dogs howling from their terrible hunger, the look in the eye of the dying caribou. He ate and wept – wept over this dreadful part of creation, its ineffable harshness, its cold beauty, heedless of all that it itself is not.[16]

Pierre as a result becomes the spokesman for a suffering creation, a curious figure in the arctic village to which Orok, the Eskimo who finds him half dead in the waste, brings him to recuperate.

> The old men, the most ancient of the village – the women, too – all often went to see this strange sight: a man, pale as the autumn snow, emaciated as a caribou's horns, who seated on his bed with his back against the wall, throughout the almost constant night and by the glow of a single candle, made pictures of the sun.
>
> Or yet again animals – the familiar animals of the muskeg: the thin-antlered caribou, the chubby bear, and others not known in these parts, for example, the great moose of the western country. And all seemed to open wide their eyes and their mouths as though in a terrible effort to speak. This, Orok by himself might perhaps not have discovered. Pierre had told him about it. He had said that he proposed to give the power of speech to beasts as well as to men – to all those who knew life's suffering.[17]

In the self-portrait which Pierre paints later in Paris, the identification between the hunter and the hunted, pursuer and pursued, is finally complete. He takes on explicitly the appearance of the great caribou he has killed. He assumes not only the horns of the slain animal but something of his knowledge as well. It is a revelation of the fundamental mystery of life. The revelation is anything but beatific. When Stanislas, a friend and fellow artist, first looks at it, the portrait makes him think of Marc Chagall's "gentle cows, of their eyes in which shone a human kindliness." But he quickly realizes that the association is inept. The expression in these eyes is entirely different.

> What, then, had Pierre tried to suggest? What close alliance of the soul to all that is primitive? Or was this not that high-pitched lament in which are commingled the anguish of killing and of being killed.[18]

It points to the sacrificial character of all life. Pierre's experience has led him to a communion through suffering not only with his fellow men, but with the animals, the mountain, the whole universe; towards a conception of life in which hunter and hunted are one, in which God is the great hunter who may be said to hunt himself through each of his creatures.

In becoming the spokesman for this world, Pierre produces a cry not of protest, but a lament. He gives expression to the suffering of the animals and of all creation, but he also gives expression to the joy or radiance of life. Just as in the arctic village he drew pictures of both suffering animals and the sun, so in his final paintings in Paris he produces first the harrowing self-portrait and then, as his last living gesture, he attempts to paint the mountain in its full glory. He too dies affirming life.

The same high-pitched lament in which are commingled the anguish of killing and of being killed is heard in Adele Wiseman's novel *The Sacrifice.** There too it leads to a compassion for all living things, to a recognition of the unity of life, and to a fuller, clearer affirmation of the world.

Set in a prairie city at the turn of the century, the book is more realistically conceived, and it unfolds in more familiar, biblical terms, within the context of a Jewish, not a Christian world. The novel turns upon the Old Testament story of Abraham and of God's command to Abraham to sacrifice his son. The central character in Miss Wiseman's story is a man called Abraham, who likewise has a son called Isaac. Isaac is the youngest of three sons, two of whom have been killed already by the Cossacks in their European homeland. Abraham hopes that in the New World Isaac will be free from such a fate and will grow old and maybe even famous among men. For a time, it looks as though his hopes might be fulfilled. Though never robust, Isaac grows into an intelligent and hard-working young man. He marries and provides his father with a grandson, Moses or Moishe, who will brighten his old age.

One evening as they sit around the table after supper, Abraham retells the story from the Bible; Moishe listens wide-eyed; Isaac is more skeptical. The old man explicates the story as he goes along. He points out how in the sacrifice is realized the identity of slayer and of slain and of their one creator, God himself. As Donald Stephens once pointed out in a paper on the sacrificial theme in Canadian literature, their unity is symbolized by the circle, the unbroken ring of the eternal. That is what it is like, says Abraham:

> "the completed circle, when the maker of the sacrifice and the sacrifice himself and the Demander who is the Receiver of the sacrifice are poised together, and life flows into eternity and for a moment all three are as one."[19]

Yet there are various ironies in this passage, in Abraham's retelling of the tale, in Isaac's comments, in the old man's confident explanation of its meaning. It is both a beautiful and a vicious circle which he spins before their eyes. Abraham does not at this point fully understand the import of the pious wisdom he so glibly dispenses. But he learns.

The skeptical Isaac is the first to see an irony within the original story. In his youth the biblical Abraham had himself rebelled against false gods who demanded the sacrifice of children; yet now in his old age Abraham was being asked to supply precisely the same sacrifice. The one true God demanded it. How, Isaac implies, is one to make sense of this? The old man merely points out that God relented, permitting Abraham to sacrifice a ram instead of his son in order to give man the future. "Kill the ram and let your son live. In him is your future." For the moment Isaac half-heartedly accepts the old man's observation. Later he develops his own more skeptical, rational, humanistic interpretation of the events. Maybe, he suggests, it was all a part of Abraham's scheme to eliminate human sacrifice: "in the end humanity is served, animal sacrifice takes the place of human sacrifice, and eventually all sacrifice ceases except for the ritual killing of creatures for food. Abraham has plotted well."[20]

As it turns out, Isaac's interpretation is much farther from the truth than that of his father. Sacrifice has not ceased: he and his father must re-enact the story to a more bitter conclusion. It was Isaac who introduced the image of the circle, and, ironically, it is Isaac who finds himself enclosed in it.

Despite his skepticism, Isaac remains the creature of his father's faith. He is driven by his father's expectations for him. When the local synagogue catches fire, Isaac automatically runs into the burning building to rescue the Torah, emerging in an aureole of flame. He never recovers from that ordeal and is thus sacrificed on the altar of his father's beliefs.

It would appear that since Isaac has already provided for the future in his son Moishe, God sees no reason to release him from his role in the ritual drama. Uncomprehending, Isaac remains caught in the circle his father has described, of the sacrifice, the one who makes the sacrifice, and God. Lying on his death-bed, Isaac dreams he is enclosed in a sphere from which he cannot escape however he struggles to break free. He dies to prove his father's point.

However, a further sacrifice is required before Abraham understands the full import of his story. Abraham himself cannot accept the death of Isaac. No more than his son can he accept the sacrifice that life demands, the sinister side of God. He remains the judge of a world he cannot wholly affirm, of the creator and his creation.

That the ritual killing of creatures for food continues, Abraham knows. He is a butcher, and though he is not a *schoichet*, who officially performs the ritual slaughter, he is familiar with the role. He had to play it once. As a youth in Europe he had been apprenticed to a butcher. One day when the *schoichet* failed to arrive, his employer decided to undertake the slaughtering himself. In the course of the proceedings he forced Abraham to take the knife and kill one of the cows. As in Pierre's encounter with the great caribou, Abraham finds himself face to face with the living creature he must kill, and he is terrified.

> Her eye was large and brown and moist, and very deep. It made me dizzy to look. I closed my eyes and fell upon her. Will I ever forget that moment? It was as though I too were sinking with the knife. It was, as I have said, as though I were somewhere between living and dying. Not until I saw that the creature was dead did I realize that I was still alive. I have wondered since if that is what our forefathers felt when they made the sacrifices to renew their wonder and their fear and their belief, before they were forbidden to make them any longer. It is a mystery too deep for man.[21]

That occasion, Abraham declares, was his initiation into manhood. "It was not until after I had been forced to take a life that I really changed and was no longer a child ... Who has to take a life stands alone on the edge of creation. Only God can understand him then."[22] However, Abraham must stand there once more – to renew his wonder and his fear and his belief. He has never really accepted the implications of that experience. Like other conventional religious figures we have met, Abraham pushes the darker side of his experience out of sight. His confidence or faith does not embrace the cruder and more painful elements in life. And it crumbles before Isaac's death.

After the death of his son, Abraham becomes preoccupied with himself and his problem; he becomes suspicious and resentful of the world; he withdraws from those around him to become the one self-righteous man in an evil world where even God, perhaps, cannot be trusted. He would like to die, but death refuses him.

It is at this point that he goes to visit Laiah, an earthy widow with a reputation for her way with men. Abraham has known her slightly for many years. Lately he has made deliveries to her apartment and has stayed to have a cup of tea. For he is an old man, exhausted by the climb to her apartment, and she, despite her bravado, is a lonely woman who has few, if any, intimate friends. Laiah has in fact long admired Abraham, for his dignity as well as for his masculinity. Now she begins to daydream: he might even marry her. Thus, when he arrives at her apartment late one night she naturally believes that he has come to relieve his loneliness, the loneliness of the flesh as of the spirit. The scene that follows develops through a series of misunderstandings as each misconceives the other's meaning. Yet it is the scene in which, ironically, Abraham arrives at a final understanding of his problem and a final affirmation of life.

Abraham is too preoccupied with his own thoughts to realize how Laiah has misinterpreted his presence and the things he says. When he remarks abruptly, thinking of his dead sons, "You have never had any children?" the woman is startled. She, naturally enough, thinks of her present loneliness and of the future, and gives to the remark quite a different interpretation. And when Abraham bursts out in a still longer speech, which seems in the end to be addressed directly to her, Laiah not unnaturally concludes that her interpretation has been confirmed – though it is indeed a strange speech.

> "All my life," he burst out, "I have wanted only one thing: to grow, to discover, to build. Of all the voices that are given to a man I took the voice of praise; of all the paths I chose the path of creation, of life. I thought that merely in choosing I had discarded all else. I thought that I could choose. One by one, with such ease, they were stripped from me. Wherever I look there is a shadow, a shadow that all my life I did not see, I tried to ignore. The shadow grows about me, filling in the corners of my emptiness, darkening my desire. You've waited for me, empty, all this time."[23]

Laiah can make of this only a declaration of Abraham's need. She holds out her arms to him offering to fill his emptiness in her own quite simple but quite human way. Abraham stands up to continue his inner inquisition and finds himself suddenly in her arms. "Like one," Laiah whispers in his ear. And we begin to see that Laiah has begun to take on a wholly new character in the old man's eyes. She has become "the other part of him – that was empty, unbelieving, the negation of life, the womb of death, the black shadow that yet was clothed in the warm, tantalizing flesh of life."[24] He begins to see her as the slaughtered animal, the darkness that he thought he could ignore, the destructiveness of life he thought he could discard simply by choosing. He sees them now, both life and death, creation and destruction, the killer and the killed, as one, inseparable, in Laiah, and in himself. Holding her there, his mind following its own independent train of thought, the hand that supports him on the table cutting itself on the butcher knife that lies there, he reflects, "Did he come at last to accept the shadow, to embrace the emptiness, to acknowledge his oneness with the fruit without seed, with death, his other self?"[25] The answer would appear to be no, not really, not yet.

As Laiah moves voluptuously against him, speaks of love, and tells him she is his to do with as he wants, she does not realize what she is saying. She does not realize that in Abraham's eyes she has become the willing sacrificial animal:

> there was something in him that ached to see how under her eyelids her eyebulbs were large and fine. Her forehead wrinkled and was somehow sad, like that of some time-forgotten creature that had crept out to seek the sun. Her hair flowed endlessly downward, falling gently over his arm. All this he could see, in the sacred place where he stood, and he could feel that it was trying to speak to him, to explain itself, for the moment was near.[26]

Trying to keep his balance Abraham has grasped the knife on the table and the whole scene begins to focus on a remembered ritual. The past holds him; he cannot let it go. The deaths of his three sons and the first death, of the animal slaughtered in his youth, command his vision. They look out from Laiah's eyes to remind him of what he fears, of what he guiltily has refused to look at and embrace. Nor can he even now accept what Laiah represents; he can only contain it in the sacrificial ritual. He escapes into the image of the eternal. The circle becomes a refuge, a release from life and not a liberation into life: "now was the time for the circle to close, to enclose him in its safety, in its peace."[27] Thus, despite the strange tenderness he feels for the creature in his arms, he cannot bring himself to love her and to affirm the sort of world which she embodies. Uttering fragments of the Hebrew ritual prayer, he slits her throat. Only then, pulled to the floor by her weight, kneeling and cradling her in his arms, does he begin, hoarsely and vainly, to plead with her to live. "Live!" he says, "live."

Abraham is taken to Mad Mountain, the asylum which, like the abattoir, is kept outside the town, but which has nonetheless brooded over the story from the start. There Abraham's new wonder, fear and belief, along with the wisdom that has grown out of his suffering, are kept locked up, until his grandson finally comes to pay the old man a visit on Mad Mountain.

Moses has grown up nurturing a demonic image of his grandfather, the butcher and murderer. He has become for Moses the embodiment of all that is to be feared and hated in this life. It is only when he meets Aaron, a youthful friend whose professed hatred of his father serves as a common bond, that Moses can speak of his grandfather. And it is in company with Aaron that Moses talks himself into going to see the old devil. But when he arrives at the asylum he is confronted with an unexpectedly gentle old man, a man he cannot fear, much less charge with all the bitter accusations he has rehearsed over the years.

Sitting on a bench in the gardens of the asylum, the old man talks, not merely to the boy, but to someone else who is not there. "And still," he says, "though something in me reached out, I did not understand. Nothing was necessary. I could have blessed you and left you. I could have loved you." Moses is a bit disturbed by his grandfather's speech, but he is not uncomprehending.

> Was he talking to – that dame? Whom he had killed? From the way he spoke he sounded almost as if he loved her, real love, not just – whatever it was. And yet Moses had the feeling that, though he was addressing someone else, his grandfather was somehow addressing him, too.[28]

He is. And shortly Abraham addresses the boy more directly. "Moishe," he says, "when a human being cries out to you, no matter who it is, don't judge him, don't harm him, or you turn away God Himself." And a little later, when the old man takes the boy by the the hand, Moses stares at their hands in wonder.

> This was the hand of a murderer. His eyes, fascinated, saw that the hands were not really different in shape, one from the other. And for a moment so conscious was he of his grandfather's hand on his own, of its penetrating warmth, of its very texture, that he felt not as though it merely lay superimposed on his own but that it was becoming one with his hand, nerve of his nerve, sinew of his sinew; that the distinct outlines had disappeared. It was with the strangest feeling of awakening that he saw their hands fused together – one hand, the hand of a murderer, hero, artist, the hand of a man.[29]

In his recognition of the two hands of man, and his acceptance of their radical identity within each man, as, perhaps, within the one great mystery of God, Moses is released from the grip of the past, from anger, bitterness, and hatred, into love. He awakens to the present to embrace the world. Returning to the city to meet his friend, he wonders if he will have the courage to tell Aaron of the change he has discovered in himself and in his feeling for his grandfather. He wonders if he will have the nerve to say straight out, "I love him." And, climbing from the streetcar, Moses, we are told, "looked curiously about him at his fellow men."[30]

There is an ironic edge to Miss Wiseman's novel. She is assuredly not recommending human sacrifice, or murder. Yet, she says, until we recognize and accept the sacrificial character of life we shall not avoid getting caught in the ritual, either as the unwitting sacrifice or as the one who unwittingly sacrifices others. She demands too that we recognize the radical identity of hunter and hunted, of killer and killed, within ourselves as within the world around us, implying that we shall be able to affirm the world only when we have accepted this identity. Our love of the world, our communion with the world, issues from our recognition that it is both our victim and our executioner. He who would have it otherwise remains consciously or unconsciously the alienated man.

The hero of Douglas LePan's *The Deserter* is a clear-cut example of the consciously, even deliberately alienated man. During a night spent with a girl named Althea, he has known complete fulfilment: sensual delight, tranquility of body and mind, a beauty which seems total and which he associates with the memory of Althea's body, her white thighs glimmering in the moonlight. Rusty, the hero of this novel, is a man who has had a glimpse of Eden and who becomes a witness of perfection in a fallen world. He becomes the self-appointed angry man whose rage for beauty, goodness, order makes him the inquisitor of a creation in which these qualities in their pristine form cannot be found, no more than the girl Althea. For Althea disappears, and though Rusty, through the whole course of the novel, searches for her, and for the perfection she represents, he never finds her again.

Rusty's desertion from society and his rejection of the social order is designed primarily to pose a metaphysical rather than a political problem. He makes the vision of perfection the source of all meaning: life, he assumes, has purpose and value only if we can hope to realize such perfection. But during his long journey through the human underworld, he discovers only life's imperfection, its ugliness, its disorder, its brutality and apparent absurdity. And how, he asks, can one live in an absurd world?

Though Rusty does not find Althea, he meets a girl named Anne, with whom he lives for a time. Unlike Althea, however, Anne embodies the imperfection of the world. Haunted by fears and guilts, hunted from within by a growing fear of madness, she has been driven into the world of shadows in which Rusty moves. Her life reveals the ugliness and sterility that Rusty cannot accept. At moments, however, her face will glimmer like a lily in the darkness, and Rusty will catch a glimpse of Althea. Intolerably, he discovers that he cannot think of Althea without thinking of Anne.

> What had become of her, he wondered, that delicate-veined apparition of flesh and blood who had transfigured him and ruined him, so that now whenever he thought of perfection he thought of judgement; whenever he thought of pursuit he also thought of being pursued; whenever he saw the face of ecstasy he saw also the hollow cheeks of pain, metallic, featureless?[31]

The ideal and the actual merge in the figure of Anne, who is precisely a figure who has been broken and, as it were, contaminated by the world. It is a process which Rusty cannot accept. When Anne leaves him because of her growing illness, Rusty realizes that he might have loved her and helped her. Yet he refuses to follow her because he refuses to let go of his vision of perfection, which is at the source of his guilt, his failure, and continues to divide him from Anne as from the world.

> She had needed him and he had failed and now she was slipping over the horizon. His eyes opened to admit her wholly and the deep draught of his own failure. It burned him as he drained it. He felt it burning, corroding round his heart, prisoning still deeper the few drops of heaven that he could never surrender.[32]

Rusty believes that if he were to surrender his vision of perfection, there would be only "waste, tundra, dying stars, apathy, meaninglessness spreading everywhere."[33] But what he discovers is that the more he measures the world against his vision of heaven, the more apathy and meaninglessness spread round him anyway.

Almost from the beginning, Rusty was aware of what he calls one of the oldest of complicities, "the magic complicity of hunter and hunted." Yet he would reject such a complicity, wishing to keep each separate. Dramatically, he becomes not only a man in pursuit of perfection but a man pursued. Hunted on the one hand by the police in an all-out attempt to round up deserters and on the other by a gang of racketeers with whom he has become inadvertently involved and who are out to kill him, Rusty flees through the city with his one remaining friend, a young man named Steve. During one of their stops to rest, Rusty dozes and dreams he is walking on the sea-floor among the foundered ships, in sunken quays of drowned cities. It is a vision of the ruins of time such as Miss Crawford presents in "Malcolm's Katie" as argument for the ultimate futility of life. In the gloom Rusty sees the crumbling walls, drowned masts, "monstrous rudders or propellers, fouled and bent." He also hears a voice which speaks to him in the words of Anne's parting letter: "a voice coiled round him accusingly, 'But your heart would have to break ...' "[34] Still, he resists the implication. And when the chase finally comes to an end, his friend dead, Rusty, standing wounded and alone in the harbour of the actual world, is again overwhelmed by a sense of apathy and meaninglessness. Looking past the shadowy rooftops, the markers in the channel, to the tangled stars, he can discover no design anywhere among them.

> No bear, or eagle, or belt, or sword, or serpent. No design you could look to or could wear on your wrist, embellished with flowers, or a wreath, or a cross, or a date, or letters that spelled out "Mother" – or any other name. Nothing but impinging darkness.[35]

Neither in the sea nor in the sky can he detect any reason for living. His whole career has led him to an acute awareness of the menace of death, guilt, and meaninglessness. Though the night smells of the sea, he finds there no trace of any "annunciation of birth and beginning, only hints of the salt water that a castaway knows must sooner or later drive him mad. ... He couldn't stir."[36]

Yet he does stir. What appears to move him first is simply hunger. Reading of his friend's death, staring, as he puts it, into the very face of death itself, he finds himself moved, not by grief, but by "sheer animal instinct, sheer animal recoil."[37] He discovers that life is prior to meaning, that value lies less in perfection than in love, above all, in the affirmation of oneself and one's world. The very friends whose lives had previously confirmed the ugliness and absurdity of the world now provide him with examples of life's power to affirm itself in the face of every negation.

Having recovered a measure of health, Rusty later reviews his experience with a cold eye. Stripped of all ties with society, having symbolically abandoned his very name by throwing his identity tag in the river, having lost his only intimate friends, whom he has failed, and having given up hope of ever finding Althea or the kind of happiness she symbolized, he is tempted by suicide. Yet it is the example of Steve and Anne, and of something inherent in himself as well, that prevents him from simply shooting himself.

He recalls the stories that Steve had told him of his earlier life during the war, in the concentration camps, of "the cold, the stench, the iron doors being slammed to, the bayonets, the cries, the thin soup with fish-heads floating in it, the dying, the dead," and yet, amid all the images of forced labour, of Steve's homeless and terrified wanderings, he recalls finally "his perfect loyalty and courage."[38] And with this he recalls Anne, who had gone away despite her loneliness and need, in order not to be a burden. "What he was left with," he concludes, "was only what they had seen in him, Anne and Steve, what they had thought of him, what they had wished for him. With that, and with something of his own that he still shared with them, although he was hardly conscious of it, a deep ultimate animal courage."[39]

This is the pre-rational foundation on which Rusty builds. It leads him to recall still other friends, the ex-dragoons and fellow deserters, Brandy and Dragon, whose animal simplicity and lack of interest in Rusty's vision of beauty, goodness, and truth had led him to dissociate himself from them. They too possessed this courage; it is their legacy to him.

> He felt half ashamed to be using this as a brazier, to be warming his hands at the memory of anything so primitive and simple; but in their animal heat was to be found conspicuously the final irreducible particles, random, unpredictable, not to be trusted, but without which nothing could be built, nothing, neither love nor justice nor a city, without which there could be no meaning nor anything but spreading tundra and despair.[40]

There is no mistaking his point: the primitive and irreducible foundation of life, prior to goodness, justice, beauty, or truth, prerational, is courage, the creature's self-affirmation in the face of all that it is not, which could find no better expression than in the phrase, the courage to be. And it is on the basis of this courage that Rusty can recognize a further wisdom conveyed in the example of Steve and in the parting letter from Anne, that if he would love he must be prepared to break his heart.

It is the implacable imperfectibility of life, in any final sense, its irreducible suffering, guilt, and threat of absurdity that have driven Rusty to the recognition that value lies in love and not in perfection. Perfection of whatever kind tends to be relatively impersonal. What makes life personal is the recognition of each individual thing or creature as unique and, however imperfect, as of value in itself. What is demanded is a reversal of the Platonic pilgrimage. Instead of moving from the love of earthly things to a love of universals, we are asked to move from the love of universals, those pure eternal forms, to the love of the evanescent and mortal particulars. The love of heaven is replaced by the love of persons, of a perishing imperfect world.

Here also the vision of the ideal was expressed in terms of the circle, of the glimmering sphere, associated at times with the luminous figure of Althea and at times with the intricately turning spheres of the great sundial in the courtyard of a government ministry. Appropriately enough, this sundial is smashed towards the end of the story. For the lesson that Rusty learns is that the perfection imaged in the glimmering sphere can enter life and become personal only if the sphere is broken. He must be willing to be broken, if he is not to imprison still further the few drops of heaven in his heart.

The point is made explicit in the final passage in the novel, which celebrates his newly-discovered communion with the world. The music of a band in a nearby park is gathered up in Rusty's reverie with all the martial music he has ever known, and his surrender, which he will register in outward terms by turning himself in, becomes exultantly transformed into a victory march. He feels that something is tearing, breaking, that the skies are falling apart; yet he is laughing. What he thought all along would be a kind of death turns out to be a kind of birth. The solution, he now sees, does not lie in trying to hold the spheres together, but in letting them break. His new confidence, his solidarity with all men and his capacity to rejoice in the whole creation are taken up in the music of the drums and bugles on a rising wind.

> Now Steve's voice and Anne's were being carried to him on the wind, their courage was being added to his, they were breathing, were shouting, through him. He was uplifted by the vehemence of their breath, he was a trumpet and was helping to tear the last vestiges of illusion to tatters ... And now finally he felt something else tearing and breaking. The crystal vial in his heart that had supported all those circling spheres – the strong muscles of his heart were breaking it at last, the precious iridescent drops were spreading, spreading, were trickling everywhere along his nerves and tissues. Still he exulted. For nothing was lost. Perfection was being broken through his common dying clay.[41]

A similar, if more temperate exultation emerges towards the end of Hugh MacLennan's *The Watch that Ends the Night*. Whereas *The Deserter* is a formal invention designed to explore a theme, MacLennan's novel is a more personal and documentary reflection of Canadian life in the years between the two world wars. One of MacLennan's persistent concerns has been to give a faithful representation of various aspects of our national life. His story begins in Montreal west, which could be characterized still, he says, as an English garrison encysted in a large French village. It begins with a hero more average, and much more familiar than Rusty. Yet it explores the same theme as LePan's book, and it leads the hero to the same kind of conclusion. And one of the things that the hero discovers in the process is that he is a Canadian.

Like David Canaan in *The Mountain and the Valley* or Philip Bentley in *As For Me and My House* or James McAlpine in *The Loved and the Lost*, George Stewart is intimidated by the world around him; he lives with reference to an external order that is not his own. An observer through much of his life, he is caught in the web of circumstance others have woven out of their passions and desires. In his youth, like his father before him, he is governed by a strong-willed aunt, representative of the *status quo*. Partly because of her influence and partly because of his own innate fear, he runs away when his childhood sweetheart, and the only woman he ever loves, offers herself to him. Defying a weak heart, Catherine goes on to live her own life. She marries her masculine counterpart, Jerome Martell, who gives her a child against the advice of his fellow doctors, both Catherine and Jerome being determined to make the fullest possible affirmation of life. It is from these two that George must finally learn, but he does so only when time and events have driven him to it.

Appropriately enough, George Stewart begins his career in a boarding school, which is little more than a museum of stuffed birds, old mottoes, and odd masters, the miscellaneous backwash of life and time. But as he moves out into the world, as a broadcaster, political commentator and, finally, as a university lecturer, he is increasingly overwhelmed by the violence, suffering, and apparent futility of people's lives, both individual and collective.

Back in Montreal, he stands helplessly by as the passions and ideals of Jerome Martell lead to the break-up of his marriage. After a losing battle with the hospital where he works, Jerome leaves his wife and daughter and goes off to continue his fight in the Spanish Civil War.

In Russia in 1939, George is again a helpless observer who stands by watching as vast irrational forces there and in Germany lead the world into war. The individual, he feels, is nothing before the blind forces of life that engulf him. Public and private are inextricably mixed, and no one is safe from the menacing sea.

So he discovers quite personally when, after years of Jerome's absence and reports of his death, George finally marries Catherine. For the menace is found to be rooted in nature itself. Catherine's weak heart begins to tell; she suffers a series of devastating attacks. And Jerome Martell turns up alive just when she faces a major operation. At this point George Stewart finds that he is at the end of his tether. He is attacked on all sides. There is no defence against the invasion of the world. What is the point, he demands, of Catherine's life or anyone's life if it only goes on to another attack, another invasion, pain and inevitable death? What is the point of the struggle when death always wins? The whole irrational sea, the subconscious world, seems to rise up against him.

> Then a man discovers in dismay that what he believed to be his identity is no more than a tiny canoe at the mercy of an ocean. Sharkfilled, plankton-filled, refractor of light, terrible and mysterious, for years this ocean has seemed to slumber beneath the tiny identity it received from the dark river.
>
> Now the ocean rises and the things within it become visible. Little man, what now? The ocean rises, all frames disappear from around the pictures, there is no form, no sense, nothing but chaos in the darkness of the ocean storm. Little man, what now?[42]

How, he asks, can a man be equal to his fate when it means being equal to "the knowledge that everything we have done, achieved, endured and been proud and ashamed of is nothing?"[43] The answer, again, is courage and it comes through the example of Catherine.

> Catherine's spirit, as her fate became more obvious and unavoidable grew larger and larger. Her courage made me feel awe; it even made the doctors feel awe. To go on like this, to struggle like this – for what? Merely to have to go through it all again at a later date. She did not seem to me like a boxer rising again and again to be punished by an invincible opponent, but more like a bird in the claws of a cat who wanted to prolong the fun. The cat was God.[44]

This is the God encountered by Alexandre Chenevert. But George has yet to arrive at Alexandre's understanding. George is like Rusty, another Job, the inquisitor of a creation without rhyme or reason, whose Creator is at best but a playful torturer.

But George does not speak for Catherine. Catherine paints, and every time she recovers from one of her attacks she returns to proclaim her joy in life in more vivid and lyrical colours. Like Alexandre, she knows that through a courageous acceptance of the struggle and of all that it implies the perspective is changed. She goes on affirming her life and the world.

MacLennan also resorts to a musical metaphor, citing the work of Bach and of Beethoven to illustrate this paradoxical shift in perspective.

> The same idea restated in the major with horns and woods becomes an exultant call to life. This, which is darkness, also is light. This, which is no, also is yes. This, which is hatred, also is love. This, which is fear, also is courage. This, which is defeat, also is victory.[45]

Under the pressure of Catherine's illness and of Jerome's unexpected return, George is gradually led to experience exactly such a transformation. Death itself, he discovers, may be seen as an ally instead of an enemy. It is Jerome who observes that George is more afraid of living without Catherine than he is of death. And Jerome explicitly tells him that by accepting and even embracing death he may overcome his fear of life.

Like the force of God, Jerome is an ambiguous figure embodying both the dark and the light. The bastard son of a scornful but powerful woman who is murdered almost before his eyes, Jerome has issued from the wilderness of the New Brunswick forest. Symbolically, he embodies the primitive *élan* of life itself. It is absorbed in the Christian culture of the civilized world when Jerome is adopted and brought up by an Anglican minister and his wife. But this primitive spirit can no longer be contained in the conventional Christian culture. Following his experience of life in the First World War, Jerome feels compelled to burst its bonds. He rejects his childhood training, turning to Communism. His career follows what Kazantzakis has called the movement of the spirit in the twentieth century. He becomes a surgeon and tries to reorganize the medical services in Montreal along Communist or socialist lines; he fails; he then goes to Spain to help in the fight against Franco, to France to help in the fight against Hitler, to China to help in the fight against Japan and a reactionary Chinese regime. There he becomes deathly ill. During the illness he reaches the end of his more or less political humanitarian faith. Had he been able to pray to any God, he says, he would have prayed for death. But, at that point, he suffers an hallucination, or a vision. The figure of Jesus appears beside him in the cell. "He wasn't," he explains, "the Jesus of the churches. He wasn't the Jesus who died for our sins. He was simply a man who had died and risen again. Who had died outwardly as I had died inwardly."[46] Symbolically, Jerome himself becomes the figure of such a Jesus, of the man who has died and risen again.

When George Stewart enters the hospital to find this man who has returned, as it were from the dead, bent over the still unconscious figure of Catherine, he is outraged. He hates Jerome and would like to kill him. Jerome has become the embodiment of death and human suffering, of the sinister side of life.

> Years of concentration camps, of beatings and starvings and hatings and killings and torturings – there he was like the memory of the human race back beside her for the end, and I thought he looked like a vulture.[47]

Yet it is this man who has embraced the whole of human suffering, and death itself, who carries with him an extraordinary gift of healing, and it is under his vulture-like gaze that Catherine first stirs, emerging from the coma in which the operation left her. The inner character of the man becomes more apparent to George Stewart when they meet outside Catherine's room.

> I had never in my life seen an expression like his. His face seemed white, very lined but the lines finely drawn, the eyes very large. His whole face seemed transparent. And in his eyes was an expression new and uncanny. They seemed to have seen everything, known everything, suffered everything. But what came out of them into me was light, not darkness. A cool, sweet light came out of them into me then. It entered me, and the murderous feeling went out, and I was not afraid any more.[48]

Jerome's expression is one we have met before in *The Hidden Mountain* and *The Sacrifice*. Here too we catch a glimpse of the harrowing enigma of existence. Jerome is another of those figures who possess a knowledge of both life and death, and this knowledge is given to George Stewart as Jerome appears to actually enter and become George himself.

More discursively, Jerome tells George that in order to command the kind of courage to live that Catherine exhibits he must follow her example; he must learn to build a shell around himself and periodically creep inside. "Two days inside and you'll come out able to face anything." In explanation he adds that the "shell is death."

> You must crawl inside of death and die yourself. You must lose your life. You must lose it to yourself.[49]

When everything becomes intolerable, one can live only by embracing death, so that one may say, what difference does it make if someone dies, if I die or am disgraced, "if everything we've done means nothing. 'Then,' says Jerome, 'you will live.'"[50]

We have clearly arrived at a variation on Christ's teaching, "He who would save his life must lose it." In this sense MacLennan's novel is a Christian novel. Yet, as we have seen, the same message is presented in a variety of terms both Christian and non-Christian. Even here, where MacLennan relies heavily on Christian imagery and Christian terminology, the point is made that the figure of Jesus is not the Jesus of the churches but, as for Alexandre Chenevert, simply a man. And the wisdom which Jerome imparts to George Stewart was learned in Auschwitz from a Jewish rabbi. Jerome adds, "A few gifted Jews seem to be the only people these days who know how to be Christians."[51] It is an existential, not a dogmatic conviction, which, here as elsewhere, emerges from the experience of suffering. It springs from the acceptance of suffering as ineradicable, as part of the essentially sacrificial process of life, and it is rooted in that affirmation of oneself and one's world which we have related to Tillich's conception of the courage to be. In a world in which most of the traditional structures of meaning have been called in question or left without any convincing foundation, it is this conviction which makes possible a triumphant celebration of life and a real sense of joy in life. This is true of George Stewart, as it is true of the characters in the other novels we have looked at. Leaving the hospital after his encounter with Jerome, he experiences a renewed sense of life's worth and of his community with the world.

> As I walked along the familiar street chipped out of the rock of Mount Royal, with the city luminous below and the sky luminous above, there was music within me, so much that I myself was music and light, and I knew then that what she had upheld from childhood was not worthless, that she was more than a rat in a trap, that the loves she had known and inspired had not cancelled one another out, were not perishable absolutely, would not entirely end with her but would be translated into the mysterious directions of the spirit which breathed upon the void.[52]

Catherine survives the operation, and although the next attack and her eventual death remain imminent, George Stewart now feels able to live with his anxiety – with the threat of the bomb in the public world and the threat of Catherine's decease in the private world of his marriage. He learns to savour to the full what may be their last autumn together in the hills of the Eastern Townships of Quebec. It is there, with the autumn rains washing the gardens and the autumn moon washing the lake, amid the slow burning of the trees on the hills, that he declares his ultimate conviction. "It came to me," he says, "that to be able to love the mystery surrounding us is the final and only sanction of human existence."[53] What the purpose of life may be beyond that, he does not know, and it does not seem to matter. All their lives, he reflects, they had wanted to belong to something larger than themselves. Now they belonged to nothing but the pattern of their own lives and fates, and perhaps to God. All he knows with conviction is that life is a gift. It is the butterfly that emerges from the rock, sprung like Yeats' fountain out of life's own self-delight, despite the hand that will crush it, the rock beneath the hand. "Our past was not dead but now the present had flowed over it, as the future would flow over the present until the time came, and we both knew it would come soon – when she would be gone and I would be left."[54] And when Catherine dies, like Alexandre Chenevert with an expression of joy illuminating her face, George Stewart finds that he loves the world around him more intensely than ever, even as, at the same time, it becomes but a shadow, a shadow perhaps of the power within the rock out of which it has sprung.

CHAPTER SEVEN

An Ancient Slang or a Modern

"Where I'm going, anything may happen," says Rachel Cameron at the end of Margaret Laurence's *A Jest of God*, and we might say the same of Canadian writing.[1] Certainly changes have occurred in the literary climate during the past decade or two. Raymond Souster's anthology of young poets, *New Wave Canada*, has at least made a ripple, which is more than could be said of *New Provinces* in 1936. Robert Kroetsch's *The Words of My Roaring* has come out of the west with a buoyant optimism unknown in the novels of Grove or Ross, the crude vitality of his hero, J. J. Backstrom, shrugging off political, social, marital, and financial problems like a summer shower. Leonard Cohen has shrugged off a Governor General's Award. And Al Purdy with his shorts and his sunglasses, a brown cigarette butt hung on one lip, has gone to Ottawa to muse in the House of Commons. Irving Layton has gone to Toronto as a full-time academic; and George Bowering has gone to cheer for the Montreal Expos, shouting, "Frappez one, Le Grand Orange!" French and English may still not be speaking in appreciable numbers, but in *Poetry '64: Poésie '64* and in A. J. M. Smith's two Oxford anthologies, not to mention a centennial volume of Canadian literature, they are at least publishing side by side. Vancouver has been invaded by American poets, and one never knows whether one may find Cohen or Layton or Purdy or Bowering or various others in Israel, Greece or Japan, in Havana, or Mexico City or Nashville, Tennessee. Gwen MacEwen has presented us poems in Egyptian hieroglyphics, and B. P. Nichol has given us poems to burn. The renewed publication of poets that began in the forties, grew through the fifties, has swelled to a flood in the sixties. New poets spring up across the country, spawning new magazines and private presses every year. Their variety as well as their numbers have greatly increased. Has the climate not radically changed? Do the older writers and the preoccupations we have discussed at such length still have some relevance for those active today? Or have they become as invisible as the winter tracks and northern trees have become for Al Purdy as he walks home through the spring snow and the night, recovering from a "winter hangover":

> while the dead underfoot whisper
> and the land stirs to life
> and nothing is impossible?[2]

The answer is yes and no. Anything may happen, but whatever it may be it will continue to reflect the past.

Rachel Cameron's statement reflects a new, more open, more adventurous mood. Yet it was born of her past experience, an experience of precisely the kind we have discussed in the previous chapters, and that we may recognize in the lines by Carl Sandburg that Miss Laurence quotes as the epigraph to her novel.

> If I should pass the tomb of Jonah
> I would stop there and sit for awhile;
> Because I was swallowed one time deep in the dark
> And came out alive after all.[3]

Rachel's experience has given her the courage to take life as it comes without exhausting herself in a continual attempt to anticipate its dangers, to make of it what she can without constantly worrying about what others might wish her to be. Anything may happen. But good, bad, or indifferent, Rachel looks forward to it with an awareness, and prefaces it with a petition that echoes the convictions of previous Canadian writers.

> I do not know how many bones need be broken
> before I can walk. And I do not know, either, how
> many need not have been broken at all.
> *Make me to hear –*
> How does it go? What are the words? I can't
> have forgotten all the words, surely, the words
> of the songs, the psalms.
> *Make me to hear joy and gladness, that the*
> *bones which Thou hast broken may rejoice.*[4]

The *Jest of God* is itself a work of the sixties. We have heard such words as these in the work of Jay Macpherson and Margaret Avison. Reaney and Cohen have expressed a similar conviction. It may not be very pronounced among others, but I suggest that it is not irrelevant to their present concern. Purdy and Nowlan, Newlove and Bowering, Atwood and MacEwen may exhibit a variety of styles and may appear to be preoccupied with new or with quite unrelated themes; yet the work of these poets is not unrelated to the perspective that we have defined. As a conclusion to this study, we may try to demonstrate something of that continuity within change.

Like Margaret Laurence or Margaret Avison, various writers continue to explore the themes we discerned. Following Jonah into the dark they discover, like Rachel, that they can contain it; they arrive at the conviction that though life may break them it is nonetheless good. Others go on from where Rachel leaves off; with the courage of that conviction they go out to explore the possibilities of life, to articulate a wilderness of inarticulate experience, to exorcise the ghosts of the dead or the mute, of all that is haunting America's attic.

The garrison vs the wilderness. There is no denying the persistent preoccupation of novelists, Grove, Ross, Callaghan, Mitchell, Buckler, Watson, MacLennan, and Laurence with the terms of this opposition. Among the poets it could be seen as early as Lampman and Scott. We may note that it also informs many poems, both ironic and sober, by F. R. Scott. It lay at the heart of Anderson's "Poem on Canada," and it runs through much of the work of his contemporary, P. K. Page. It has spurred Irving Layton to rage and to utter obscenities. And it continues to occupy writers today.

Enormous changes have occurred in Canadian life since the Second World War. The solitudes, of English and French, Catholic and Jew, Italian, Ukrainian, Negro or white, can never again be quite so complete. Nor can the whole fabric of community life be entirely controlled by a small, officially Anglican, Baptist, or Presbyterian élite. It is hard to imagine the profound isolation of a Philip Bentley today. Yet the problem persists. The older colonial attitudes may die, but the garrison mentality lives on. As Cohen suggests, extending the insights of Lampman and Grove in his *Beautiful Losers*, it persists in the highly aggressive but essentially very exclusive spirit informing much of our modern world, and it may be all the more sinister in that it appears to serve all those aspects of our nature that were previously excluded, extending our comfort, our leisure, the means and the desire for sensual pleasure. It wars upon death; yet only complicates dying. It would make the world a new Eden; yet more often pollutes and destroys it. It may now profess secular rather than religious ideals; it may speak with an American rather than a British accent; but it often remains a garrison culture. The American look often gives to the commercial, industrial, and military establishment the air of a continental Titanic which would wall out the sea. Meanwhile familiar, traditional forms of defensive behaviour continue to breed fear and exclusiveness, alienation and lives wholly lacking in authenticity. *Five Legs*, a novel by Graeme Gibson, is one of the most intense and original of the recent developments of this theme. More broadly, it continues to generate curious and original forms of expression in the poetry of Margaret Atwood, concerned as she is with the circle games of both children and adults, the closed-in worlds of the rented room, the photograph album, the museum, the car, the train, the capsule in space, the progressive insanities of her symbolic pioneer. The theme is still far from exhausted.

To escape from the garrison and from the alienation it breeds, one must go into the wilderness, as Lampman and Scott quite early advised. There one may discover a more vital community, a larger and more inclusive view. That, I propose, is exactly what many of the poets who emerged in the sixties have done – though the wilderness they are intent on exploring has little to do with snowstorms or Indians, the actual forest or prairie or sea. It is rather the wilderness of everyday life, the town and the country created by man as much as by God.

It is the wilderness of Alden Nowlan's "Shack Dwellers" or "Stoney Ridge Dance Hall," where he tells us, "They don't like strangers./ So be careful how you smile." It is a world of maritimers who, when they tire of dancing, go down the road to drink white lightning, wearing their spiked logging boots and home-made brass knuckles, a world where one finds "men ... who have never heard of Canada."[5]

It is equally the wilderness of Raymond Souster's Toronto, which Etienne Brulé discovers when he is pictured returning up the Humber River only to go aground on the shallows before the Bloor Street Bridge, "across which the latest convertibles fling themselves." Throwing out their nets for fish, his men haul in "a strange collection of used condoms,/aspirin bottles, tomato cans." It is a world that Brulé quickly abandons, "crowding all sail to lose/sight of such putrefaction."[6]

What many of the poets of the past decade have undertaken is precisely the role of the nth Adam. They have set out to take an inventory of the world but scarcely uttered, the world of the excluded or ignored. It would comprehend whatever is crude, whatever is lonely, whatever has failed, whatever inhabits the silence of the deserted streets, the open highways, the abandoned farms. It is the wilderness of experience that does not conform to the cultural maps of the history books, sermons, political speeches, slick magazines and ads. And it is the wilderness of language in which the official voices of the culture fail to articulate the meaning or the actual sensation of living and tend to become gibberish. This is the wilderness Leonard Cohen describes in "Lines from my Grandfather's Journal."

> Doubting everything that I was made to write. My dictionaries groaning with lies. Driven back to Genesis. Doubting where every word began. What saint had shifted a meaning to illustrate a parable. Even beyond Genesis, until I stood outside my community, like the man who took too many steps on Sabbath. Faced a desolation which was unheroic, unbiblical, no dramatic beasts.
>
> The real deserts are outside of tradition.[7]

Here lies the difference between a Leonard Cohen and a Jay Macpherson. Miss Macpherson's poems recommend an inclusive view, embracing the whole of life, even to the engulfing sea. But they do so in a highly formal way. She remains confident that there are still traditional words and images that may convey an excluded reality, the biblical images of Adam and Eve in the wilderness, of lion and snake and Leviathan. But for others she does not actually enter and make an inventory of the immediate wilderness of daily experience, the desolation that Cohen describes as "unheroic, unbiblical, no dramatic beasts."

Those who inhabit the deserts that lie outside tradition are faced with a problem of language. As Cohen says further, "Desolation means no comparisons." Therefore, he resolves, "let me refuse solutions, refuse to be comforted."[8]

Such an impulse informs John Newlove's "At this Time," though here the poem is so simple, so lacking in explanatory comment, we might well be puzzled to discover the motives of the speaker's refusal, or the point of his poem.

> It is my refusal to make comparisons
> this time that keeps me silent. There
> is this snow, and me,
>
> I saw on the dry snow, which was
> grey, a bird sitting as if he would
> eat bread or seeds.
>
> And I saw an eaten melon; it was
> this and it was that and red
> with black seeds.
>
> I spat them out. What keeps me silent
> is not the bird on the dry snow,
> but my continuous refusal.[9]

No comparisons. The scene is not violent, but it is part of the crude actuality of place, the isolated moment of experience that the speaker refuses to gloss or distort by referring it to some social or moral or metaphysical idea. There may be an ironic ambiguity in the speaker's refusal, but first and foremost the poem would appear to say, here is what strikes me, here are the significant elements of my experience at this moment, the bird, the seeds, the speaker himself, and the dry snow, which I refuse to betray by some imposing comparison.

No ideas except in things, said William Carlos Williams. The current influence of American poetry on the younger generation of Canadian poets is not merely a fad, but stems from a common conviction. In varying degrees Bowering or Newlove, Nowlan or Purdy share with Williams a common distrust of conventional forms, rhythms, diction, and imagery, and a common desire to explore and articulate those aspects of their experience that are ignored or denied or simply distorted by the traditional matrix of language. Here is the reason for the continuing vitality of imagism – and for the resistance to Frye and to poets like Reaney and Macpherson – among a number of the more recent Canadian writers. To tell it as it is, to name and define a world of inarticulate feeling, to reveal the significance of those elements of their experience that do not conform to conventional ideas of what is significant, the imagist program provides a basic method. Avoid the dictionaries groaning with lies; present an image, the thing in itself; use rhythms that correspond to the emotion felt, the rhythms especially of actual speech.

Much of the recent poetry is concerned with gathering up fragments of experience and is characterized by a distinctly colloquial diction and rhythm. Listen again to John Newlove in "That's the Way Everything Is:"

> That's the way everything is now,
> sweetheart. And we are too.
>
> Beat to hell and we love it. Not
> beatitude. Tired. Too tired
>
> to find a handkerchief. You litter
> the bed with little bits of toilet paper.
>
> I litter the bed with toilet paper too.
> Have a cigarette. Or go to sleep, you.[10]

As much as anything it is the tone, the tone of the talk, that here reveals the precise character of the speaker's experience: a little tired, a little banal or crude, but not risqué; neither glamourous nor sordid but rather domestic; affectionate not passionate, ordinary not romantic.

Carl Klinck has argued that the distinctly Canadian element in our literature will reveal itself less in the imagery, subject or theme than in the rhythms and syntax, the tone of the talk. Certainly Newlove is always talking. That is his way of taking possession of his world in all its immediacy. He must make his own personal inventory and he is concerned about the appropriate tone, precisely what tone he should take. All this he explains in the poem "I Talk to You."

To whom shall I talk except
my exhaustive self? To whom indicate
the shape of the house I inhabit,
or the brain and the leg, the pressures
behind the bony skull, the leg's hairs,
the moulding of the front-door stairs.
To talk to myself expecting an answer,
expecting a credence, confessing
insaneness in this dialogue –

is this to be mad? To sound foolish,
to sound foolishness, to be mad to say,
to say the convulsive illegible world
is how? and demand a reply.

To be mad, to be mad, unangry, to sit
sour in the old wooden chair
and run across the unmoving world
without pity, with only the wild regret
at not to know? To be mad for an answer
knowing there is no answer, except
in peculiarities and particularities?

The chair: what sort of sunny wood
its back is made of; the leg's shape
and not the brain's. And whom to talk to;
and whether it is fit to whisper or to shout.[11]

It is the same voice that we hear in poem after poem by Al Purdy, that of a man talking, of a man mad for an answer who nevertheless finds no answer, except in peculiarities and particularities, and who doesn't know often whether it is fit to whisper or to shout. Witness the opening lines of his poem on Percy Lawson, contract negotiator for the Vancouver Upholsterers' Union:

Sitting with Lawson in 1954
          sitting with Percy Lawson

ill at ease in the boss's panelled office
after work hours talking of nothing
talking of practically almost nothing
a lousy nickel raise that is
        haggling over a lousy nickel
and maybe besides the long and hourly
bearable toil of an almost lifetime[12]

Purdy's is also the voice of a man talking to possess the moment, the actual elements of the world he moves through that do not fit into conventional patterns of poetry, or any convincing or clearly recognizable pattern of meaning. It is the voice of a man who is lost in a wilderness and who tries to determine *what* his position is, even if he cannot determine *where* it is. Thus in his poem "In the Wilderness," he tries to comprehend what is happening in the world around him in Agassiz, the center of the Doukhobour activities in the early sixties:

Sitting at Agassiz with Big Fanny
in 1963
talking with Big Fanny at Agassiz
while the Mounties' "D" squad
drives by in Chevys and Pontiacs
continually hovering
talking of young Podmoroff who died
in Agassiz mountain prison and
was buried home in the Kootenays
talking of 100 men fasting and dying
in Agassiz mountain prison
and the sons of mothers and daughters of husbands
and Big Fanny:
"I was 15 days on water and lemon and
now apple and prune juice"
(40 days and 40 nights in the wilderness
while the "D" squad looked and hovered
and the Pillar of Fire by day
stood over the Sons of Freedom at Agassiz)
Talking with Big Fanny
about mystic Lebedoff
comic-opera-satan-Lebedoff
Judas-enemy of Peter Verigin's people
who plots against them in the far mountains
schemes at Wynndel
        for the people's destruction

accepting another 30 pieces of silver smiling and
the Mounties' "D" squad cruising and hovering –
(Talking to Big Fanny
making notes for an article ... [13]

Whatever the meaning of these events, it is to be found only in the particularities that are gathered up as the speaker goes over and over the ground, talking – only in the particularities and in the rhythms and colour of the talk.

Purdy's are poems that go round and round, as Gwen MacEwen put it, and where they stop nobody guesses. The meaning is all in the tone of the talk and the gathering up of the detail, not in the ending, not in a conclusion. After describing his old '48 Pontiac and telling us how he finally had it dragged off to the auto wrecker's, where he makes a last visit to polish it up and renew old associations, Purdy continues:

I turned the speedometer back to 5000 miles
changed the oil
polished the headlights to look at death
adjusted the rear-view mirror to look at life
gave it back its ownership card
and went away
puzzled by things[14]

The past may be as puzzling as the present. One of the characteristic preoccupations of contemporary poets is a concern to possess, or to re-possess, the actuality of their childhood, of their father's or grandfather's world. Such poems are often more intimate than those we find in earlier Canadian poetry. The poets are concerned with articulating and so with affirming those individual lives in all their puzzling, crude, and even absurd actuality. For frequently they conform to no desirable model. The lives of his ancestors, even their convictions and aspirations, may well have a grotesquely ironic character for the poet himself, something out of a tragi-comedy or an opera-bouffe rather than a heroic romance of pioneer life.

George Bowering reveals this concern in several of the poems in *Points on the Grid*. His grandfather crossed the ocean from England to Canada at the age of twelve, and he gradually made his way across a continent, and a lifetime, to Vancouver and an ironic conclusion. The poem "Grandfather" begins with a view of his life in mid-career:

Grandfather
        Jabez Harry Bowering
strode across the Canadian prairie

hacking down trees
        and building churches
delivering personal baptist sermons in them
leading Holy holy holy lord god almighty songs in them
red haired man squared off in the pulpit
reading Saul on the road to Damascus at them.

This is the heroic, or mock-heroic version. But after reaching Brandon, Manitoba, shovelling coal to heat Brandon College, building more churches, marrying a sick girl who gave him two children and died, "leaving several pitiful letters and the Manitoba night," grandfather moved on to a different end.

He moved west with another wife and built children
        and churches
Saskatchewan Alberta British Columbia Holy holy holy
lord god almighty
        struck his laboured bones with pain
and left him a postmaster prodding grandchildren with
        crutches
another dead wife and a glass bowl of photographs
and holy books unopened save the bible by the bed
Till he died the day before his eighty fifth birthday
in a Catholic hospital of sheets white as his hair.[15]

"Was there power where I sprang from?" Bowering asks in another poem called "Family," whereupon he is led to make a descent through the "tangled rime of time," a vague vision of ancestral life in Angle Land, of the slow growth of Church and Nation and Clan in another time on another continent, back to the present and the answer to his question:

To where we are, now.
        No power but the delta of time.
No past unfogged on the Island.
        No family but me.[16]

The title poem of John Newlove's book *Moving in Alone* is also an attempt to acknowledge and possess his own past, his childhood, his parents, the roots of his own vitality despite its banality, its occasional violence, its incoherence. It is literally a *recollection* of childhood in the small western town of Verigin, of a boy "fatherless, 250 people/ counting dogs and gophers . . . mother/principal of the 2-building/ 3-room 12-grade school." It is the recollection of fragments that made up his life, of trying to shoot crows with an air-gun, of shooting wild dogs in the winter, of leaping in the fresh grain in summer, into snowbanks in the winter, of swimming in Dead Horse Creek in the cold spring, getting the strap at school for watching a fight; and:

> coldly holding back tears
> and digging for drunken father's
> rum-bottle, he had finally
> arrived, how I loved him,
> loved him, love him, dead, still.

The poem can lead to no moral except the one that George Stewart announces at the end of MacLennan's novel: that to be able to love the mystery surrounding us is the final and only sanction of human existence. So Newlove is concerned with articulating and confessing his love for his father, despite his desertion, his drunkenness, the fact he can provide no model by which to live. Newlove affirms the facts of his singular fate, though the various elements fail to resolve themselves into any larger or final pattern of meaning. He remembers the isolated fragments, his brother, his sister, the cry of a gull, the corpse of a horse turning "slowly and sweetly to bone," his friends, his peers, his enemies, "till everything breaks down."[17]

The disintegration of traditional or conventional patterns of meaning may reveal themselves in the syntax of such poems. The vernacular may reveal at once the essential colouring of life in a particular time and place and also its lack of connection, its distance from the traditional or publicly accepted conventions of behaviour or language. Whether the tone is ironic or straightforward, whether the voice is the author's or somebody else's, whether it is the voice of the past or of the present, it is the vernacular we hear again and again in the poems of the sixties. Even earlier Raymond Souster needed only to report what he heard in "Girl at the Corner of Elizabeth and Dundas" to reveal with brutal precision one corner of the wilderness in which he lives. This too, he insists, must be part of the poem of our time:

> You want it or you don't
> You got five bucks or no
> I'm twenty-one I ain't
> Got any time to waste
> You want it or you don't
> Make up your jesus mind.[18]

More intimately, Alden Nowlan reveals something of both present and past in a mixture of baby talk drawn from a letter and his own tough fantasy. What we hear in his "Money" is nonetheless colloquial speech, and must almost be read aloud before we can disentangle the syntax, the punctuation or lack of punctuation the poem presents.

> My sister writes from Halifax.
> "Dear Bruddie ..."
> Sure enough, she wants money.
>
> Money! Why she and I
> had been reared naked
> were clothes money –
> teeth coins ours had been knocked out,
> eyes dollars hers and mine
> snipped off with a razor.
>
> Breakfast was dollar bills
> sprinkled with ground dimes
> washed down with melted pennies
> brown as coffee, but richer, sugared
> with silver – if we had any.
>
> As I remember it, our house
> was roofed in banknotes woven together.
> Rain blew in on my bed. The roof leaked.
> Father said: there's no money.
>
> "Dear Bruddie ..."
> Sistie wants money.
> She and I
> write baby talk about money.
> "don't be silly, we wore
> gold, azure and purple underpants
> because papa stole
> that cloth from the cotton mill,
> flour bag shirts and madeover pants and dresses.
> We ate beans until they came out of our ears
> and mama saved even the salt from her tears.
>
> But, p.s., I need money."[19]

As a final example we may cite Al Purdy's "My Grandfather Talking – 30 Years Ago." Here especially, it is the accent, the rhythm, the syntax of colloquial speech that reveals a world of the past – and something of its incoherence.

Not now boy not now
some other time I'll tell ya
what is was like
the way it was
without no streets
or names of places round
an nothin but moonlight boy
nothin but that

Why ain't there woods no more;
I was usta woods an
how far was anywhere was
as far as the woods went
ceptin up
        an I never went

They put a road there
an a girl on the road
in a blue dress
an given a place to go
from I went
into the woods with her
it bein the best way
to go an never get there.[20]

As the poem continues the syntax disintegrates completely, and the old man himself loses track of the subject.

Here the past speaks for itself in its own tongue, obscurely but suggestively. It speaks for itself a little differently in the "found poems" of F. R. Scott or John Robert Colombo, or in the short quotations scattered, along with the poems, through the pages of Bowering's *Rocky Mountain Foot*. Isolated from its formal context and a whole set of conventional assumptions, the text of an Indian treaty may discover new meanings: governmental eloquence may become pompous hypocrisy; native simplicity may become honest eloquence. The fragments of the past, even the most recent past, may suddenly reveal with irony or dignity its authentic voice. In the case of Purdy's poem it is a voice that is seldom recorded in official papers, the voice of the land and a world that is almost lost. It comes from "the country of defeat," as Purdy calls it in "The Country North of Belleville, a world:

... where the farms have gone back
to forest
        are only soft outlines and
        shadowy differences –

Old fences drift vaguely among the trees
　　a pile of moss-covered stones
gathered for some ghost purpose
has lost meaning under the meaningless sky
　　– they are like cities under water and
the undulating green waves of time are
　　laid on them.

Sometime, says Purdy, we may go back there, to the country of our defeat, "But it's been a long time since/and we must enquire the way/ of strangers."[21]

It is not simply the wilderness of a rural past gone back into bush, but all the drowned cities of our inarticulate experience that Purdy and Nowlan, Newlove and Bowering would raise into the light and air of consciousness. It is the same impulse that has increasingly informed the work of James Reaney, in such poems as "Le Tombeau de Pierre Falcon" and "Twelve Letters to a Small Town," and in plays such as "The Kildeer." Despite the Spenserian apparatus of "A Suit of Nettles," his concern to explore the world of southwestern Ontario has led him more and more to make his lines flow like the Avon he knew around Stratford when he was a boy, and which he says, "did not taste English to me."[22] It is the impulse behind not a few of the poems of Raymond Souster and of such a poem as Cohen's "Lines from my Grandfather's Journal." For it is an exercise by no means restricted to those whose roots go back to the farm or the small town, but an exercise rather to be undertaken by all who live in those real deserts that lie outside tradition. As Eli Mandel suggests in "The Meaning of the I CHING," it leads back endlessly into the world of the past:

before I was: the dead who speak to me
　　　　arranged themselves in me[23]

And as he also suggests in "Manner of Suicide," it leads out endlessly into the world of the present, a world of incredibly various and very particular forms of frustration, suffering, despair, and death.

These poets exhibit the courage to be. Mandel, Cohen, Souster, Nowlan, Newlove, and Purdy are constantly facing their own inadequacies, the disorder, guilt, and mortality they find in the world around them. They may be said to have faced a desolation, "unheroic, unbiblical, no dramatic beasts." Yet they are concerned with digesting that desolation and affirming the world despite it. "Let me swallow it whole and be strong," says Newlove.[24] "Let me be gay for the girls and boys/broken before me," sings Mandel, "Who else will remember their joys?"[25] And through that acceptance, through their articulation of the imperfect world, they would discover a new communion. In the process their world may again become biblical, though in an unconventional, unorthodox way. Eli Mandel's catalogue in "Manner of Suicide," though drawn from a psychiatrist's study, becomes in effect a litany for the dead, which Mandel ironically contrasts with an orthodox prayer from "EVENING SERVICE FOR THE SABBATH: THANKSGIVING FOR GOD'S UNFAILING MERCIES."[26] It is a much less ironic, yet strangely biblical voice that we hear in a late song of Cohen's:

I stepped into an avalanche
It covered up my soul
When I am not a hunchback
I sleep beneath a hill
You who wish to conquer pain
Must learn to serve me well

The figure who speaks somewhat obscurely here is the God of Leviathan become anonymous Christ, a God who has been broken, incarnate in his creation. And he is to be served by love of that incarnate and mortal world.

You who wish to conquer pain
must learn what makes me kind
The crumbs of love you offer me
are the crumbs I've left behind
Your pain is no credential
It is the shadow of my wound

I have begun to claim you
I who have no greed
I have begun to long for you
I who have no need[27]

In "Lines from my Grandfather's Journal" Cohen remarks, "It is strange that even now prayer is my natural language." Many of these poems might be considered a kind of prayer, an incantation to recapture one's past life, a method for calling up ghosts, as Purdy entitles one of his poems: ghosts of the present as well as the past; prayers for the dead and prayers for the living, and prayers to effect a communion with all the inarticulate experience that remains unheard and invisible beneath the slogans and conventional formulas of the day. It need not have a rural accent, nor need it always be crudely colloquial or fragmented in syntax; yet it tends to be the vernacular, the spoken word that carries the breath of the spirit however removed from the formal, hieratic language of the traditional liturgies.

This aspect of language has a more explicit or poignant interest for a writer like Cohen, whose very name means "priest." But what he says in the following passage speaks not only for him and for his grandfather but in varying degrees, I suspect, for many contemporary poets.

> The language in which I was trained: spoken in despair of priestliness.
>
> This is not meant for any pulpit, not for men to chant or tell their children. Not beautiful enough.
>
> But perhaps this can suggest a passion. Perhaps this passion could be brought to clarify, make more radiant, the standing Law.
>
> Let judges secretly despair of justice: their verdicts will be more acute. Let generals secretly despair of triumph; killing will be defamed. Let priests secretly despair of faith: their compassion will be true. It is the tension ...

Let us affirm an order, but let us not make of the Law a garrison against life, a garrison that would know nothing of guilt, doubt, or the defeat of inevitable death. Let us order and celebrate the world in a language that can comprehend its imperfections and yet find it good.

Of the poets who speak in this spirit we may say, they remain in this wilderness ministers of the word who secretly despair of faith and yet are concerned to articulate the life of the spirit. For them, as for Cohen:

> Prayer makes speech a ceremony. To observe this ritual in the absence of arks, altars, a listening sky: this is a rich discipline.

For some of these poets, at least, the recovery of the past extends to the recovery of older conventions, of much that may yet remain vital in the traditional patterns of cultural and spiritual life, though it has dangers as Cohen remarks:

> It seems that nothing is lost that is not forsaken: The rich old treasures still glow in the sand under the tumbled battlement; wrapped in a starry flag a master-God floats through the firmament like a childless kite.
>
> I will never be free from this tyranny.
>
> A tradition composed of the exuviae of visions. I must resist it. It is like the garbage river through a city: beautiful by day and beautiful by night, but always unfit for bathing.[28]

Yet Cohen himself cannot resist it entirely, will not leave it forsaken.

In the popular "Suzanne Takes You Down," which has been heard across North America, Cohen takes us down to the river, which is both Souster's river, filled with the garbage of the present, and Cohen's river, filled with exuviae of visions. Half saint and half prostitute, Suzanne will take you to her place down by the river, where you may stay the night beside her:

> Suzanne takes your hand
> and she leads you to the river,
> she is wearing rags and feathers
> from Salvation Army counters.
> The sun pours down like honey
> on our lady of the harbour
> and she shows you where to look
> among the garbage and the flowers,
> there are heroes in the seaweed
> there are children in the morning,
> they are leaning out for love
> they will lean that way forever
> while Suzanne she holds the mirror.[29]

We may recognize in Suzanne a more contemporary and more successful version of Sinclair Ross's Judith, who sang in the choir with the feral energy of the prairie wind, or of Callaghan's Peggy Sanderson, who held in a single vision both the church and the leopard. Suzanne offers the same conviction as Miss Macpherson, but without benefit of arks, altars, a listening sky. Nothing is lost that is not forsaken, but it is the idiom of the popular ballad, of Judy Collins or Cohen himself that here gives it new life, conveys for many its authenticity, ensures the recovery of a drowned kingdom.

Margaret Avison would also recover the exuviae of visions in a more contemporary speech. It is a sunken image of Christ, "a giant, sort of," who emerges in "A Story":

> Tall, sunburnt, coming
> not hurried, but as though
> there was so much power in reserve
> that walking all day and night
> would be lovelier than sleeping if
> sleeping meant missing it, easy
> and alive, and out there.[30]

He comes on a mythical clamback, which is nonetheless ordinary earth; he comes as a gardener into a wilderness. This vision is presented to people spending the day at the beach by a man in a boat. It comes to us through the mouth of a girl who recounts the events to a skeptical mother.

We have already remarked Miss Avison's renewed approach to biblical themes, her explicitly Christian perspective. We may also remark that she has been one of the most meticulous in making an inventory of her immediate, highly urban, and technical world. Her rhythms are tense, often abrupt, highly nervous rhythms of her thought and of a complex, mechanized world. Theme, image, and rhythm insist on the immediate fact, the detail, the distinctly individual character of every life, and death. She appeals to traditional myth, but would gloss over nothing, leave out none of the dark, refractory world.

Gwen MacEwen is another who cannot resist the appeal of old visions, and her language becomes hieratic, incantatory. Yet she does not abandon her immediate world or the intonations, the accent of contemporary speech. She too would suggest that the concern to be inclusive, to take an inventory, to make a dumb wilderness vocal, and in a speech that is true to its time and its place, cuts across the division frequently drawn between myth-makers and realists. All eloquence need not be lies, all myths academic.

If anyone sounds academic at moments, it is George Bowering, a most obvious disciple of Williams and Olson, and never more academic than when quoting his lessons in the midst of a poem, as in the passage from *Cadence*:

> *Rhythm; measured move-*
> *ment, esp. of sound; fall of voice, esp. at*
> *end of period; intonation; close of musi-*
> *cal phrase.*[31]

If anyone sounds colloquial, it is Gwen MacEwen, and never more so than when engaged with Cartaphilus, a figure of distinctly mythical proportions – and what she has to say may be more to the point than Bowering's quotation.

> Your words, Cartaphilus, are not profound,
> it is mouths that are profound, not words;
> then out of your profound mouth bring forth sounds –
> Egyptian hipster, an ancient vernacular –
>
> O baby, get out of Egypt –
> This history is not for you ...

As she says in conclusion, "An ancient slang speaks through me like that."[32] An ancient slang or a modern: either or both may serve to illumine the actuality of her world. Thus the mythical figure of Icarus helps to articulate the immediate wilderness of her "Poem Improvised around a First Line," which expresses the frustration and violence of personal relationships, sex, and the life style of many young people today. The imagery and language, the phrasing and tone, give it an hallucinatory vividness. Formal and informal, classical and contemporary are strangely woven together in urgent speech.

> the smoke in my bedroom which is always burning
> worsens you, motorcycle Icarus;
> you are black and leathery and lean and
> you cannot distinguish between sex and nicotine
>
> anytime, it's all one thing for you –
> cigarette, phallus, sacrificial fire –
> all part of that grimy flight
> on wings axlegreased from Toronto to Buffalo
> for the secret beer over the border –
>
> now I long to see you fullblown and black
> over Niagara, your bike burning and in full flame
> and twisting and pivoting over Niagara
> and falling finally into Niagara
> and tourists coming to see your black leather wings
> hiss and swirl in the steaming current –
>
> now I long to give up cigarettes
> and change the sheets on my carboniferous bed;
> O baby, what Hell to be Greek in this country –
> without wings, but burning anyway.[33]

Miss MacEwen evokes, and would also reject, the crude violence of place. It is a cry of exasperation, but also, finally, of sympathy. She would move beyond this Hell. Yet it is only by entering and taking possession of it that we may be able to do so. Only by digesting our world, in all its crude, complex, or repugnant particularity, can we hope to transform it. "I believe," she says in her introduction to *A Breakfast for Barbarians*:

> I believe there is more room inside than outside.
> And all the diversities which get absorbed can
> later work their way out into fantastic things,
> like hawk-training, IBM programming, mountain-
> climbing, or poetry.
>
> It is the intake, the refusal to starve.
> And we must not forget the grace.[34]

It is not by shutting things out or destroying them that we shall turn the wilderness into a garden, but by taking them in and giving them human articulation. We shall remain haunted by the one word which has never yet been said.

It is the myth of the word that ultimately occupies Miss MacEwen's attention, which is equally the myth of identity, of the dancer whose body becomes the "first letter/of an unknown, flawless alphabet,"[35] the word incarnate that contains us all. Only in myth, the symbolic or ritual gesture, can we grasp that flawless alphabet, the total order in which everything has a life of its own and is yet one life. In practice we can only approach it, or contribute to it, by taking in the mortal peculiarities and particularities of our lives and by letting them work themselves out in a language appropriate to their time and place. We are fated to be always barbarians speaking a demotic Greek, an ancient slang or a modern. Yet, as the poet says in her "Breakfast for Barbarians," we shall also suffer from a hunger that is not for food; we can never forget the visions of some "fabulous sandwich,/the brain's golden breakfast/eaten with beasts/with books on plates."[36]

Miss MacEwen's is also a sacrificial view of life. The great hook that descends to hoick in the unwitting modern man who would catch Leviathan in Jay Macpherson's "The Fisherman" is transformed into a gigantic universal spoon in Gwen MacEwen's "Ultimately, Said the Saint, We Are All of Us Devouring Each Other." A consumers' society has provided its own image of the universe. The process, however, is a spiritual as well as a physical one, and if we accept it and affirm it as good we may join in the communion to which Miss MacEwen invites us in "Breakfast for Barbarians." The invitation is not couched in very priestly or traditional terms, but it is a sacramental communion nevertheless, and the language is in many respects a vernacular peculiarly suited to the world of our time. "My friends, my sweet barbarians," she says:

> let us make an anthology of recipes,
> let us edit for breakfast
> our most unspeakable appetites –
> let us pool spoons, knives
> and all cutlery in a cosmic cuisine,
> let us answer hunger
> with boiled chimera
> and apocalyptic tea,
> an arcane salad of spiced bibles,
> tossed dictionaries –
>   (O my barbarians
>   we will consume our mysteries)

and can we, can we slake the gaping eye of our desires?
we will sit around our hewn wood table
until our hair is long and our eyes are feeble,
eating, my people, O my insatiates,
eating until we are no more able
to jack up the jaws any longer –

to no more complain of the soul's vulgar cavities,
to gaze at each other over the rust-heap of cutlery,
drinking a coffee that takes an eternity –
till, bursting, bleary,
we laugh, barbarians, and rock the universe –
and exclaim to each other over the table
over the table of bones and scrap metal
over the gigantic junk-heaped table:
by God that was a meal.[37]

We are invited once more to rejoice, to celebrate life in its mortal variety. The world is a wilderness; guilt, isolation, the menace of death are inherent in the human condition. Yet the problem of how to affirm such a world, posed over and over again in the work we have studied, is resolved by accepting these conditions. That acceptance effects a real transformation: the alienation produced by attempts to exclude or destroy every menace is replaced by a larger communion. As MacLennan suggests, what was the condition of our defeat is now also the condition of our victory; what was a wilderness is now also a garden.

The view at which we arrive provides the basis for the individual's affirmation of his actual world, his own authentic reality; he need not conform to an external order to justify his life or possess an identity. And in Miss MacEwen's view that authentic reality in all its individual variety demands to be made articulate. Only thus will we arrive at what F. R. Scott terms the full culture of occupation. For Gabrielle Roy, as for Frye or Buckler or Layton, it is especially the role of the artist to give it a voice, to celebrate the actual, to reveal to nature's divided things their uniqueness and their oneness, their cause for rejoicing. And not a few of the writers have deliberately set about giving such a voice to a heretofore largely inarticulate world of experience.

We cannot speak for the whole of Canadian literature, even less for Canadians generally. But in the course of this study we have examined the work of a significant number of Canadian writers over a period of several generations. They give evidence of the possibility, at least, that Canadians, English as well as French, have arrived at the first days of Creation, that life is now a matter of naming and discovering, of finding words for the obscure features of our own identity.

And some of the writers have arrived at a fundamental view of life that could provide the basis for such an identity. Inclusive, affirmative, yet essentially sacrificial, such an identity would not be a peculiarly national one; yet it would not be inappropriate for Canadians either. Though revolutionary in the light of many of the dominant western attitudes, especially as they reveal themselves south of the border, the view we have characterized here is radically conservative.

However that may be, what we can conclude with certainty from this study is that Canadian writers have been engaged in a more profound and increasingly original exploration of life than is frequently assumed. They have stepped into the desert to discover the North America that John Newlove sees lying, "remote/in the night/ /among the trees/and flowers ... unused."[38] They may send back messages occasionally, like Eli Mandel, saying, "we have not learned/what lies north of the river/or past those hills that look like beasts."[39] Yet others continue to set out on the journey to discover a land that is neither Canada nor Egypt, to explore a continent that is neither America nor Africa, but that unmapped continent in which Miss MacEwen invokes the dancer whom the landscape has designed:

> Life, your trillions people me,
> I am a continent, a violated geography,
> Yet still I journey to this naked country
> to seek a form which dances in the sand
> This is my chosen landscape.
> Hear my dark speech, deity.[40]

We may look to Canadian literature with every expectation of learning more about that obscure landscape that is our life and the world's.

Notes

INTRODUCTION

1 John Newlove, *Black Night Window* (McClelland and Stewart 1968), 110.
2 Louis Dudek, "Nationalism in Canadian Poetry," *Queen's Quarterly*, LXXV, 4 (Winter 1968), 557-67.
3 John Newlove, *Black Night Window*, 110.
4 Margaret Atwood, *The Animals in That Country* (Oxford University Press 1968), 38.
5 Louis Fréchette, *The Oxford Book of Canadian Verse*, ed. A. J. M. Smith (Oxford University Press 1960), 43.
6 Gatien Lapointe, *Ode au Saint-Laurent: précédée de j'appartiens à la terre* (Editions du Jour 1962), 61-2.
7 Anne Hébert, "Poésie, Solitude Rompue," *Poèmes* (Editions du Seuil 1960), 71.
8 Yves Préfontaine, "Indices," *Pays sans parole* (Editions de l'Hexagone 1967), 9.
9 F. R. Scott, *Selected Poems* (Oxford University Press 1966), 39.
10 Gilles Marcotte, *Une Littérature qui se fait* (Les Editions HMH 1962), 67.
11 Irving Layton, *Collected Poems* (McClelland and Stewart 1965), 282.

CHAPTER ONE: THE SLEEPING GIANT

Epigraph: James Reaney, *The Oxford Book of Canadian Verse*, ed. A. J. M. Smith (Oxford University Press 1960), 392.
1 Quoted in *The Globe and Mail*, Toronto, the week of 4 July 1964.
2 Earle Birney, "Can. Hist.," *Near False Creek Mouth* (McClelland and Stewart 1964), 31.
3 Earle Birney, "Can. Lit.," *Ice Cod Bell and Stone* (McClelland and Stewart 1962), 18.
4 Leonard Cohen, *The Favourite Game* (The Viking Press 1963), 124.
5 André Rossinger, "Ou Mourir ou Grandir," *Cité Libre*, XV, 77 (Mai-Juin 1965), 18.
6 W. P. Wilgar, "Poetry and the Divided Mind in Canada," *Masks of Poetry*, ed. A. J. M. Smith (McClelland and Stewart, NCL Series 1962), 69.
7 Margaret Avison, *The Book of Canadian Poetry*, 3rd ed., ed. A. J. M. Smith (W. J. Gage 1957), 472-3.
8 Jay Macpherson, *The Boatman* (Oxford University Press 1957), 12.
9 *Ibid.*, 32.
10 James Reaney, *The Red Heart* (McClelland and Stewart 1949), 31.
11 P. K. Page, *Cry Ararat* (McClelland and Stewart 1967), 100.
12 Phyllis Webb, *The Oxford Book of Canadian Verse*, 400.
13 Charles G. D. Roberts, *Selected Poems* (Ryerson 1955), 56.
14 Archibald Lampman, *Poets of the Confederation*, ed. Malcolm Ross (McClelland and Stewart, NCL Series 1960), 70.

15 Jay Macpherson, *The Boatman*, 33.
16 *Ibid.*, 41.
17 *Ibid.*, 56.
18 Duncan Campbell Scott, *Selected Poems*, ed. E. K. Brown (The Ryerson Press 1951), 51.
19 Jay Macpherson, *The Boatman*, 61.
20 Earle Birney, *Selected Poems* (McClelland and Stewart 1966), 90.
21 Phyllis Webb, *The Sea Is Also a Garden* (The Ryerson Press 1962), #17.
22 A. M. Klein, *The Rocking Chair* (The Ryerson Press 1948), 56.
23 *Ibid.*, 55.
24 Irving Layton, *Collected Poems* (McClelland and Stewart 1965), 64-5.
25 *Ibid.*, 85-6.
26 Earle Birney, *Selected Poems*, 117.
27 Irving Layton, *Collected Poems*, 16.
28 Ernest Buckler, *The Mountain and the Valley* (McClelland and Stewart, NCL Series 1961), 200.
29 *Ibid.*, 281.
30 *Ibid.*, 292.
31 *Ibid.*, 298.
32 *Ibid.*, 300.
33 Gabrielle Roy, *The Hidden Mountain* (McClelland and Stewart 1962), 186.
34 Patrick Anderson, *A Tent for April* (First Statement 1945), no page number.
35 Patrick Anderson, *The White Centre* (The Ryerson Press 1946), 43.
36 *Ibid.*, 35 and 37.
37 Robert Frost, "The Gift Outright," *Complete Poems* (Henry Holt 1949), 467.
38 William Toye, "Introduction," *A Book of Canada* (Collins 1962), 16-17.
39 Warren Tallman, "Wolf in the Snow," *A Choice of Critics* (Oxford University Press 1966), 73.
40 James Joyce, *The Portable James Joyce* (The Viking Press 1947), 518.
41 *Ibid.*, 525.
42 Ortega y Gasset, "In Search of Goethe from Within," *The Dehumanization of Art and Other Essays* (Doubleday Anchor Books 1956), 139.
43 André Rossinger, "Ou Mourir ou Grandir," *Cité Libre*, xv, 77 (Mai-Juin 1965), 12.
44 Margaret Avison, *Poetry of Mid-Century, 1940-1960*, ed. Milton Wilson (McClelland and Stewart 1964), 108-9.
45 Alfred Purdy, *Poems for All the Annettes* (Contact Press 1962), 48.
46 Gwen MacEwen, *The Rising Fire* (Contact Press 1963), 79-80.

CHAPTER TWO: EVE IN DEJECTION

Epigraphs: F. R. Scott, *Overture* (The Ryerson Press 1945), 40; Patrick Anderson, *The White Centre* (The Ryerson Press 1946), 1.

1 Patrick Anderson, *The White Centre*, 36-7.
2 Northrop Frye, "Conclusion," *Literary History of Canada*, ed. Carl F. Klinck *et al.* (University of Toronto Press 1965), 830.
3 Thomas Raddall, *At the Tide's Turn* (McClelland and Stewart, NCL Series 1959), 51-2.
4 Patrick Anderson, *The White Centre*, 1.
5 Sinclair Ross, *As For Me and My House* (McClelland and Stewart, NCL Series 1957), 99-100.

6 *Ibid.*, 95.
7 *Ibid.*, 43.
8 *Ibid.*, 38.
9 *Ibid.*, 161.
10 Margaret Laurence, *The Stone Angel* (McClelland and Stewart 1964), 17.
11 Patrick Anderson, "Poem on Canada," *The White Centre*, 32.
12 Duncan Campbell Scott, *Selected Poems*, ed. E. K. Brown (The Ryerson Press 1951), 24-8.
13 Howard O'Hagan, *Tay John* (Clarkson N. Potter, Inc. 1960), 264.
14 Archibald Lampman, *The Oxford Book of Canadian Verse*, 78.
15 Patrick Anderson, "Landscape," *The White Centre*, 1.
16 Anne Wilkinson, *The Collected Poems*, ed. A. J. M. Smith (Macmillan 1968), 47.
17 Morley Callaghan, *The Loved and the Lost* (Macmillan 1951), 33.
18 *Ibid.*, 233.
19 *Ibid.*, 208-9.
20 Margaret Laurence, *The Stone Angel*, 292.

CHAPTER THREE: THE DICTATORSHIP OF MIND

Epigraphs: E. J. Pratt, *The Collected Poems of E. J. Pratt* (Macmillan 1958), 300; John Newlove, *Black Night Window* (McClelland and Stewart 1968), 82.
1 Loren Eiseley, *The Firmament of Time* (Atheneum 1960), 128.
2 Stephen Leacock, "The Rival Churches of St. Asaph and St. Osoph," *Canadian Anthology*, ed. Carl F. Klinck and R. E. Watters, rev. ed. (W. J. Gage 1966), 189.
3 *Ibid.*, 194.
4 E. J. Pratt, *The Collected Poems*, 244.
5 Susanna Moodie, *Roughing It in the Bush* (McClelland and Stewart, NCL Series 1962), 221.
6 Sinclair Ross, *As For Me and My House* (McClelland and Stewart, NCL Series 1957), 3.
7 *Ibid.*, 31.
8 Hugh MacLennan, *Each Man's Son* (Little, Brown and Company 1951), 200.
9 *Ibid.*, 189.
10 *Ibid.*, 219.
11 F. R. Scott, *Selected Poems* (Oxford University Press 1966), 89.
12 E. J. Pratt, *The Collected Poems*, 295-6.
13 Patrick Anderson, *The White Centre* (The Ryerson Press 1946), 38.
14 Howard O'Hagan, *Tay John* (Clarkson N. Potter, Inc. 1960), 188.
15 *Ibid.*, 184.
16 *Ibid.*, 211.
17 E. J. Pratt, *The Collected Poems*, 197.
18 Duncan Campbell Scott, *Selected Poems*, ed. E. K. Brown (The Ryerson Press 1951), 38-9.
19 E. J. Pratt, "The Roosevelt and the Antinoe," *The Collected Poems*, 199, 203.
20 Howard O'Hagan, *Tay John*, 222.
21 Archibald Lampman, *The Oxford Book of Canadian Verse*, 81.
22 Frederick Philip Grove, *In Search of Myself* (Macmillan 1946), 448.
23 Frederick Philip Grove, *The Master of the Mill* (McClelland and Stewart, NCL Series 1961), 225.
24 *Ibid.*, 227.

25 *Ibid.*, 280.
26 *Ibid.*, 287.
27 *Ibid.*, 194-5.
28 *Ibid.*, 188.
29 *Ibid.*, 229.
30 *Ibid.*, 234.
31 Frederick Philip Grove, *The Fruits of the Earth* (McClelland and Stewart, NCL Series 1965), 132.
32 Frederick Philip Grove, *Our Daily Bread* (Macmillan 1928), 131.
33 Frederick Philip Grove, *The Settlers of the Marsh* (McClelland and Stewart, NCL Series 1966), 112.
34 *Ibid.*, 163.
35 *Ibid.*, 217.
36 Leonard Cohen, *Beautiful Losers* (McClelland and Stewart 1966), 210.
37 *Ibid.*, 222.
38 *Ibid.*, 236.
39 *Ibid.*, 241-2.
40 *Ibid.*, 158.
41 *Ibid.*, 137.
42 *Ibid.*, 141-2.

CHAPTER FOUR: THE PROBLEM OF JOB

Epigraphs: James Reaney, *The Red Heart* (McClelland and Stewart 1949), 20; F. R. Scott, *Selected Poems* (Oxford University Press 1966), 65; Irving Layton, *Collected Poems* (McClelland and Stewart 1965), 55.

1 Frederick Philip Grove, *The Master of the Mill* (McClelland and Stewart, NCL Series 1961), 226.
2 John Grube, "Introduction," Sheila Watson, *The Double Hook* (McClelland and Stewart, NCL Series 1966), 11.
3 *Ibid.*, 84, 85.
4 *Ibid.*, 7.
5 *Ibid.*, 28.
6 *Ibid.*, 61.
7 *Ibid.*, 114.
8 *Ibid.*, 134.
9 Charles Mair, *The Oxford Book of Canadian Verse*, ed. A. J. M. Smith (Oxford University Press 1960), 32.
10 Aldous Huxley, *Island* (Harper and Brothers 1962), 41.
11 Charles G. D. Roberts, *Selected Poems* (The Ryerson Press 1955), 10.
12 Charles G. D. Roberts, *The Penguin Book of Canadian Verse*, ed. Ralph Gustafson (Penguin Books 1967), 69-70.
13 Joseph Gold, "The Precious Speck of Life," *Canadian Literature*, No. 26 (Autumn 1965), 27.
14 *Ibid.*, 25.
15 Charles G. D. Roberts, *Canadian Anthology*, rev. ed., ed. Carl F. Klinck and R. E. Watters (W. J. Gage 1966), 104.
16 Charles G. D. Roberts, *The Last Barrier* (McClelland and Stewart, NCL Series 1958), 150.
17 Charles G. D. Roberts, *Selected Poems*, 92.
18 Joseph Gold, "The Precious Speck of Life," *Canadian Literature*, No. 26 (Autumn 1965), 26.

19 Bliss Carman, "Windflower," *The Selected Poems* (McClelland and Stewart 1954), 34-5.
20 *Ibid.*, 76.
21 Archibald Lampman, *Poets of the Confederation*, ed. Malcolm Ross (McClelland and Stewart, NCL Series 1960), 82.
22 *Ibid.*, 83.
23 *Ibid.*, 76.
24 *Ibid.*, 81.
25 *Ibid.*
26 *Ibid.*, 77.
27 *Ibid.*, 65.
28 *Ibid.*, 63.
29 Archibald Lampman, *The Oxford Book of Canadian Verse*, 73.
30 Archibald Lampman, *Canadian Anthology*, 130.
31 Desmond Pacey, *Ten Canadian Poets* (The Ryerson Press 1958), 164.
32 Duncan Campbell Scott, *Selected Poems*, ed. E. K. Brown (The Ryerson Press 1951), 134.
33 *Ibid.*, 133.
34 *Ibid.*, 134.
35 *Ibid.*, 62-4.
36 *Ibid.*, 146-7.
37 E. K. Brown, "Memoir," Duncan Campbell Scott, *Selected Poems*, xxvii.
38 Duncan Campbell Scott, *Selected Poems*, 57-8.
39 Duncan Campbell Scott, *The Oxford Book of Canadian Verse*, 94-5.
40 Duncan Campbell Scott, *Selected Poems*, 42-3.
41 Leonard Cohen, *Beautiful Losers* (McClelland and Stewart 1966), 147.

CHAPTER FIVE: THE COURAGE TO BE

Epigraphs: John Newlove, *Moving in Alone* (Contact Press 1965), 74; Ralph Gustafson, *Sift in an Hourglass* (McClelland and Stewart 1966), 24.
1 Gwen MacEwen, "The Sperm King," *Breakfast for Barbarians* (The Ryerson Press 1966), 43.
2 Paul West, "E. J. Pratt's Four-Ton Gulliver," *A Choice of Critics* (Oxford University Press 1966), 103, 106.
3 E. J. Pratt, *The Collected Poems* (Macmillan 1958), 2.
4 *Ibid.*, 22-3.
5 *Ibid.*, 242.
6 Paul West, *A Choice of Critics*, 107.
7 E. J. Pratt, *The Collected Poems*, 155, 160, 180.
8 E. J. Pratt, "From Stone to Steel," *ibid.*, 41.
9 Paul West, *A Choice of Critics*, 107.
10 *Ibid.*, 108.
11 A. J. M. Smith, "Introduction," *The Oxford Book of Canadian Verse* (Oxford University Press 1960), xliii-xliv.
12 E. J. Pratt, *The Collected Poems*, 37.
13 A. J. M. Smith, *Collected Poems* (Oxford University Press 1962), #31.
14 *Ibid.*, #12.
15 *Ibid.*, #57.
16 *Ibid.*, #97.
17 *Ibid.*, #95.

18 *Ibid.*, #99.
19 *Ibid.*, #85.
20 *Ibid.*, #96.
21 Earle Birney, *Selected Poems* (McClelland and Stewart 1966), 100.
22 *Ibid.*, 133-41.
23 *Ibid.*, 142.
24 *Ibid.*, 77.
25 *Ibid.*, 75.
26 *Ibid.*, 148.
27 *Ibid.*, 111.
28 *Ibid.*, 56-7
29 *Ibid.*, 142.
30 *Ibid.*, 18.
31 Jay Macpherson, *The Boatman* (Oxford University Press 1957), 51.
32 *Ibid.*, 52.
33 Earle Birney, *Selected Poems*, 206.
34 Isabella Valancy Crawford, "Malcolm's Katie," *The Collected Poems* (William Briggs 1905), 203.
35 Earle Birney, *Selected Poems*, 89.
36 Irving Layton, *Collected Poems* (McClelland and Stewart 1965), 136.
37 *Ibid.*, 103.
38 "Seven O'Clock Lecture," *ibid.*, 56.
39 *Ibid.*, 48.
40 *Ibid.*, 99-100.
41 *Ibid.*, 65.
42 *Ibid.*, 33.
43 *Ibid.*, 335-8.
44 Paul Tillich, *The Courage to Be* (Yale University Press 1952), 190.
45 *Ibid.*, 185.
46 *Ibid.*, 36.
47 Isabella Valancy Crawford, *The Collected Poems*, 190.
48 Earle Birney, *Selected Poems*, 212.
49 Paul Tillich, *The Courage to Be*, 179.
50 Earle Birney, *Selected Poems*, 212.
51 John Newlove, *Moving in Alone*, 74.
52 Margaret Avison, *The Book of Canadian Poetry*, 3rd ed., ed. A. J. M. Smith (W. J. Gage 1957), 474.
53 Paul Tillich, *The Courage to Be*, 188.
54 Margaret Avison, *The Dumbfounding* (W. W. Norton 1966), 56.
55 Irving Layton, *Collected Poems*, 281-2.
56 Jay Macpherson, *The Boatman*, 55.

CHAPTER SIX: THE SACRIFICIAL EMBRACE

Epigraphs: Louis Dudek, "Groundhog among the Stars," *A Choice of Critics* (Oxford University Press 1966), 182; Ralph Gustafson, "The Exhortation," *Sift in an Hourglass* (McClelland and Stewart 1966), 14.

1 Hugh MacLennan, *The Watch that Ends the Night* (Macmillan 1959), 343.
2 Northrop Frye, *The Return of Eden* (University of Toronto Press 1965), 143.
3 George Whalley, "Literary Romanticism," *Queen's Quarterly*, LXXII, 2 (Summer

1965), 241.
4 Colin McDougall, *Execution* (Macmillan 1958), 218.
5 *Ibid.*, 222.
6 *Ibid.*, 226-7.
7 Gabrielle Roy, *The Cashier* (McClelland and Stewart, NCL Series 1963), 211.
8 *Ibid.*, 208-9.
9 *Ibid.*, 216.
10 *Ibid.*, 214.
11 Gabrielle Roy, *The Hidden Mountain* (McClelland and Stewart 1962), 96.
12 *Ibid.*, 97.
13 *Ibid.*, 95.
14 *Ibid.*, 98.
15 *Ibid.*
16 *Ibid.*, 98-9.
17 *Ibid.*, 104-5.
18 *Ibid.*, 178.
19 Adele Wiseman, *The Sacrifice* (Macmillan 1956), 178.
20 *Ibid.*, 179.
21 *Ibid.*, 38.
22 *Ibid.*, 37.
23 *Ibid.*, 299.
24 *Ibid.*, 300.
25 *Ibid.*
26 *Ibid.*, 303.
27 *Ibid.*
28 *Ibid.*, 344.
29 *Ibid.*, 345.
30 *Ibid.*, 346.
31 Douglas LePan, *The Deserter* (McClelland and Stewart 1964), 210
32 *Ibid.*, 246.
33 *Ibid.*
34 *Ibid.*, 276.
35 *Ibid.*, 284-5.
36 *Ibid.*, 285.
37 *Ibid.*, 287.
38 *Ibid.*, 293.
39 *Ibid.*, 294.
40 *Ibid.*, 297.
41 *Ibid.*, 297-8.
42 Hugh MacLennan, *The Watch that Ends the Night*, 343.
43 *Ibid.*, 340.
44 *Ibid.*, 341.
45 *Ibid.*, 344.
46 *Ibid.*, 330.
47 *Ibid.*, 360-1.
48 *Ibid.*, 361.
49 *Ibid.*, 365.
50 *Ibid.*, 366.
51 *Ibid.*
52 *Ibid.*, 370.

53 *Ibid.*, 372.

54 *Ibid.*

CHAPTER SEVEN: AN ANCIENT SLANG OR A MODERN

1 Margaret Laurence, *A Jest of God* (McClelland and Stewart 1966), 201.

2 A. W. Purdy, "I Guess A Poem," *Wild Grape Wine* (McClelland and Stewart 1968), 11.

3 Epigraph to Laurence, *A Jest of God*, v.

4 *Ibid.*, 201.

5 Alden Nowlan, *The Things Which Are* (Contact Press 1962), 30.

6 Raymond Souster, "Etienne Brulé Re-enters the Humber River, October 1958," *A Local Pride* (Contact Press 1962), 79.

7 Leonard Cohen, *Selected Poems: 1956-1968* (McClelland and Stewart 1968), 82.

8 *Ibid.*, 83.

9 John Newlove, *Moving in Alone* (Contact Press 1965), 68.

10 *Ibid.*, 64.

11 *Ibid.*, 71.

12 Alfred Purdy, "Percy Lawson," *The Cariboo Horses* (McClelland and Stewart 1965), 17.

13 *Ibid.*, 36-7.

14 A. W. Purdy, "My '48 Pontiac," *Wild Grape Wine*, 49.

15 George Bowering, *Points on the Grid* (Contact Press 1964), 52-3.

16 *Ibid.*, 49.

17 John Newlove, *Moving in Alone*, 82-3.

18 Raymond Souster, *The Selected Poems* (Contact Press 1956), 128.

19 Alden Nowlan, *The Things Which Are*, 34.

20 Alfred Purdy, *The Cariboo Horses*, 105.

21 *Ibid.*, 75.

22 James Reaney, "First Letter: To the Avon River Above Stratford, Canada," *Twelve Letters to a Small Town* (The Ryerson Press 1962), 1.

23 Eli Mandel, *An Idiot Joy* (M. G. Hurtig 1967), 11.

24 John Newlove, "Resources, Certain Earths," *Moving in Alone*, 74.

25 Eli Mandel, "Song," *An Idiot Joy*, 59.

26 *Ibid.*, 56.

27 Leonard Cohen, *Selected Poems: 1956-1968*, 217.

28 *Ibid.*, 80-3.

29 *Ibid.*, 210.

30 Margaret Avison, *The Dumbfounding* (W. W. Norton and Company 1966), 27.

31 George Bowering, *The Silver Wire* (The Quarry Press 1966), 51.

32 Gwen MacEwen, "Cartaphilus," *A Breakfast for Barbarians* (The Ryerson Press 1966), 47.

33 *Ibid.*, 16.

34 *Ibid.*, vii.

35 "The Aristocracies," *ibid.*, 53.

36 *Ibid.*, 1.

37 *Ibid.*

38 John Newlove, "The Big Bend: By-Passed Highway," *Black Night Window* (McClelland and Stewart 1968), 104.

39 Eli Mandel, "From the North Saskatchewan," *An Idiot Joy*, 67.

40 Gwen MacEwen, "Finally Left in the Landscape," *A Breakfast for Barbarians*, 52.

Index

This book

was designed by

ANTJE LINGNER

under the direction of

ALLAN FLEMING

and was printed by

University of

Toronto

Press